The Social Cost of Carbon

Ethics and the Limits of Climate Change Economics

J. PAUL KELLEHER

OXFORD
UNIVERSITY PRESS

Oxford University Press is a department of the University of Oxford.
It furthers the University's objective of excellence in research, scholarship,
and education by publishing worldwide. Oxford is a registered trade mark of
Oxford University Press in the UK and in certain other countries.

Published in the United States of America by Oxford University Press
198 Madison Avenue, New York, NY 10016, United States of America.

© Oxford University Press 2025

All rights reserved. No part of this publication may be reproduced, stored in a retrieval system, transmitted, used for text and data mining, or used for training artificial intelligence, in any form or by any means, without the prior permission in writing of Oxford University Press, or as expressly permitted by law, by license or under terms agreed with the appropriate reprographics rights organization. Inquiries concerning reproduction outside the scope of the above should be sent to the Rights Department, Oxford University Press, at the address above.

You must not circulate this work in any other form and you must
impose this same condition on any acquirer

CIP data is on file at the Library of Congress

ISBN 9780197687796

DOI: 10.1093/9780197687826.001.0001

Printed by Marquis Book Printing, Canada

The Social Cost of Carbon

PHILOSOPHY, POLITICS, AND ECONOMICS

Ryan Muldoon, Carmen Pavel, Geoffrey Sayre-McCord,
Eric Schliesser, Itai Sher
Series Editors

Published in the Series

The Open Society and Its Complexities
Gerald Gaus

A Theory of Subjective Wellbeing
Mark Fabian

Intelligent Democracy
Jonathan Benson

The Social Cost of Carbon
J. Paul Kelleher

For Jackie

Contents

Series Editors' Foreword   xi
Preface   xiii
Acknowledgments   xxi

PART I. ECONOMICS

1. Integrated Assessment and Policy Optimization: A Brief Introduction   3
   1.1 Constrained Optimization   3
   1.2 Beyond the Surface Logic of Objective Functions   7

2. The Social Cost of Carbon in Social Choice Climate Economics   10
   2.1 Social Welfare Functions and Optimal Growth Theory   10
   2.2 Two Crucial Background Assumptions   15
   2.3 The SCC in the Social Choice Framework   18
   2.4 An Alternative (but Equivalent) SCC Formula   20
   2.5 Incorporating Intratemporal Consumption Inequality   25
   2.6 The Relevance of Financing   29
   2.7 Optimal Social Choice SCCs   31

3. The Social Cost of Carbon in General Equilibrium Climate Economics   35
   3.1 Two Types of Optimization   35
   3.2 Pareto Efficiency   35
   3.3 The Two Welfare Theorems   36
   3.4 Utility Functions   39
   3.5 Aggregating Utilities in a General Equilibrium Framework   41
   3.6 Pareto Weights   42
   3.7 Negishi's Method   46
   3.8 Public Goods   48
   3.9 Externalities   51
   3.10 The Lindahl-Pigou Pricing Scheme   54
   3.11 Negishi's Method and Pareto-Improving Climate Policy   57
   3.12 Optimal General Equilibrium SCCs   60

3.13 The Ramsey-Koopmans-Cass Model	66
3.14 An Overlapping Generations Model	70
3.15 Baseline General Equilibrium SCCs	74

PART II. PHILOSOPHY

4. A Foundation for (Discounted) Utilitarian Social Welfare Functions	89
4.1 Koopmans's Axiomatic Utilitarianism	90
4.2 The Trouble with Infinite Paths	97
4.3 Harsanyi's Axiomatic Utilitarianism	99
4.3.1 Harsanyi's Aggregation Theorem	100
4.3.2 Interpersonal Comparisons of Well-being	111
4.3.3 Same-Number Aggregation	114
4.3.4 Same-Lifetime Aggregation	115
4.3.5 Complete Aggregation	119
5. Normative Abridgement and Pure Time Discounting	122
5.1 The Concept and Possibility of Normative Abridgement	122
5.2 Examples of Normative Abridgement	125
5.3 Interlude: Harsanyi's Impartial Observer Argument	130
5.4 Normative Abridgement and Pure Time Discounting	135
5.5 Should SWFs Be Temporally Impartial and Normatively Abridged?	140
5.6 Normative Abridgement and Evaluative Humility	144
6. Distribution	148
6.1 Axiomatic Prioritarianism	149
6.2 Prioritarianism under Risk	156
7. Population	174
7.1 The Zero Level of Lifetime Well-being	175
7.2 Population Ethics	176
7.3 Population Ethics and Normative Abridgement	180

PART III. POLICY ANALYSIS

8. The Social Cost of Carbon in Applied Climate Change Policy Analysis	191
8.1 Summary	192

 8.2 Climate Change Cost-Benefit Analysis 196
  8.2.1 The Interagency Working Group and the EPA 197
  8.2.2 Biden's Executive Order and OMB's New Circular A-4 208
  8.2.3 The Peer Reviewers Strike Back 209
  8.2.4 Discounting, Revisited 224
  8.2.5 The Future of Federal SCCs in the United States 226
 8.3 Carbon Taxes and Climate Targets 227

References 233
Index 243

Series Editors' Foreword

Philosophy, Politics and Economics (PPE) is coming of age as a distinct area of research of high social relevance. Modern societies face numerous complex challenges, including those associated with immigration, inequality, trade, environmental degradation, pluralism, and technological change. These cannot be completely understood through any single disciplinary lens. By fostering a more robustly interdisciplinary approach to these challenges, PPE as a field of study will help uncover opportunities that have been missed due to existing disciplinary blinders.

OUP and the editors aim for the series to be a home for scholarly monographs at the cutting edge of PPE research as well as for books aimed at broader audiences looking to learn about PPE and the perspectives it brings to pressing questions and issues. We are interested in research that integrates the disciplines of philosophy, political science, and economics to tackle or solve important policy and research problems. We are also interested in work that develops new theories and approaches that *synthetize* the different fields and offer a means to integrate them into something new.

We welcome original, boundary crossing new work that incorporates insights from all the social sciences, not just political science and economics. We intend for work in the series to be ecumenical about its potential scope and rigorous about its methods. We believe that an integrated approach to PPE can range very broadly , and we are excited to explore its frontiers.

Preface

Climate change economists have called it "the most important number you have never heard of" (Ackerman and Stanton 2010, p. 2), "the single most important variable for [climate] policy analysis" (Pearson 2011, p. 78), the "holy grail of climate economic analysis" (Wagner 2020), and "the one number that rules them all, the one number that every government across the globe should use" (Auffhammer 2017, at 4m26s). William Nordhaus concurs, calling it "[t]he most important single economic concept in the economics of climate change" (Nordhaus 2017, p. 1518). It is the *social cost of carbon dioxide*, and its purpose is to reflect in one dollar figure the total amount of harm caused by emitting an additional ton of carbon dioxide into the earth's atmosphere. Many people just call it "the social cost of carbon"—hence the title of this book.

Economists use the social cost of carbon (SCC) in cost-benefit analyses of climate change mitigation projects. If the cost to abate a ton of carbon dioxide is larger than the monetized harm done by that ton, then from a standpoint of weighing costs against benefits, it is better to let the damage be done. But if the harm caused by a unit of emissions is greater than the costs of preventing that unit, then the benefits of abatement exceed the costs of prevention, and cost-benefit analysis should rank abatement above the status quo. In other contexts, the SCC has been used as an indicator of the optimal level of atmospheric CO_2 concentrations, as well as the optimal level of the tax that should be imposed on each ton of carbon dioxide that humans emit into the atmosphere.

Partially in response to a 2008 ruling by the United States Ninth Circuit Court of Appeals that stated "the value of carbon emissions reductions is certainly not zero," the Obama administration established the federal Interagency Working Group on Social Cost of Carbon (IWG) to establish a standardized range of SCC figures to be used in federal cost-benefit analyses (U.S. Ninth Circuit Court of Appeals 2008). In 2016, the IWG's "central" SCC estimate for 2020 was $42 (in 2007 dollars). Shortly after taking office, however, President Trump issued an executive order that dissolved the IWG, barred federal agencies from using the Obama-era SCC figures, and permitted these agencies to make profound changes to federal SCC methodology. As a result, the Trump administration authorized the use of SCC values as low as $1 (Armstrong 2017). This diminished the chances that climate change–related regulations would pass a cost-benefit test. In President Biden's first month in office, a reconstituted IWG reinstated the Obama-era numbers, adjusted for inflation. Most recently, the U.S. Environmental Protection Agency finalized its own range of updated SCC figures in November 2023 (EPA 2023). EPA's headline central SCC estimate for 2020 came in at $190 per ton of CO_2 (in 2020 dollars).

Prior to becoming a political football in the U.S., the academy hosted some rather acrimonious battles over the SCC's theoretical foundations. In response to Nordhaus's criticism of a 2007 U.K. government report for which John Broome served as a consultant, Broome (a former economist turned leading moral philosopher) told a journalist:

> I actually got rather angry . . . it is so obvious that these economists are applying ethical principles without noticing. Something needed to be done about it, they shouldn't get away with this. It was no longer a sideline [in my own research], this is a challenge. (quoted in Miller 2013)

And in a bitter exchange with the economist–cum–political philosopher John Roemer over discount rates, which are key components of any SCC calculation, the doyen of environmental economics, Partha Dasgupta, wrote in the journal *Environmental and Resource Economics* that "'Social discount rates' often bring out the intellectually worst among moral and political philosophers writing on the subject" (Dasgupta 2011, p. 489).

Nor is this just economists versus philosophers. For it is hard to name a higher-profile intra-disciplinary debate than the one in climate economics between Nordhaus and Nicholas Stern on the theoretical foundations of social cost of carbon calculations. Quite possibly, no academic debate has ever been more consequential for the future of life on this planet than the Stern-Nordhaus debate. Stern is a former World Bank chief economist and lead author of the report Broome consulted on, namely *The Economics of Climate Change: The Stern Review* (Stern 2007), and Nordhaus won the 2018 Nobel Prize in economics for his trailblazing work in climate economics. What is remarkable about this debate is that each participant has declared that the other's *whole approach* to climate economics is flatly irrelevant to the problem it aims to address (see Nordhaus 2007, p. 692; and Stern 2010, p. 51).

The Stern-Nordhaus dispute is only the most extreme version of a general trend: virtually everyone writing on the theoretical foundations of the social cost of carbon believes that virtually all the others are badly mistaken on crucial matters. This makes it hard to persuade others of one's own idiosyncratic views. And as Dasgupta's remark suggests, the hill is perhaps steeper if one is—like me—a moral philosopher, rather than a card-carrying economist.

Nevertheless, I aim in this book to bring new conceptual clarity to disputes over the SCC, and over the foundations of climate change economics more generally. Although I became interested in the SCC in part because of the high-profile debates I have referred to, the book is not organized around those debates. Instead I proceed analytically, by disentangling four distinct SCC concepts and sorting them into two families. The families correspond to the two main branches of welfare economics, social choice theory and general equilibrium theory. In the course of explaining each SCC concept and its theoretical basis, I shall relate each to the distinct analytical task in climate economics that it is best suited to address.

At a fundamental level, none of the four SCC concepts conflicts with any of the others: each can be linked to one of four distinct analytical tasks. This does not mean that each is *well-suited* for the task it has been used to address; nor does it mean that philosophers, economists, and other analysts have avoided using the various SCC concepts in problematic ways. For example, whereas two of the SCC concepts are often treated as bearing on the topic of efficient CO_2 pollution taxation, in fact only one of these concepts can properly serve in that role. Likewise, a different pair of SCC concepts has been treated as relevant to the question of whether a marginal abatement project is a good thing from the standpoint of aggregate social welfare, when in fact only one member of this pair can properly serve in *that* role. The good news is that these conflations and confusions can be cleared up, and that three of the four SCC concepts really do have important roles to play in climate change policy analysis. The bad news is that the fourth, policy-*ir*relevant SCC concept is the concept that largely underlies the SCC estimates that have been produced by the federal government in the United States. As chapter 8 discusses, there is reason for hope that this could change in the future. But as of this writing it seems unlikely to change very soon. This book is in part an argument for making that change.

I hope, therefore, to show that three of the four SCC concepts I identify are theoretically well-founded and relevant to ethically responsible climate change policy analysis. The real difficulty is that it is hard to say exactly *how* or *to what degree* these concepts are relevant. This is because none of the three SCC concepts can justify carbon dioxide mitigation policies on its own. Each is, as I shall put it, *normatively abridged*: however theoretically sound these SCC concepts are, there are important policy-relevant ethical values and principles that are external to—and thus abridged from—the theoretical frameworks underlying them. The normative abridgement that afflicts the three defensible SCC concepts severely limits the evaluative power of climate change economics—hence the subtitle of this book. Even if their SCC figures were impeccably derived, and even if these were combined with an infallible schedule of marginal abatement costs (MAC), economists still should not conclude that we ought to mitigate right up until the SCC (i.e., the benefit of mitigation) equals the MAC (i.e., the cost of mitigation). In other words, quantitative cost-benefit reasoning cannot justify climate policies all on its own. Or so I shall argue.

I should note that the types of normative abridgement I will focus on do not concern the intrinsic value of nature or the well-being of non-human animals. It is true that these two considerations are typically ignored in SCC estimates, and this is absolutely an important limitation that I do not wish to downplay. But I shall principally be concerned with different limitations, and with the question of whether and how to rectify these additional limitations in calculating SCC values. This latter question would arise even if nature and animal welfare were somehow adequately included.

Finally, this book is also a study of the basis and analytical role in climate change economics of ethical ideas generally, and of utilitarianism more specifically. Climate change economists often invoke a framework they call *discounted utilitarianism*, which virtually no moral philosopher accepts. Meanwhile, philosophers engaged with climate economics often endorse a *non*-discounted utilitarian framework, which climate change economists routinely criticize for having absurd policy implications. This certainly looks like a disagreement, but in fact it need not be. Instead, these two frameworks—economists' discounted utilitarianism and philosophers' utilitarianism—can arise from distinct and mutually consistent theoretical foundations. Moreover, if my claims concerning normative abridgement are correct, neither framework on its own entails anything decisive about the proper targets of climate policy. I shall argue that the economists should not reject utilitarian climate economics if they do so because of its putative policy implications, and the philosophers should not reject economists' discounted utilitarianism if they do so because they assume it is at odds with their philosophical utilitarianism.

The book is structured as follows. After the introductory chapter 1, the rest of Part I explains each of the four SCC concepts, their theoretical bases in either social choice theory or general equilibrium theory, and the respective analytical tasks they address. Part II then examines more deeply the philosophical foundations of social choice climate change economics and the two SCC concepts that belong to it. This branch of climate economics is, at bottom, an applied branch of moral philosophy. Part II argues that while social choice SCC concepts are genuinely relevant to climate change policy, there are good reasons to treat them as normatively abridged and therefore as offering incomplete answers to climate policy questions. If this is right, then a comprehensive analysis of climate policy must take account of considerations that are external to the social choice framework that gives rise to the SCC concepts.

The sole chapter in Part III then puts normatively abridged climate economics to work. First, I explain why one of the normatively abridged social choice SCC concepts offers important and practicable improvements over the normatively *ir*relevant SCC concept that is currently used by the U.S. federal government to evaluate greenhouse gas regulations. Second, one of the normatively abridged general equilibrium SCC concepts is important because it is an essential component in the design of greenhouse gas abatement policies that could be undertaken without anyone's having to make a sacrifice. Whether the world *ought* to pursue sacrifice-free climate policy is not something that climate economics alone can establish. Nor will I examine that question in detail. But in light of the roadblocks that still impede climate action, the possibility should be taken seriously.[1]

Of course I expect and welcome pushback on my claims concerning the various SCC concepts' relevance for climate change policy analysis. With respect to the social choice SCC concepts in particular, I certainly cannot claim to have proved my normative abridgement thesis beyond all reasonable doubt. Doing that would require a much longer book, and I wanted to write a philosophy book that non-philosophers might read in full. Yet even if I am mistaken that a theoretically correct social choice climate economics will be normatively abridged, there is an important further reason to take

---

[1] For further discussion and advocacy on this point, see Foley (2009), Posner and Weisbach (2010), Broome (2012), Broome and Foley (2016), and Kotlikoff et al. (2021).

the phenomenon seriously. The reason is that the most important institution for which a social choice SCC concept might make a difference, the U.S. federal government, is (at best) decades away from being comfortable with unabridged social choice SCC figures. Indeed, it is already official U.S. policy to treat SCC figures as theoretically incomplete and in need of supplementation by ethical considerations that are excluded from the SCC estimation process. So even if my arguments for normative abridgement in social choice climate economics are mistaken at the level of theory, it remains important to examine the implications of abridgement for applied climate change policy analysis of the sort undertaken by federal agencies in the U.S. That is a main task of Part III.

I am much more confident about the importance of disentangling the four different SCC concepts and then mapping each to the task it addresses in climate economics. I have sometimes had economists respond to this project by noting that, barring outliers, published SCC estimates do not differ much, even when the studies' methodologies clearly focus on different SCC concepts. (This is one of the findings of a recent meta-analysis by Tol (2023a, see pp. S7, S25)). On this basis, these economists have suggested that the conceptual distinctions I stress in this book are not important enough to fuss over. But this is a bad argument. The correct approach would compare SCC figures that have been constructed by those who grasp and are responsive to the relevant conceptual distinctions. Moreover, if some of the SCC concepts are inherently normative, then at least some models in climate economics should be informed by philosophical argumentation and analysis. Yet philosophers are rarely central members of a modeling team or otherwise meaningfully consulted by the economists who construct and run the models. And even when philosophers *are* consulted and heeded, as was the case with the *Stern Review*, the analysis becomes liable to economists' ridicule as one that "takes the lofty vantage point of the world social planner, perhaps stoking the dying embers of the British Empire" (Nordhaus 2007, p. 691), or one that is "paternalistic and at risk of intolerance, authoritarianism and totalitarianism" (Tol 2019, p. 152). When conceptually and ethically important aspects of a quantitative indicator are dismissed or jeered at within climate economics, one cannot draw inferences from published figures to what SCC levels *would be* if those aspects were taken seriously.

This book is principally addressed to numerate philosophers and economists, and to the graduate students they train. I have come to believe that much disagreement between climate economists and moral philosophers (and between economists themselves) stems from the fact that two radically different analytical frameworks can give rise to exactly the same mathematical formalism. To explain this, and to explore its implications for climate economics, I have had to explain the conceptual and mathematical bases of two fundamentally different branches of welfare economics. The result is a more technical book than I had expected to write on an already technical topic. Much as I tried, I could find no way around this. Still, I hope much of the book will be comprehensible and useful to any patient reader who is not immediately put off by the symbols and formulae.[2]

---

[2] Two excellent primers for those entirely new to welfare economics are Feldman and Serrano (2006) and Adler (2019). But again, I hope my exposition will be accessible even to the uninitiated.

Acknowledgments

I am immensely grateful to so many people who helped me as I worked on this book. I am sure I cannot name everyone who helped in discussion or in written comments, or both. For that I am very sorry. Still, I am eager to thank Frank Ackerman, Matthew Adler, Scott Ashworth, Spencer Banzhaf, Simon Beard, Truman Bewley, Geoff Brennan, R. Daniel Bressler, Daniel Bromley, Simon Caney, Beatrice Cherrier, Marc Davidson, Simon Dietz, Moritz Drupp, Steven Durlauf, Marc Fleurbaey, Hilary Greaves, Ben Groom, Lauren Hartzell Nichols, Geoffrey Heal, Garth Heutel, Avram Hiller, Richard Howarth, Niko Jaakkola, Ravi Kanbur, Noah Kaufman, Timothy Kehoe, David Kelly, Laurence Kotlikoff, Nils Kupzok, Simon Lang, Douglas MacLean, Christopher McKelvey, Antony Millner, Kian Mintz-Woo, Frances Moore, David Morrow, John Mullahy, Frikk Nesje, William Nordhaus, David O'Brien, Charles Pearson, Matthew Rendall, Armon Rezai, Dominic Roser, Jeff Round, Felix Schaumann, Gernot Wagner, and David Weimer.

I owe special debts of gratitude to Partha Dasgupta and John Broome. Around 2015 they answered emails in which I asked if they might comment on a draft of a paper I had written on discounting in climate economics. They each generously replied with constructive comments, and patiently responded to follow-up questions, as indeed they have several times since. Just as important to me has been the example set by their published writings on climate economics and on the foundations of welfare economics. I have returned to this work again and again for instruction in the subject matter and in the difficult art of writing clearly about it. In 2016 I finally met Dasgupta in Oxford at an interdisciplinary workshop on discounting, and his kindness and sincere interest in my ideas on that day meant a great deal to me. Broome has generously read and commented on other papers I have sent to him, and he also provided extensive and extremely valuable written comments on a full draft of this book as a (voluntarily de-anonymized) referee for the Press. His comments saved me from innumerable errors and impelled me to overhaul and greatly improve chapter 3. In general, his published work, judicious comments, and penetrating questions about my arguments have been the single largest influence on my approach to the topics in this book. I cannot thank him enough.

I am grateful as well to three other, anonymous referees for the Press, and to the PPE Book Series editors. Their criticisms and suggestions led to many improvements. I also want to thank my excellent editors at OUP, Peter Ohlin and Alex Rouch, and my copy editor Judith Hoover. It was a pleasure to work with each of them.

In spring 2019 I was able convene a small workshop on a first, incomplete draft of the manuscript, and there I received extremely helpful criticism and advice from David Anthoff, Mark Budolfson, Maddalena Ferranna, Dan Hausman, Kian Mintz-Woo, and Thomas Rutherford. Their enthusiasm and advice on that day was particularly valuable. I should also like to thank Rutherford and the students we taught together in a seminar on ethics and climate economics at UW–Madison in spring 2023, in which portions of this book served as assigned reading and the basis for class discussion.

I wish to thank the University of Wisconsin–Madison and its School of Medicine and Public Health for supporting my work on this book through a paid research leave and through its commitment to faculty research generally. I was also supported in 2018 by a Summer Humanities Research Fellowship from the university's Institute for Research in the Humanities, for which I am very grateful. This fellowship generously funded the 2019 book workshop I mentioned above, and it also helped to arrange external mentorship of my project from Marc Fleurbaey during an early stage. I am indebted to Fleurbaey for agreeing to share his time and expertise in this capacity, and I thank the Institute's director, Steven Nadler, and its (now retired) assistant to the director, Ann Harris, for helping me make the most of this valuable opportunity.

I am grateful as well to the faculty and staff in the Department of Medical History & Bioethics and in the Department of Philosophy at UW–Madison. I am fortunate to have kind and brilliant colleagues. None is more kind, more brilliant, or more supportive of early-career faculty than Dan Hausman. I could not hope to express how important his encouragement, advice, and example were for me in the eleven years that we spent as colleagues in these two departments. He has been sorely missed on our campus since his departure for Rutgers University in the summer of 2020.

Much of this book was written during the COVID-19 pandemic. When schools shut down, and for some time after that, our small child was at home every minute of every day of every week. My progress would have been completely halted had it not been for our small pod of rotating caregivers that joined forces to enable parents to work while two best friends played together. I will forever be grateful to Ann McCall, Alejandra Pilarz, Mike Pilarz, and (Grandma) Debbie Ward for collectively caring for Leo and Jackie. And while those months were not easy, I will cherish the unplanned time I spent watching two intrepid toddlers fix the Root Tree and explore the Mini Arboretum.

For their friendship and general moral support, I warmly thank Paul Audi, Merlin Chowkwanyun, Bill Gardner, Kristen Hoffmann, Steve Shulman-Laniel, and David Wilcher (who are human beings), and Maddie, George, Teddy, and Charlie (who are Labrador retrievers).

Lastly, I wish to express my heartfelt gratitude to my wife, Ann, and to our kiddo, Jackie. Their love and encouragement, and their patience with this project, have meant absolutely everything to me.

PART I
ECONOMICS

1
Integrated Assessment and Policy Optimization: A Brief Introduction

1.1 Constrained Optimization

There are several types of climate change integrated assessment model (IAM). All of these bring together methods and results from multiple disciplines to help analyze one or more aspects of climate change. One type of climate change IAM is focused exclusively on empirical "what-if" questions concerning "how the future will evolve under a particular set of conditions and how the system will change under the influence of external factors" (Calvin et al. 2019, p. 678). Some IAMs in this family address certain dimensions of specific sectors, like demand in the energy sector or the availability of fresh water in a given global region. Other IAMs in this family, like the widely used GCAM model, combine many sector-specific models into one empirical IAM concerned with "questions at the intersection of energy, water, land, socioeconomics, and climate" (Calvin et al. 2019, p. 677). IAMs of this sort can be very large; for example, GCAM involves more than 100,000 lines of computer code. Sometimes these complex what-if IAMs are called "detailed process IAMs" (Weyant 2017, p. 117).

In contrast to pure what-if IAMs, *policy optimization IAMs* combine what-if modules with an *objective function*. An objective function is a ranking function: it takes all the possible ways the world could be according to the what-if part of the policy optimization IAM, and ranks them against one another. To perform this ranking procedure, policy optimization IAMs must be able to aggregate together the features of a given feasible outcome, so that each such outcome can be given its own single ranking score. In part because of the processing power needed to perform this sort of optimization exercise, early policy optimization IAMs adopted highly simplified what-if modules. It is still not uncommon for policy optimization IAMs to represent in just a few lines of code what the more detailed non-optimization models represent in hundreds or even thousands of lines. In the PAGE policy optimization

IAM, for example, the entire global carbon cycle is represented by a single simple equation (Hope 2005, p. 85). But there are now also some policy optimization IAMs whose what-if modules would place them in the detailed process IAM camp if the model did not also feature an objective function. Examples include the REMIND and WITCH IAMs (Baumstark et al. 2021; WITCH Team 2019). And since any policy optimization model includes at least some representation of empirical relationships between social and physical phenomena, even policy optimization models can be run in a what-if mode (Nordhaus 2013, p. 1080).[1]

Sometimes policy optimization IAMs are called "cost-benefit IAMs" (Weyant 2014, p. 386). This is because the role of the objective function is to weigh the benefits of possible changes in world outcomes against the costs of bringing those changes about, and then to identify the specific intertemporal outcome—the way the world could be from now into the distant future—whose net benefits are greatest. The net-benefit-maximizing outcome is often labeled by policy optimization modelers as the "optimal" outcome. An optimal intertemporal outcome is one whose *marginal* benefits exactly equal its marginal costs. Thus, if a policymaker in an already optimal scenario attempts to produce a few more benefits by changing the world slightly, the costs of doing so will exactly offset the benefits. It is as if one has so thoroughly wrung out a wet piece of clothing that the benefits of any further wringing would be exactly offset by the costs of further wrist pain. It was out of this concern to identify intertemporal outcomes whose marginal costs and benefits exactly offset that William Nordhaus, a leading policy optimization climate change modeler, titled his most well-known book *A Question of Balance: Weighing the Options on Global Warming Policies* (Nordhaus 2008). "Policy optimization" can refer either to the whole process of finding and characterizing the highest-ranked outcome, or to the process of actually placing the world onto an optimal intertemporal path with public policy instruments.

When economists "run" a policy optimization model, they are engaging in a mathematical exercise known as *constrained optimization*. In this process the what-if part of the model determines a set of feasible outcomes that can be brought about by adjustments to *decision variables*. The most important decision variables in climate change policy optimization IAMs are the levels of conventional and "green" investment undertaken in different years, and

---

[1] I thank Felix Schaumann for very useful discussion about how to taxonomize existing integrated assessment models.

the various policy instruments, such as a carbon tax, that would induce individual agents to choose one sort of investment over the other. In Nordhaus's famous DICE model, for example, green investment takes the form of an abstract abatement technology that mitigates the degree to which economic production creates emissions, and in turn the degree to which present economic production impacts the level of goods and services available for future generations to enjoy. In DICE, the specific relationships between degrees of present abatement and levels of future economic output are determined by equations that link present economic phenomena to greenhouse gas emissions levels; emissions levels to atmospheric concentrations of CO_2; atmospheric concentrations to the atmospheric trapping of the sun's energy (also known as *radiative forcing*); radiative forcing to global mean temperature increases; and finally temperature increases to future "economic damages" in the form of reductions in the goods and services that future generations are able to enjoy. By adjusting today's levels of green and conventional investment (the latter coming in the form of individuals' private savings), the empirical relationships expressed by the model's what-if equations determine the resulting course of the intertemporal global economy.

Different models specify their what-if components differently and with different degrees of precision. For example, some policy optimization IAMs break the world into several regions with different baseline wealth levels, and then allow climate change to impact the regions in very different ways. Some also characterize greenhouse gas–induced damages in a very granular and precise way—for example, *this* specific amount of damage from sea level rise in *this* specific region. Others (like DICE) treat the world as one region and characterize damages simply as a warming-induced reduction in aggregate global economic output.

More generally, exercises in constrained optimization employ three components (Gilboa 2012, p. 25): (1) the what-if module that specifies empirical linkages between societal and climatic phenomena, with the module's result being an outcome specified for every feasible combination of those phenomena; (2) a set of decision variables that can be used to influence economic and climatic phenomena, and thus used to bring about a given feasible outcome; and (3) an objective function that assigns a ranking score to each feasible outcome.[2] The what-if module is the part of the model that specifies

---

[2] Here I am (falsely) describing the method of optimization as if risk is irrelevant—that is, as if modelers always assume that a given feasible outcome can be brought about with certainty by

its constraints, while the objective function determines which of the model's feasible outcomes is "optimal"—that is, ranked the highest. The "policy" part of policy optimization modeling enters when one runs the model and it spits out the changes that must be made in the decision variables in order to achieve the outcome the model deems optimal.

The leading policy optimization models are highly aggregated and make use of very simplified representations of the relationships belonging to their what-if modules. For example, none of these models attempts to incorporate the biodiversity-, human migration-, or wildfire-related impacts of climate change. This means that when optimization is used to rank feasible climate policy outcomes from best to worst, this is done completely ignoring these important impact categories and their upshot for the life prospects of people around the world and across generations. Moreover, even for impact categories that are standardly incorporated into policy optimization IAMs, such as the impacts of temperature increases on per capita gross domestic product, the equations specifying these relations rest on extremely limited data and are best treated as conjectural. For example, Nordhaus has written:

> I think we do not have sufficient evidence to extrapolate reliably above 3 degrees C [of warming] ... While damage estimates at high temperatures are necessary for modeling purposes ... they are placeholders subject to further research and should be used with sensitivity analysis to indicate their importance for the key result, such as estimates of current policy or the current social cost of carbon. (quoted in Stern 2015, pp. 346–347n26)[3]

For all of these reasons, it is important to understand the role that a policy optimization IAM's what-if module plays, and why it may be of limited reliability in empirical forecasting. But this book is concerned with conceptual, theoretical, and policy questions raised primarily by policy optimization IAMs' objective functions, and with related questions concerning social cost of carbon estimates that derive from interactions between a model's objective function and its empirical projections. I will therefore mostly ignore

---

adjusting the decision variables. In fact, many models do seek to capture risks. But I will be abstracting from considerations of risk until Part II.

[3] These remarks were expressed by Nordhaus in written correspondence with Nicholas Stern, who published them with Nordhaus's permission.

these empirical issues in order to focus on other aspects of policy optimization IAMs that raise particularly important foundational questions about the point and policy-relevance of constrained optimization in climate change economics.

1.2 Beyond the Surface Logic of Objective Functions

Objective functions are at the center of much debate in climate economics. Among economists, this debate has primarily focused on the choice of specific parameters within a *discounted utilitarian* function. (I will introduce such functions formally in chapter 2.) One side in this debate is exemplified by Nordhaus, who insists that ethics is irrelevant to the calibration of parameters within discounted utilitarianism (Nordhaus 2007, p. 692); on the other side is Nicholas Stern, who claims that calibration within discounted utilitarianism involves "unavoidable ethical issues" (Stern 2008, p. 12). Owing almost entirely to this disagreement, Stern and Nordhaus arrived at very different evaluations of proposals to take costly action in 2007 to prevent climate damages decades and centuries in the future. As Nordhaus put it, Stern's

> results are dramatically different from earlier economic models [such as the DICE model] that use the same basic data and analytical structure. One of the major findings in the economics of climate change has been that efficient or "optimal" economic policies to slow climate change involve modest rates of emissions reductions in the near term, followed by sharp reductions in the medium and long term. We might call this the *climate-policy ramp*, in which policies to slow global warming increasingly tighten or ramp up over time. (Nordhaus 2007, p. 687, emphasis in original)

In contrast, Stern drew "a simple conclusion: the benefits of strong and early action far outweigh the economic costs of not acting" (Stern 2007, p. xv).

Within moral philosophy, meanwhile, discounted utilitarianism is roundly rejected as ethically flawed. Despite this, moral philosophers have viewed the use of discounted utilitarianism in climate economics as an opening to shape climate change policy analysis, since philosophers have made important contributions to a broader methodology in which discounted utilitarianism is but one of several prominent options. This broader methodology is what

Matthew Adler and Nicolas Treich call the social welfare function (SWF) methodology (Adler and Treich 2015, p. 282). As they explain it, an exercise within the SWF framework "maps a given outcome onto a vector [i.e., a list] of well-being numbers, one for each person in the population"; then it "ranks outcomes via some rule M for ranking vectors of well-being numbers. This outcome ranking, in turn, generates a ranking of the *policies* (choices) available to the decisionmaker" (Adler and Treich 2015, pp. 281, 282, emphasis in original). Adler and Treich then add:

> Although some economists are skeptical about SWFs ... this is not true of economists working on climate change. The SWF methodology is pervasive in this literature. For example, both the *Stern Review* and Nordhaus' book *A Question of Balance* employ an SWF as the fundamental tool for evaluating carbon-reduction policies. Their policy differences are profound—but because of a disagreement about the parameters of the SWF ... and not because of a disagreement about the methodology itself. (Adler and Treich 2015, p. 282)

Part I of this book provides reasons to question Adler and Treich's key assumption here. For it explains how one can employ a discounted utilitarian objective function in climate economics without doing so within the SWF framework. Chapters 2 and 3 together show how the discounted utilitarian formalism that Stern and Nordhaus both employ can be derived from within two radically different analytical frameworks. The SWF framework is only one of these. Philosophers have generally failed to see that the other framework is also used in climate economics to address questions that the SWF framework may be unfit to answer. Yet a main reason for philosophers' misapprehension is the fact that some climate economists mistakenly act as if the other framework really can answer a question philosophers are very much interested in—namely, "From a normative perspective concerned with improving the world by adding well-being to it, which climate change policies are most desirable?"

The dual foundations for discounted utilitarianism are not dueling foundations, however: two climate economists could adopt very different discounted utilitarian objective functions without any inconsistency, so long as these functions are rooted in different theoretical frameworks and so long as they are addressed to different analytical questions. It will also turn out to be perfectly consistent to reject discounted utilitarianism *as a method for ranking vectors of well-being* while embracing or remaining agnostic on the use of discounted utilitarianism to perform certain other important tasks in climate economics. These other tasks are the focus of chapter 3.

My central goal in this part is to explain how discounted utilitarianism can be derived in two very different ways, and to link each of these derivations to distinct tasks in climate economics. The two theoretical frameworks I shall describe are not interchangeable, and it is absolutely crucial to understand how they differ and what they can and cannot be used to do in climate economics. This will provide the theoretical basis for making cognate qualifications about the four distinct SCC concepts.

2

The Social Cost of Carbon in Social Choice Climate Economics

2.1 Social Welfare Functions and Optimal Growth Theory

In *The Economics of Climate Change: The Stern Review*, a 2006 report produced for the British government, Nicholas Stern and his team employed the welfare economic framework that David Cass, one of its pioneers, calls the *optimal growth* framework (Stern 2007; Spear and Wright 1998, p. 538). A very simple idea underlies the optimal growth framework as Cass and Stern conceive of it. It is this: in a normative ranking of all the possible ways the economy could unfold over the indefinite future—of all possible economic *growth paths*—some of these should be ranked above others. Assuming for the moment that just one feasible growth path sits atop the ranking, that is the optimal growth path. Optimal growth theory, so conceived, is centrally concerned to describe various characteristics of this optimal path and the ranking procedure that identifies it.

Optimal growth theory in this sense is a specific application of the broader analytical framework of *social choice theory*. Unfortunately, it is very common for economists to use "optimal growth theory" to refer to an analytical framework whose concerns are very different from those of social choice theory. That second framework is the subject of chapter 3. There I will adopt further terminology that will help prevent confusion between them. For now, I shall use "the social choice approach to climate economics" to refer to the broad approach adopted in the *Stern Review* and set out in this chapter.

To carry out the main task of the social choice approach to climate economics, one must possess both a way to identify the economy's feasible set of intertemporal paths and a method for constructing a normative ranking of the items in that set. Social choice theory as a modern discipline traces back to Arrow (1950, 1951). Arrow explored the possibility of constructing a social ranking of outcomes by aggregating individuals' preference rankings of those outcomes. He proved that the only social ranking that satisfies certain independently plausible axioms is a dictatorial ranking that allows a single individual's preferences to determine the social ranking. A systematic study by Amartya Sen showed that Arrow's so-called "impossibility theorem" can be evaded if social rankings are responsive to individuals' interpersonally comparable indicators of well-being, rather than solely to individuals' personal rankings of outcomes (Sen 2017). Social choice climate change economics adopts this well-being-oriented strategy.

In a seminal paper whose influence upon social choice climate economics is profound, Frank Ramsey adopted classical utilitarianism as his general approach to ranking. Ramsey did not know about the threat of climate change, but his framework is general enough to incorporate it. His approach first looks to the bundle of goods, services, and amenities—that is, "consumption bundles"—that contribute to the well-being of each individual who will ever live if the economy is on a given growth path; it then determines the levels of well-being that each individual's bundle affords her; finally, it sums together each person's lifetime level of well-being to arrive at an overall sum. Intertemporal paths of consumption are then ranked according to these sums (Ramsey 1928, p. 543).[1] A utilitarian framework of this sort requires that individuals' well-being functions exhibit a form of interpersonal comparability that was ruled out by Arrow's social choice framework. (I shall return to these details in section 2.2.)

Ramsey adopted four important assumptions. First, he assumed a constant population, both across times along the same growth path and at the same times across different paths. Second, he assumed perfect *temporal equality*. That is, while a given growth path may involve people tomorrow being richer than people today, Ramsey assumed that no growth path involves some people being richer than others at the same point in time.[2] Third, he assumed that in at least some possible scenarios, the human species will live on forever. Finally, he assumed that the goods, services, and amenities that are consumed by an individual i in a given time period t can be expressed as a single numerical indicator of that person's *generalized consumption*, c_{it}. The idea is that the consumption of many different goods can

---

[1] I am interpreting Ramsey's term "enjoyment" to refer to what philosophical utilitarians mean by "well-being." Ramsey also used the term "utility," but in this book "utility" will mean something very specific that is *not* synonymous with "well-being." I shall introduce my definition of "utility" in section 3.4.
[2] At the end of his original paper Ramsey relaxed this assumption, but the canonical presentation of his discussion retains it.

be expressed as a total level of expenditure on them, say in terms of dollars. The typical assumption in models that use indicators of generalized consumption is that consumers keep their expenditures proportional across time, so that if they spend 5 percent of their income in one year on bread, they will spend that same proportion on bread in the next year, regardless of how much their disposable income might have changed in absolute terms. This enables an analyst to express a consumer's entire consumption bundle with a single indicator of total expenditure, with higher levels indicating larger amounts of each type of good in the bundle. Generalized consumption indicators are then just these indicators of total expenditure (Deaton 1992, pp. 7–10).

Under Ramsey's assumptions, the growth paths at issue can be expressed as *consumption paths* of the form:

$$C = (c_t, c_{t+1}, ..., c_\tau, ...)$$

where c_t is an indicator of *per capita* consumption at time t. Per capita consumption at t is equal to aggregate consumption at t, which we denote by C_t, divided by the total size of the population at t, which we denote by N_t. Ramsey's assumptions entail that all N_t's take the same value and that consumption at any time is always distributed equally to those who are alive at that time. In that case, the following two *social welfare functions* yield exactly the same ranking of paths of per capita consumption:

$$V(C) = \sum_{t=0}^{\infty} w(c_t) \qquad (2.1)$$

$$V(C) = \sum_{t=0}^{\infty} N_t \cdot w(c_t) \qquad (2.2)$$

In each of these social welfare functions (SWFs), the function w converts a level of (generalized) consumption into its associated level of well-being. Then each time's well-being total—starting at $t = 0$ and extending out into an infinite future—is added together with that of all other times, and this sum is the consumption path's ranking score.[3] Each SWF then ranks paths by these

---

[3] I shall use discrete time formulations rather than continuous time formulations in this book. The one exception comes in section 4.1.

scores. The two SWFs above yield the very same ranking under Ramsey's assumptions, because the scores assigned by (2.2) will differ from the scores assigned by (2.1) only by a factor equal to the constant value of the population indicators, N_t.

Ramsey actually used neither (2.1) nor (2.2) for the purpose of constructing a utilitarian ranking of consumption paths. For when one's time horizon is infinite and consumption remains positive across time, the scores assigned to many consumption paths by these social welfare functions will be infinite as well. And this makes it impossible to rank all consumption paths by their SWF score. I will discuss this problem further in chapter 4. For now I introduce a solution—the most common solution in the economics literature—that raises issues we will return to frequently. This solution is to insert some degree of *pure time discounting* into equations (2.1) and (2.2). Here, for example, is equation (2.2) supplemented by a pure time discount *factor*:

$$V(C) = \sum_{t=0}^{\infty} N_t \cdot w(c_t) \cdot \frac{1}{(1+\delta)^t}, \text{ with } \delta > 0 \qquad (2.3)$$

The heart of a pure time discount factor is its pure time discount *rate*, denoted in (2.3) by δ. A useful way to think of a discount rate within the social choice framework is as a "rank-preserving rate of return." Let me explain.

Set aside the worry about infinite sums for the moment and suppose that the social welfare function (2.2) assigns a score V to a given consumption path. That social welfare function does not involve any pure time discount factor, which means that if we traded this path for one that was identical to it except that one unit of well-being is delayed from any given time, t, to the very next time period, $t+1$, then we would be trading one path for another with exactly the same score, V. This would *not* be so, however, if the social welfare function included a pure time discount factor whose pure time discount rate is positive, as it is stipulated to be in (2.3). (2.3) imposes the requirement that when well-being in one period is decreased by one unit so that well-being in the next period can be increased, the two paths will have the same ranking score *if and only if* well-being in the next period is increased by $1+\delta$ units. For example, suppose we set δ equal to 0.03, or 3 percent, and we stipulate that one consumption path C is identical to a second path C' except that C'

generates one fewer unit of well-being than path C at t and generates somewhat higher well-being at time $t+1$. Then the social welfare function in (2.3) would assign the same score to paths C and C' if and only if well-being in time $t+1$ along C' is 1.03 units higher than it is along C. In other words, for (2.3) to treat C' as at least as good as C, the rate of return on the one-unit "well-being investment" must be at least 3 percent. And for the investment to be such that it moves the economy from one path to a second, *higher-ranked* path, the investment's rate of return must surpass, or "hurdle over," the pure time discount rate, δ. This is why discount rates are sometimes also called *hurdle rates*.

So a discount rate specifies the rate of return on a marginal investment that would leave the post-investment consumption path having the same social welfare score as the pre-investment path. The positive discount rate built into (2.3) is called a "pure time" discount rate because it seems to discriminate against future well-being simply because it is in the future: if the pure time discount rate is 3 percent, then delaying a unit of today's well-being until tomorrow renders that unit less valuable—at least as far as rankings represented by (2.3) are concerned.

Since (2.3) ranks consumption paths by adding up the well-being that each path affords to its intertemporal population, it must find a way to compare future units of well-being with present units, so that their relative values are properly reflected in the path's single overall V-score. This is where the pure time discount *factor* enters. By convention, the first period's pure time discount factor is set equal to 1. ((2.3) achieves this by multiplying initial-period well-being by $\frac{1}{(1+\delta)^0}$, which equals 1.) Well-being in the next period (period 1) is then multiplied by the discount factor $\frac{1}{(1+\delta)^1}$, which equals 0.97 if $\delta = 0.03$. So units of well-being in period 1 are given only 97 percent the weight they *would have* been given if they had been enjoyed in period 0 instead. Likewise, units of well-being in period 2 are treated as worth only 94 percent as much as period 0 well-being, and units of well-being in period 24 are treated as worth less than half of what exactly similar units are worth in period 0. Increase the pure time discount rate to 0.05, and it would take just over 14 periods for a unit of well-being to have half the value as its period 0 counterpart. Such is the profound impact of pure time discounting.

It turns out that if the pure time discount rate is large enough (and if consumption growth is not exponential), then discounted utilitarian sums expressed by the social welfare function (2.3) will converge to finite values. This enables a meaningful comparison of all paths' social welfare scores, and is a reason why some climate economists endorse a positive pure time discount rate. Still, many of these economists believe that its value should be as low as possible, to avoid significantly discriminating against the well-being of future generations. I will discuss in chapter 5 whether pure time discount rates should be positive, and what the answer to this question implies for social cost of carbon computations and for how they should influence climate policy. For now, note that one's choice of pure time discount rate—sometimes also called the *well-being discount rate*—can be a major determinant of how a given social welfare function ranks consumption paths. Change the pure time discount rate, and you change both the social welfare function itself and the ranking it yields.[4]

2.2 Two Crucial Background Assumptions

To play this role in aggregating well-being across individuals, (2.3)'s well-being function, w, must exhibit two important properties. First, w must make it legitimate to talk meaningfully about the relative magnitudes of changes in well-being. This is possible when w represents individual well-being *cardinally*: if w_i is a cardinal well-being function for an individual i, then when $w_i(c_a) - w_i(c_b) = w_i(c_c) - w_i(c_d)$, it follows that the change in well-being the individual experiences in moving from consumption level c_a to c_b is equal to the change she would experience in moving from c_c to c_d.

A well-being function w_i is cardinal if it is *unique up to a positive affine transformation*. This means that w_i is actually a member of a family of well-being functions, each of which represents individual i's well-being ordering equally well. The family is comprised of functions that can be constructed out of w_i by applying to it a transformation of the form

---

[4] Strictly speaking, an SWF *represents* a ranking, in the sense that it assigns a number to each argument (e.g., each consumption path) such that the number it assigns to one argument is larger than the number it assigns to a second argument just in case the first argument comes higher in the ranking than the second. On this more accurate definition, the ranking is logically prior to the function that represents it. But for our purposes it is useful to talk as if the function itself *generates* the ranking. See Broome (1992, p. 51n37).

$aw_i + b$, for any positive number a and any number b. If a well-being function f_i can be arrived at in this way from w_i—that is, if $f_i = aw_i + b$—then both functions belong to the family of well-being functions that all equally well represent an ordering of consumption bundles in terms of their capacity to benefit i. Moreover, it will be true that the *ratios of differences* between well-being levels will not change when w_i is replaced by f_i. This is the feature of cardinal well-being functions that licenses meaningful talk of the relative magnitude of well-being changes. For example, if f_i is a positive affine transformation of w_i, then the following will be true for any selection of consumption levels c_w, c_x, c_y, and c_z:

$$\frac{w_i(c_w) - w_i(c_x)}{w_i(c_y) - w_i(c_z)} = \frac{f_i(c_w) - f_i(c_x)}{f_i(c_y) - f_i(c_z)} \tag{2.4}$$

Strictly speaking, "i's cardinal well-being function" refers to the whole family of functions, each of which is a positive affine transformation of the others. By convention it is standard to refer to this family by referring to one of its members, and then by noting that this single function is *unique up to a positive affine transformation* (Kreps 1988, p. 46).[5]

Cardinality is one property that (2.3)'s well-being function must exhibit if it is to facilitate the ranking of consumption paths by first converting each consumption path into an intertemporal path of well-being. In addition to this, it must also be possible to make comparisons of well-being *across* people. Specifically, each individual's well-being function must be at least *unit comparable* with the others'. What is distinctive about this form of interpersonal comparability is that it does not require the ability to compare well-being *levels* across individuals. All that is required is the ability to make interpersonal comparisons of the *differences* in well-being of the sort I just mentioned in the context of a single individual who moves from consumption level c_w to c_x, or from c_y to c_z.

To illustrate, suppose that both Ann's and Bob's well-being is cardinally measurable, and that w_A and w_B are members of their respective families of cardinal well-being functions. Furthermore, suppose that w_A and w_B are

---

[5] Sometimes the phrase used is "unique up to a positive *linear* transformation," as for example in Sen (2017, p. 93) and Broome (1991, p. 71).

unit comparable but not level comparable. So we cannot say that Ann and Bob enjoy the same level of well-being when they each enjoy consumption level c_x. This is true *even if* $w_A(c_x) = w_B(c_x)$. Different individuals' well-being levels simply cannot be compared meaningfully when the only sort of interpersonal comparability is unit comparability. Yet unit comparability does allow one to determine whether *as much* well-being would be generated if one gave a certain extra amount of consumption, Δ_c, to one person rather than to another. For instance, if w_A and w_B are cardinal and unit comparable well-being functions, we could determine this by asking whether the following is true:

$$w_A(c_A + \Delta_c) - w_A(c_A) \geq w_B(c_B + \Delta_c) - w_B(c_B)$$

where c_A and c_B are Ann's and Bob's respective status quo consumption levels.

It might be hard to imagine a scenario in which we feel confident we have unit comparable well-being functions that do not also permit comparisons of levels. Even so, only unit comparability is required by (discounted) utilitarian approaches to ranking consumption paths. To see why, suppose we had a set of cardinal and unit comparable lifetime well-being functions for a group of people indexed by $1, 2, 3, \ldots, N$. Now use these functions to translate two different consumption paths into corresponding interpersonal vectors of lifetime well-being, $(w_1, w_2, w_3, \ldots, w_N)$ and $(w'_1, w'_2, w'_3, \ldots, w'_N)$. In a non-discounted utilitarian SWF framework, one can determine the relative ranking of these two paths by asking whether the following is true:

$$\sum_{i=1}^{N} w_i \geq \sum_{i=1}^{N} w'_i \qquad (2.5)$$

Now note that (2.5) may be rewritten as follows:

$$\sum_{i=1}^{N} w_i - w'_i \geq 0 \qquad (2.6)$$

One can see from this second formulation that since the individual-specific well-being *levels* get subtracted out, they are irrelevant in the utilitarian approach to ranking vectors of well-being (Weymark 2016, pp. 141–142).

All that matters are the *differences* between the levels that appear in the formulae.

The same is true of discounted utilitarianism. Like a utilitarian SWF, discounted utilitarian SWFs rank vectors of well-being against one another by first computing the differences in well-being that they exhibit at each time. These time-specific differences are then discounted to account for their placement in time, and then the evaluation sums over times. There is no need in this procedure to compare well-being levels across individuals. But the ability to compare units across people is essential: discounted utilitarian SWFs entail that a one-unit increase in an individual's well-being today is more valuable than a *same-sized* increment in a *different* person's well-being next year.

So the (discounted) utilitarian SWF methodology requires cardinal and interpersonally unit comparable well-being functions. An implication is that if we begin with a set of such functions, and if we wish to rank paths using a (discounted) utilitarian social welfare function, then if we apply a positive affine transformation to any one of these well-being functions, we must apply one to the others as well. Since we must preserve unit comparability, the only allowable transformations will be of the form $aw_i + b_i$, with a positive and the same for all individuals, but where the b_i values may vary across individuals (since the b_i constants affect levels and levels are irrelevant).

The discounted utilitarian SWF given by (2.3) presupposes that all individuals' well-being orderings can be represented by the same family of cardinal and unit comparable well-being functions, one member of which is w.

2.3 The SCC in the Social Choice Framework

We can now define the SCC in the social choice approach to climate economics. SCC figures are always defined relative to a given consumption path and a specific time along that path. This is one reason why there is no such thing as "the" SCC: there is an SCC for every time period along every feasible consumption path. I shall state the definition in formal terms, and then walk through what it means. Here is the formal definition:

$$SCC_{t,C} = \frac{\Delta V/\Delta e_t}{\Delta V/\Delta c_t}\bigg|_C \qquad (2.7)$$

In words, the SCC at time t along path C is equal to the ratio of the change in the social welfare function's value caused by the emission at t of an extra ton of CO_2—this is the numerator of (2.7)—to the change in the social welfare function's value caused by a one-unit change in consumption in time period t—this is (2.7)'s denominator. The vertical bar and letter to the right of the fraction convey that the computations embedded in the fraction must be performed using the values that pertain to the designated intertemporal consumption path—in this case the arbitrary path I have labeled C.

To illustrate, suppose that (2.7)'s V function is the discounted utilitarian social welfare function (2.3). Then, (2.7) tells us to compute the $SCC_{t,C}$ in the following way. First, find the score that V assigns to path C. Next, determine which consumption path would result if the circumstances underlying C changed in only the following respect: there is one extra ton of carbon dioxide emitted in the first period. Call this the *emissions-perturbed path*, or PER_e. This is the path that includes all of the climate damages that would be engendered by the emission of that extra ton of CO_2. Next, compute the score that V assigns to PER_e. Find now the difference in the two scores you have calculated. This difference is the $\Delta V / \Delta e_t$ part of (2.7): it is the change in V's value engendered by a one-unit change in period t emissions. Next, perform a parallel calculation in which, instead of imagining that an extra ton of CO_2 is emitted at t, we imagine that an extra unit of consumption is taken away at t. Call this slightly different path the *consumption-perturbed path*, or PER_c. Find now the score that V assigns to PER_c, and compute the difference between $V(C)$ and $V(PER_c)$. This difference is the $\Delta V/\Delta c_t$ part of (2.7): it is the change in V's value engendered by the loss of one unit of consumption. Then, (2.7) is equivalent to the following formula:

$$SCC_{t,C} = \frac{V(C) - V(PER_e)}{V(C) - V(PER_c)} \qquad (2.8)$$

The social choice SCC is therefore the ratio of the V-based difference made by a marginal unit of present emissions to the difference made by a marginal unit of present consumption. It expresses the marginal impact that present CO_2 emissions make on social welfare, and it denominates that impact in terms of the marginal impact that present consumption makes.

This computation tells us how bad the effects of marginal emissions are, and it expresses that degree of badness in terms of the loss in present consumption it is equivalent to—as judged by V and its underlying ranking of consumption paths. This SCC figure can then be used to determine whether a mitigation project today would move the world onto a higher-ranked path: if the marginal cost of CO_2 abatement is higher than today's SCC, then in paying for abatement, one moves the world onto a path that is ranked lower than the prevailing baseline path. But if the cost of abatement is below today's SCC, then in paying for that abatement one moves the world onto a path that V ranks higher than the baseline path. In this way the social choice SCC is a key ingredient in climate change–related cost-benefit analysis.

2.4 An Alternative (but Equivalent) SCC Formula

There is a second method for calculating the SCC that employs *consumption discount factors*. Recall that pure time discount factors are constructed using a pure time discount rate. Future increments of well-being are then multiplied by a set of pure time discount factors to convert those units of well-being into their "present value well-being-equivalents." Consumption discount factors are likewise constructed using *consumption discount rates*; the consumption discount factors are then multiplied by changes in future consumption to convert those changes into their present value consumption-equivalents. This offers a sort of shortcut: instead of using a social welfare function to perform the threefold conversion described in section 2.3—that is, converting future climate damages into changes in future well-being, changes in future well-being into their present well-being-equivalents, and then these present well-being-equivalents into their present consumption-equivalents—the alternative method constructs consumption discount factors that perform these conversions in just one step.[6]

Like pure time discount rates, consumption discount rates are rank-preserving rates of return.[7] For any time t along a given consumption path C,

---

[6] The two methods are equivalent in the context of Ramsey's simplifying assumptions. If we relax some of those assumptions, we must use section 2.3's method instead.

[7] It is to consumption discount rates that economists typically refer when they use the term "social discount rates."

the consumption discount rate ρ_t gives the rate of return on a *consumption* investment required for the underlying social welfare function to give C the same ranking it gives to an alternative path, C', that is identical to C except for involving one fewer dollar of consumption at t (this is the "investment") and somewhat higher consumption at $t+1$ (this is the "return"). Suppose the consumption discount rate at t along C is $\rho_t = 0.03$. Then C and C' are level in the underlying social welfare function's ranking if and only if C' is identical to C except for involving one fewer dollar of consumption at t and $1.03 more in consumption at $t+1$. Moreover, as with pure time discount rates, we can use each period's consumption discount rate to construct a consumption discount factor, $\frac{1}{1+\rho_t}$, which, when multiplied by changes in consumption in time $t+1$, converts those changes into their time t consumption-equivalents. Thus assuming once again that $\rho_t = 0.03$, it follows that the underlying social welfare function treats a consumption increase of $1 at $t+1$ as equivalent to a consumption increase at t of 97 cents.

Why would a dollar of consumption at $t+1$ be worth less than a dollar of consumption at t? The answer must come from the social welfare function that underlies the derivation of consumption discount rates. Assuming an SWF of the form expressed by equation (2.3), we know that the future well-being arising from future consumption is already discounted by the positive pure time discount rate denoted by δ. So that is one reason this SWF treats future consumption as less valuable than present consumption.

Furthermore, a standard tenet of classical utilitarianism is that the amount of well-being one derives from the consumption of the same goods and services declines as one becomes richer in consumption. Most of us are well-acquainted with this phenomenon of *declining marginal well-being*; for example, while we take pleasure in a second glass of iced tea on a hot day, the amount of pleasure so derived is usually less than the amount derived from the very first glass. Thus the increase in well-being one experiences from an increase in consumption becomes smaller and smaller as one consumes more and more.

It is standard in social choice climate economics to incorporate the declining marginal benefit of consumption into a social welfare function by adopting a *strictly concave* well-being function. A well-being function with this property is depicted visually by the curved line in figure 2.1.

22 THE SOCIAL COST OF CARBON

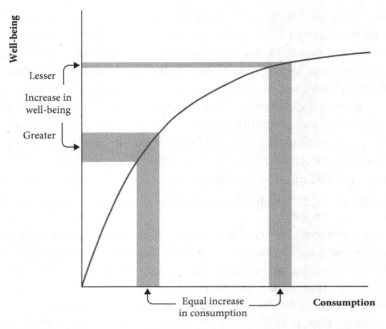

Figure 2.1 A strictly concave well-being function. Adapted from Kolstad et al. 2014, p. 223.

When a well-being function is strictly concave, the marginal well-being of consumption declines as the consumer becomes richer and richer, so that equal incremental increases in consumption generate less and less well-being as one's consumption level rises.

Social choice climate change economists often use the following mathematically convenient *isoelastic* well-being function:

$$w = \frac{c_t^{1-\eta}}{1-\eta} \tag{2.9}$$

In this well-being function, η is the *elasticity of the marginal well-being of consumption*.[8] When $\eta = 0$, increasing a poor person's consumption by one

---

[8] Strictly speaking, it is the *absolute value* of the elasticity of the marginal well-being of consumption.

dollar creates the same increase in well-being as does increasing a rich person's consumption by one dollar. In that case, the *w* function is *linear* rather than strictly concave, and the resulting well-being function fails to reflect the declining marginal well-being of consumption. When $\eta = 1$, the *w* function is strictly concave and *logarithmic*, which implies that equal *proportional* increases in consumption generate equal increases in well-being.[9] For example, increasing a poor person's consumption by 10 percent will yield the same increase in well-being as increasing a rich person's consumption by 10 percent, even though the *absolute* increase in consumption is much greater for the rich person. Thus as η gets larger and larger, people become less and less efficient at converting consumption into well-being as they become richer and richer. Higher values of η therefore give higher priority to improvements in the consumption of a poor person over that of a rich person. If per capita consumption levels are expected to grow steadily over time, that would be another reason why equivalent changes in consumption may be deemed less valuable when enjoyed in the future versus the present.

When one's social welfare function takes the form of equation (2.3), there is a formula for deriving a consumption discount rate for every time period along any given consumption path. These rates, which are sometimes called *Ramsey discount rates*, reflect the pure time discounting of future well-being (represented by a positive δ in (2.3)) and the declining marginal well-being of consumption (represented by a positive η in what I shall assume is (2.3)'s isoelastic *w* function). They are called Ramsey discount rates because they are computed using mathematical techniques that Ramsey introduced into the economics literature. Here is the standard formula, which I shall call the *Ramsey formula*:

$$\rho_t = \delta + \eta \cdot g_t \qquad (2.10)$$

Here ρ_t is the consumption discount rate for *t* along whichever consumption path one is investigating. In line with the definition given earlier, ρ_t is the rank-preserving rate of return on an investment made in period *t* and paying a return in period $t+1$. The parameters δ and η come straight from the social welfare function (2.3) in the manner described just above, and g_t is the rate

---

[9] That this well-being function is logarithmic is a consequence of L'Hôpital's rule in the context in which η approaches 1.

of per capita consumption growth from t to $t+1$ along the relevant consumption path. This rate of growth is essential for deriving rank-preserving rates of return on consumption investments, because one needs to know whether an investment's return would be consumed by people whose consumption level is below, equal to, or greater than the level of those who would be called upon to finance the investment.

With such discount rates in hand, one can construct the consumption discount factors needed to express marginal changes in consumption in any period in terms of the change in any other period's consumption that it is equivalent to—equivalent, that is, as judged by the social welfare function.[10] This gives us a new way to construct the social cost of carbon.

To explain, suppose the time path of consumption discount rates along an arbitrary consumption path C is $(\rho_0, \rho_1, ..., \rho_\tau, ...)$. Since the discount rate for time t determines the discount factor to be applied to consumption changes at time $t+1$, the time path of consumption discount rates can be used to construct a corresponding series of consumption discount factors, $(\beta_1, \beta_2, ..., \beta_\tau, ...)$:

$$\beta_1 = \frac{1}{1+\rho_0}$$

$$\beta_2 = \frac{1}{1+\rho_1}$$

$$\vdots$$

$$\beta_\tau = \frac{1}{1+\rho_{\tau-1}}$$

$$\vdots$$

Note that each of these discount factors can be used only to translate one period's consumption changes into its immediately prior period's equivalent consumption changes. Thus to translate one period's consumption changes into the equivalent changes in a time period that is not just prior to it, one must multiply several discount factors together. To see how this works, suppose an extra ton of CO_2 is emitted along path C at time $t = 0$ and that this causes consumption damages at some future time τ of quantity Δ_τ. To express these consumption losses in terms of the loss in period 0 consumption

---

[10] Crucially, this is so only if the changes in consumption are genuinely marginal in the technical sense explicated by Dietz and Hepburn (2013).

it is equivalent to, we use the time path of consumption discount factors to translate consumption damages at time τ into their equivalents in the previous period, $\tau-1$, and so on back to time 0:

$$\Delta_\tau \cdot \left(\beta_\tau \cdot \beta_{\tau-1} \cdot \ldots \cdot \beta_1\right)$$

This is equivalent to:

$$\Delta_\tau \cdot \left(\prod_{j=0}^{\tau-1} \frac{1}{(1+\rho_j)}\right)$$

This formula multiplies period τ's damages by the product of a series of discount factors, beginning with the discount factor constructed using period 0's consumption discount rate, ρ_0, and ending with the discount factor constructed using the consumption discount rate associated with the period immediately preceding period τ, period $\tau-1$.

The general formula for the social choice SCC at any arbitrary time t along a given path C is regrettably cumbersome, but it is only an application of the weighted aggregation procedure I have just described. The SCC at t along C is the sum of every future year's weighted consumption damages, with each weight's being the product of the appropriate sequence of consumption discount factors:

$$SCC_{t,C} = \sum_{i=1}^{\infty} \Delta_{t+i} \cdot \left(\prod_{j=0}^{(t+i)-t-1} \frac{1}{(1+\rho_{t+j})}\right) \qquad (2.11)$$

So long as the consumption discount rates in (2.11) are derived from the same underlying SWF, V, this formula will be mathematically equivalent to (2.7) and (2.8).

2.5 Incorporating Intratemporal Consumption Inequality

I have noted that one of the simplifying assumptions behind Ramsey's original analysis is that there is no intra-temporal consumption inequality. This assumption is implicit in the social welfare functions discussed in section 2.1. Because of time constraints, the *Stern Review* team also abstracted from intra-temporal inequality by attending only to *global* per capita consumption levels, rather than to more fine-grained consumption data (such as regional per capita levels) (Yale Center for the Study of Globalization 2007, p. 16).

One could incorporate intra-temporal inequality across regions using the following social welfare function instead of those used in section 2.1:

$$V = \sum_{r}\sum_{t=0}^{\infty} N_t^r \cdot w(c_t^r) \cdot \frac{1}{(1+\delta)^t}, \quad \delta \geq 0 \qquad (2.12)$$

This social welfare function still abstracts away from intra-temporal inequality *within* regions, by assuming that everyone within any region r at a given time t has the same consumption level c_t^r. But it allows for consumption levels to differ at the same time *across* regions. One could then use this informationally richer social welfare function to derive social choice SCC figures using suitably adjusted versions of equations (2.7) and (2.8). The adjustment is required because, while climate science says that a ton of CO_2 will have the same *effects* regardless of where it is emitted, this is clearly not true of marginal reductions in consumption: owing to the diminishing marginal well-being discussed in section 2.4, more well-being is lost if per capita consumption is reduced in China by $1 than if it is reduced by that same amount in the United States. We therefore need to adjust equations (2.7) and (2.8) so that it is explicit which region will sustain the small change in consumption referenced in their respective denominators:

$$SCC_{t,C}^R = \left.\frac{\Delta V/\Delta e_t}{\Delta V/\Delta c_t^R}\right|_C \qquad (2.13)$$

$$SCC_{t,C}^R = \frac{V(C)-V(PER_e)}{V(C)-V(PER_c^R)} \qquad (2.14)$$

When it is normalized to a specific region R in this way, the resulting SCC is the value to be used in a social choice cost-benefit analysis of a mitigation project that will be financed by reducing current consumption in that region.

Recall that consumption discount factors were introduced to provide a shortcut around having to run three distinct consumption paths through the underlying social welfare function, as is required by (2.13) and (2.14). As I explained in section 2.4, one can begin instead with a projection of CO_2-induced marginal changes in consumption and then weight and aggregate these using an appropriate sequence of consumption discount factors. The consumption discount rates that featured in these discount factors were derived from the underlying social welfare function (2.3) and an empirical projection of the baseline consumption path. A similar shortcut is available when the analysis incorporates intra-temporal regional inequalities in consumption, as it will when the underlying SWF is (2.12). When we were using the inequality-insensitive SWF (2.3), the formula for the SCC was equation (2.11). That formula weights future consumption damages by an appropriate sequence of consumption discount factors, which in turn feature Ramsey discount rates (i.e., the ρ_{t+j} terms in (2.11)). When we move to the inequality-sensitive SWF (2.12), the SCC formula must be tailored for the specific region that will pay the abatement costs. This is again because the question is whether the total international and intertemporal benefits of abatement are greater than the costs that would be borne by whoever would pay the abatement costs today. Fankhauser et al. (1997, pp. 256–257) and Tol (2019, pp. 175–176) derive the required formula:[11]

$$SCC_{t,C}^{R} = \sum_{r} \left(\frac{c_t^R}{c_t^r}\right)^{\eta} \sum_{i=1}^{\infty} \Delta_{t+i}^{r} \cdot \left(\prod_{j=0}^{(t+i)-t-1} \frac{1}{(1+\rho_{t+j}^{r})} \right) \qquad (2.15)$$

Observe that the computations governed by the second summation symbol in equation (2.15) reproduce the SCC formula for a context without consumption inequality, given by (2.11). This is because the relevant summations are region-specific aggregations of within-region damages, and we are still supposing that there is no intra-temporal consumption inequality within regions. Each of these region-specific aggregations is performed using region-specific sequences of Ramsey discount rates, given by the ρ_{t+j}^{r} terms,

---

[11] I have amended their formula to make it consistent with the notation I have used to express equation (2.11).

and the aggregations give the period t loss in region-specific consumption that would have the same impact on the SWF as all of the climate damages that will be suffered in that region. Next, because we are assuming that consumption levels differ across regions, these region-specific SCC values must be weighted once more to reflect regional differences in the marginal well-being of period t consumption. This is the job of the weights expressed by $\left(c_t^R/c_t^r\right)^\eta$ in (2.15). These weights do two things simultaneously: first, they take account of the regional differences in the marginal well-being of period t consumption; second, they normalize the resulting global SCC values to whichever reference region will subsequently use the global SCC figure in its cost-benefit analyses of mitigation projects. Thus in the weights, c_t^R is a constant given by per capita consumption in the reference region R, and r is a variable ranging over all regions such that c_t^r is per capita consumption in region r. If, for example, the reference region is rich, then the weight given to its region-specific SCC is 1, whereas the weight given to a poor region q's SCC will be greater than 1, since the fraction $\left(c_t^R/c_t^q\right)$ will be greater than 1, and this quotient is then raised to the power of η, which is positive if the well-being function (2.9) exhibits declining marginal well-being of consumption (as it always does in social choice climate economics).

Economists sometimes call these region-specific weights *equity weights* (Fankhauser et al. 1997; Tol 2019). A moral philosopher would not have used that term, since the weights' job is merely to account for differences in the *well-being impacts* of consumption, rather than anything philosophers would associate with the concepts of fairness, equity, or justice.[12] "Welfare weights" is a superior term that is used in some studies (e.g., in Stern 1977), and it is the term I will use.

An SCC value computed using equation (2.15) will be equivalent to an SCC produced using equations (2.13) and (2.14), so long as the same reference region is employed in each calculation. Each of these gives a formula for an SCC that can be used in a social choice cost-benefit analysis to determine whether a greenhouse gas mitigation project that is financed out of consumption in the reference region will move the world onto a consumption path that the social welfare function (2.12) ranks higher than the prevailing

---

[12] Adler and Posner (2006, p. 157) make this same point in response to another common term for equity weights, namely "distributive weights." The Intergovernmental Panel on Climate Change (IPCC) used "distributional weights" when it wrote, "Ethical theories based on social welfare functions imply that distributional weights, which take account of the different value of money to different people, should be applied to monetary measures of benefits and harms" (IPCC 2014, p. 5).

baseline path.[13] I shall refer to social choice SCC figures that pertain to the prevailing, real-world baseline path as *social choice baseline SCCs*, or *SC-BASE SCCs* for short.

2.6 The Relevance of Financing

One way to pay for reductions in greenhouse gas emissions is to decrease current consumption to free up funds for mitigation. My description of social choice cost-benefit analysis has assumed this method of paying for mitigation. But another way is to reduce the amount that is currently devoted to more traditional investments, and then to divert those funds into climatic investments. This would have no impact on current consumption, since current investment finances future consumption, not present consumption. So if one chose to pay for the mitigation of one ton of CO_2 by reducing the current portfolio of non-climatic investments, a cost-benefit analysis of this project should not compare the cost of present mitigation with the social choice SCC. Instead, it should compare the SCC with the present value of the future consumption that would be forgone if funds were diverted from the baseline investment portfolio into mitigation. And to work out this present value, one must discount those forgone benefits using the very same baseline time path of consumption discount rates that one uses to construct the SCC itself (Dasgupta et al. 1972, ch. 14; Lind 1982, pp. 39–55).

Here is an example (which reinstates the assumption of perfect intratemporal equality, thereby omitting the need for welfare weights). Suppose a public CO_2 mitigation project today would offer benefits in each of the next two time periods, valued at $100 per period. And suppose the consumption discount rate is a constant 3 percent. Then the present value of the benefits created by the project are:

$$\frac{\$100}{1.03^1} + \frac{\$100}{1.03^2} = \$191.35$$

---

[13] Using the FUND IAM and setting $\eta = 1$ (so that the well-being function is logarithmic), Errickson et al. (2021, p. 569) calculated the expected social choice social cost of methane as US$8,290 when the United States is the reference region, and US$134 when the normalization is instead done with respect to per capita consumption in sub-Saharan Africa. Since sub-Saharan Africa is so much poorer than the U.S., the *same* amount of global, intertemporal harm done by a ton of methane is equivalent to the well-being loss associated with a relatively small consumption loss in sub-Saharan Africa and a relatively large consumption loss in the U.S.

If the mitigation project is financed out of present consumption, and if its present cost is $185, then the project will pass a social choice cost-benefit test: undertaking it would move the world onto a consumption path that the underlying SWF ranks higher than the status quo path.

But now imagine that instead of being financed out of present consumption, the project will be financed by canceling an existing non-climatic investment that has a rate of return of 6 percent per period. Thus if the non-climatic investment were *not* diverted, the prospective $185 in CO_2 mitigation costs would be able to finance $185 \cdot 1.06^2 = \$207.87$ worth of consumption two years from now. To know whether this investment-financed project passes a similar social choice cost-benefit test, we must discount that $207.87 by the consumption discount factor $\frac{1}{1.03^2}$, which yields a present value of $195.94. This cost—the present value of the consumption forgone if the mitigation project is financed by diverting funds from non-climatic investments—is larger than the present value of the project's consumption benefits. So the project passes a cost-benefit test if it is financed by reducing present consumption by $185, but not if it displaces $185 in preexisting non-climatic investments.[14]

This example is highly stylized. Importantly, it assumes that the impact of the non-climatic investment is fully reflected in its 6 percent rate of return. Suppose we adjust the example so that in addition to providing $207.87 in consumption benefits two periods from today, the industry offering the investment opportunity *also* emits CO_2 as a byproduct of its activities. And suppose this CO_2 would create climate damages equal to $2 per year for eight straight years beginning thirty years in the future. In that case, instead of displacing $195.94 in discounted consumption benefits, diverting $185 in non-climatic investments into the CO_2 mitigation project would actually displace just $189.98 in discounted consumption benefits (assuming, again,

---

[14] Note that this example implicitly assumes a status quo in which the ongoing non-climatic investment finances consumption two periods from now, rather than consumption in *each* of the next two periods. Suppose, by contrast, that if $185 were not diverted from the non-climate investment, 90 percent of its return would be consumed in the next period, with the remainder reinvested to finance consumption the period after that. That works out to $176.49 in consumption in the next period and $20.79 in the following period. Discounted once again at the hypothetical constant discount rate of 3 percent, this yields a present value of $190.94. Since that is less than the $191.35 in discounted benefits created by the mitigation project, this project passes a social choice cost-benefit test when the non-climatic investment it displaces involves this specific blend of consumption and reinvestment in future time periods. This again shows the importance of attending to how a proposed mitigation project will be financed. See Broome (1992, pp. 80–81) for more on this point.

a constant 3 percent consumption discount rate). And this is less than the $191.35 in benefits created by the mitigation project:

$$\frac{\$207.87}{1.03^2} - \frac{\$2}{1.03^{30}} - \frac{\$2}{1.03^{31}} - \frac{\$2}{1.03^{32}} - \frac{\$2}{1.03^{33}} - \frac{\$2}{1.03^{34}} - \frac{\$2}{1.03^{35}}$$
$$- \frac{\$2}{1.03^{36}} - \frac{\$2}{1.03^{37}} = \$189.98$$

This second example shows that while it is important to attend to how a mitigation project will be financed, it is equally important to attend to the external costs of non-climatic investments (Broome 1992, p. 91). Because the social choice framework is first and foremost concerned to rank consumption paths, cost-benefit analyses within this framework must convert all effects—direct and indirect—into consumption effects and then discount them using the appropriate consumption discount rates.[15]

2.7 Optimal Social Choice SCCs

When an SCC value is computed along the feasible consumption path that is ranked highest by a social choice social welfare function, I shall call it an *optimal social choice SCC* (or *SC-OPT SCC* for short). Adopting the formalism from section 2.3, and abstracting from regional inequalities, we can express SC-OPT SCCs in these two equivalent ways:

$$SCC_{t,OPT} = \left.\frac{\Delta V / \Delta e_t}{\Delta V / \Delta c_t}\right|_{OPT}$$

$$SCC_{t,OPT} = \frac{V(OPT) - V(PER_e)}{V(OPT) - V(PER_c)}$$

with PER_e and PER_c referring to consumption paths that are identical to the optimal path, except for including the effects of an extra unit of carbon dioxide and the loss of one dollar of period t consumption, respectively.

---

[15] This undercuts a common "opportunity cost"-based argument for discounting future consumption using prevailing interest rates. See Kelleher (2017a, pp. 962–964).

The social choice SCC for each time period along the top-ranked consumption path will equal the marginal costs of abating a unit of carbon dioxide in the corresponding time period along that same top-ranked path. The reason is simple: if that path really is the top-ranked path, then it cannot be possible to move the world onto a higher ranked path by adjusting the level of abatement in any time period; but if the SCC differs in any time period from that period's marginal cost of abatement, it would be possible to move to a higher-ranked path by adjusting the level of abatement—adjusting it up if the SCC is greater than the marginal abatement cost, and adjusting it down if the SCC is less than the marginal abatement cost. The optimal set of SCC values therefore gives us the optimal set of abatement costs, which in turn indicate the period-specific abatement efforts required to place the world onto the top-ranked path.

A similar line of reasoning leads to a proposition known as the *Ramsey rule*. This says that along the top-ranked path, each time period's consumption discount rate equals that period's rate of return on investment. The reasoning underlying this proposition is again intuitive, especially when we recall that consumption discount rates are rank-preserving rates of return. Call the top-ranked path C^*. If period t's consumption discount rate along C^* is ρ_t^*, this tells us that any period t investment whose return in $t+1$ is greater than ρ_t^* is an investment that would move the world onto a higher-ranked consumption path (assuming the investment imposes no external costs). If the corresponding interest rate were greater than ρ_t^*, that would tell us that C^* is not in fact the top-ranked path, for we would be able to climb to a higher-ranked path by undertaking an investment whose rate of return is greater than the rank-preserving rate of return, ρ_t^*. Nor can the relevant interest rate be lower than ρ_t^*; if it were, we could climb to a still higher-ranked path by *dis*investing a small amount. This would increase consumption in period t and decrease consumption in period $t+1$, which would lower g_t and thus the consumption discount rate (according to formula (2.10)). Disinvestment of this sort would then continue to move the world onto a higher-ranked path right up until the consumption discount rate for period t declined to equal the corresponding rate of return on investment. Hence the Ramsey rule, with r_t denoting the marginal rate of return in period $t+1$ of an investment made in period t:

$$r_t = \delta + \eta \cdot g_t \qquad (2.16)$$

One consequence of the Ramsey rule and the line of reasoning underlying it is that the optimal social choice social cost of carbon can be computed by discounting consumption damages using the time path of real interest rates that pertains to the top-ranked consumption path. But in the social choice framework, this connection between consumption discount rates and interest rates holds only along the top-ranked path. As we have seen, a time path of SCC values can be computed for any arbitrary consumption path, and when computing SCC values along a non-optimal path—for example, when computing SCCs along the real-world baseline path—it is equation (2.10) that must be used, not equation (2.16) (Dasgupta 2008, pp. 153–154). In other words, the path of consumption discount rates that corresponds to a given non-optimal consumption path has *no necessary conceptual connection whatsoever* to the path of rates of return on investment that corresponds to that consumption path.

* * *

The social choice framework is concerned to rank feasible consumption paths. The leading approach to this task in the climate economics literature adopts a discounted utilitarian social welfare function, and we have seen how two SCC concepts arise within this framework: the baseline social choice SCC (SC-BASE SCC) is an ingredient in project-level cost-benefit analysis, while the optimal social choice SCC (SC-OPT SCC) is an indicator of the level of greenhouse gas abatement required to place the world onto the consumption path ranked highest by the underlying social welfare function.

Owing to the very structure of policy optimization IAMs, it is common for both their architects and those who use or study them to interpret them in this way—that is to say, as applied tools for doing social choice theory. For example, in his book *A Question of Balance*, climate economist William Nordhaus stresses the need to construct a framework for "weighing alternative options for dealing with climate change" and for finding "the appropriate balance between costly emissions reductions and climate damages" (Nordhaus 2008, pp. 4, 36). Nordhaus helped to pioneer the field of climate change economics and the use within it of policy optimization IAMs. And one would be forgiven for concluding that Nordhaus's work falls squarely within the social choice framework, for he structures his policy optimization IAMs around what he explicitly calls a social welfare function, which (he says) "ranks different paths of consumption" (Nordhaus 2008, p. 33). His models are then used, he says, to identify "an idealized policy that we label the 'optimal' economic response [to climate change]" (Nordhaus 2008, p. 14).

Elsewhere, however, Nordhaus paints a very different picture of the fundamental aims of his efforts in climate economics. For example, he distinguishes between *positive* and *normative* policy optimization IAMs, associating the latter with the aims of social choice theory. In contrast, he says that positive optimization models are to be used as "descriptive" tools for "simulating... the behavior of a system of interacting competitive markets" and for "estimating the equilibrium of a market economy" (Nordhaus 2013, pp. 1110–1111):

> As such, [optimization] does not necessarily have a normative interpretation. Rather, the maximization [of an objective function] is an algorithm for finding the outcome of efficient competitive markets. (Nordhaus 2013, p. 1111)

Unfortunately, Nordhaus does not say much more about how, exactly, policy optimization models are to be used for these "descriptive" or "positive" purposes. And his willingness to draw policy recommendations from the results of his modeling reasonably leads readers to conclude that, despite his claims to the contrary, his models are normative social choice models. For example, when Nordhaus insists that philosophical considerations are "irrelevant" to the calibration of parameters in a policy optimization model's objective function (Nordhaus 2007, p. 692), moral philosopher John Broome infers that Nordhaus must be adhering to a flawed "democratic" conception of ethics on which the values to be embedded in optimization models "should be derived from the preferences people reveal in the market" when they make choices to buy, sell, consume, and invest (Broome 2012, p. 11).[16] Undoubtedly, some climate change economists endorse this ethical stance, and it accounts for why they wish to calibrate a social choice optimization model by reference to empirical facts about how people actually choose in the real world.[17] But I am not sure this is the correct interpretation of Nordhaus. Indeed, I doubt that it is. Yet rather than pursue this exegetical question, I shall turn next to the theoretical foundations of the "market-simulating" brand of optimization to which Nordhaus refers in the block quotation above. We shall see that this brand of optimization leads to two entirely new SCC concepts that are disconnected from the social choice framework's ambition to rank all feasible consumption paths from best to worst.

---

[16] Here Broome is commenting more specifically on the view of the economist Martin Weitzman, but he makes it clear in context that he takes this to be Nordhaus's broad view as well. See also Broome (2008).

[17] For example, this is how I read Anthoff et al. (2009, p. 2).

3
The Social Cost of Carbon in General Equilibrium Climate Economics

3.1 Two Types of Optimization

The branch of economics that provides foundations for the connection between optimization and market simulation is general equilibrium theory. Whereas social choice theory is concerned with normative rankings of outcomes, general equilibrium theory is concerned to study the outcomes that would arise in a market economy satisfying precise assumptions about the economy's agents, its markets for goods and services, and its physical and technological possibilities. As we shall see, this is the theoretical framework that underwrites the so-called Fundamental Theorems of Welfare Economics. While many philosophers associate the term "welfare economics" with social choice theory, and especially with the branch of social choice theory that ranks outcomes by aggregating the well-being of the people who would exist in them, the Fundamental Theorems can be proved without the assumptions about interpersonal comparisons of well-being that are required by a social choice approach to the SCC. To be clear: it is not that general equilibrium theory is inherently hostile to interpersonal comparisons. It is just that none of the results I shall discuss in this chapter *depends* upon the ability to make them.

3.2 Pareto Efficiency

Before I turn to the textbook general equilibrium model and relate it to the tools of optimization, I must introduce the single normative property of interest to general equilibrium theory. This is the property of Pareto efficiency. An outcome is *Pareto efficient* if improving the situation of any person would require making someone else worse off. In the general equilibrium framework, whether someone has been made better or worse off is determined on the basis of that person's preferences. Thus suppose there are just two people, A and B, in an outcome, O. And suppose there is just one feasible alternative outcome, O', which A prefers to O but which B disprefers to O. Then O is Pareto efficient, since in O it is impossible to make a change that at least one person prefers to O and that no one disprefers to O. However, if A prefers O' to O, and B is indifferent between the two outcomes, then we say that O is Pareto *inefficient*, and that O' *Pareto dominates* (or is *Pareto superior* to) O.

In the real world, as well as in applied general equilibrium models, there are many more than two possible outcomes. Some outcomes will Pareto dominate many others. Still other outcomes will be Pareto efficient. Different Pareto efficient outcomes will involve different distributions of goods and services among people in the model. The normative criterion of Pareto efficiency is of no use in comparing different efficient outcomes, for neither of two Pareto efficient outcomes is Pareto superior to the other. Instead, they are *Pareto noncomparable*. In order to compare Pareto efficient outcomes, one needs a normative ranking of them. And that is something that the general equilibrium framework (as I am defining it in this chapter) cannot itself supply.

If an analytical framework's only normative property is Pareto efficiency, then it lacks the resources to conclude that any one of the many Pareto efficient outcomes is singularly "optimal," or that it ought to be a focus of public policy. Many economists, however, regrettably use the terms "Pareto efficient" and "Pareto optimal" interchangeably. In this book I shall follow Arrow and Hahn's lead:

> We use the term "Pareto efficient" instead of the more common "Pareto optimal" because the latter term conveys more commendation than the concept should bear, since a Pareto-efficient allocation might ... not be optimal in any sense in which distributional ethics are involved. (Arrow and Hahn 1983, p. 91)

3.3 The Two Welfare Theorems

The simplest general equilibrium models, the ones economics students tend to encounter first, model *exchange economies* in which there is no production. Instead, the only agents are consumers who are endowed with different types and amounts of the economy's goods (apples and oranges, say). These consumers are imagined to engage in mutually beneficial trading until no pair of them can better satisfy their preferences by agreeing to further trades. The outcome of this process is, therefore, Pareto efficient.

The next step is to extend the simple exchange model to include production. In the canonical model involving production, it is still supposed that each consumer begins with a definite endowment of goods (which can include their labor); but the model assumes further that at least some consumers own shares of productive firms, from which they derive income. Consumers are once again interested in obtaining the bundle of goods and services they most prefer out of the set of bundles they can afford given their initial endowment and whatever income they earn from the firms they partially own. We will return to the relevant concept of affordability in a moment.

A further standard assumption in this model with production is that all goods and services in the modeled economy are *private*, in the sense that (1) when a good or service is consumed by one individual, it cannot also be consumed by another; and (2) one person's consumption impacts other people in one way only, namely by precluding others from consuming it, and thereby helping to drive up the price of that type of good.

We are now in a position to state the two Fundamental Theorems of Welfare Economics. Each of these theorems requires some assumptions beyond the ones I have set out in describing the so-called *private ownership economy*. These include physical assumptions concerning each consumer's set of possible consumption bundles, as well as assumptions concerning each consumer's preferences. The assumptions required for the First Fundamental Theorem are quite minimal, while the Second Fundamental Theorem requires stronger assumptions, including ones about the productive side of the economy. Yet since many of these assumptions are rather technical and are in any case universally embedded into climate change policy optimization IAMs, I will not rehearse them here.[1]

Each of the two welfare theorems is a proposition relating the property of Pareto efficiency to the general equilibrium concept of a *competitive equilibrium*. This concept combines two others. A perfectly *competitive* economy is one in which all agents are *price-takers*, that is, an economy in which no agent's behavior on its own can influence market prices. When it comes to consumers, for example, the price-taking assumption entails that there are so many

---

[1] For details, see Varian (1992, ch. 17).

consumers that no single consumer's refusal to pay a prevailing price will induce a seller to lower that price. In the case of producers, it is assumed that there are enough producers of any given commodity that no one of them can adopt monopolistic pricing policies without going bankrupt. For the two theorems to be true, the economy at issue must be such that markets are complete—there are markets for each and every good—and perfectly competitive.[2]

A competitive *equilibrium* is a specific type of outcome from trading within complete and competitive markets. It is defined in terms of (1) an allocation of goods and services among consumers, (2) a production plan for each producer, and (3) a single list (or *vector*) of market prices that is known to all agents in the economy. An outcome is a competitive equilibrium if and only if, in the outcome, each consumer consumes the bundle of goods and services they most prefer out of the set of bundles they can afford at the equilibrium's prices; each firm's production plan maximizes profits at those prices; and the quantities of goods and services that consumers enjoy exactly match the quantities supplied either by consumers who were initially endowed with the goods or by producers who use some goods as inputs in order to produce others as outputs. In short, a competitive equilibrium is an outcome in which consumers maximize preferences (at prevailing prices), producers maximize profits (at prevailing prices), and all consumption and production plans are feasible (in the sense that the goods and services demanded equal the goods and services supplied).

We can now state the two Fundamental Theorems of Welfare Economics, which are true of private ownership economies in which all consumption is private and every good or service is traded in a perfectly competitive market:

First Fundamental Theorem of Welfare Economics: If an outcome is a competitive equilibrium, then it is Pareto efficient.

Second Fundamental Theorem of Welfare Economics: If an outcome is Pareto efficient, then it is also a competitive equilibrium for some initial distribution of endowments.

The First Theorem says that if there is a prevailing price vector and an allocation of goods such that all consumers and producers are doing the best they can given those prices, and if the set of goods that consumers and producers

---

[2] Remember that we are supposing for now that every good is "private" in the sense defined above.

wish to buy at those prices is equal to the set of goods that consumers and producers wish to supply at those prices, then that outcome is Pareto efficient; that is, there is no alternative outcome that some prefer and that no one else disprefers.

The Second Theorem says that from any status quo allocation of goods, any Pareto efficient outcome in the private ownership economy can be achieved as a competitive equilibrium by redistributing consumers' endowments in a suitable way and then letting trade take place in the economy's free, complete, and competitive markets. This theorem is sometimes said to concern equity, since different Pareto efficient outcomes will feature different distributions of consumption among consumers, and since the theorem explains how to achieve any one of these using the market mechanism. And to that extent it does concern equity. But importantly, there is nothing in either theorem that *recommends* any specific Pareto efficient outcome and its particular distribution of goods. For that one needs normative tools and techniques of the sort supplied by the social choice framework discussed in chapter 2.

3.4 Utility Functions

In discussing the aggregation of well-being in the social choice framework, I made reference to "well-being functions." An individual's well-being function is a function that represents a betterness ordering of alternatives, with betterness defined in terms of what is better or worse with respect to the individual's well-being. An individual's *utility function* also represents an ordering of alternatives; but the ordering relevant to a utility function is the individual's *preference* ordering. Economists often assume that there is nothing to well-being beyond the satisfaction of actual preferences, and thus that an individual's well-being function just is her utility function. In moral philosophy, by contrast, it is commonly assumed that a person can prefer something that is, in fact, bad for her. To be sure, the view that well-being is nothing over and above preference satisfaction is definitely one of several conceptions of well-being on offer in the philosophical literature. But in philosophy that conception is very much a minority view.

Debreu (1954) proved that if a preference ordering meets certain technical conditions that I pass over here, then the ordering can be represented by a numerical function. Since I wish to distinguish strongly between a function that faithfully represents preferences and a well-being function that, possibly, represents what economists would call "paternalistic" betterness orderings for individuals, I shall use "utility function" solely for the former purpose.[3]

So let us suppose that each consumer i in our private ownership economy has a preference ordering, denoted by the symbol $\succeq_i$, for which one can construct a utility function, U_i, that represents it. This means that for any two possible outcomes a and b,

$$U_i(a) \geq U_i(b) \quad \text{if and only if } a \succeq_i b \tag{3.1}$$

In words: a's utility for i is at least as large b's if and only if a is ranked at least as highly as b in i's preference ordering.

Recall now what I said earlier in this chapter about interpersonal comparisons: the general equilibrium framework need not assume they are possible. To drive this point home, I will be supposing that the utility functions I refer to are not interpersonally comparable. Further, I will assume for now that utility functions are not cardinal. Thus, I will suppose that the only significance had by the numerical values assigned by a utility function to items in a set of alternatives is the numerical *order* of those values. When a utility function and its values have this significance only, the utility function is said to be *ordinal*. An ordinal utility function cannot license inferences concerning the sizes of benefits conferred by various alternatives in the way that a cardinal utility function can. Thus, unlike cardinal utilities, the ratios of differences between ordinal utilities have no significance whatsoever. For any ordinal utility function U, infinitely many other functions represent the same underlying preference ordering just as well. Each of these is an *increasing function* of U: V is an increasing function of U when $V(U(x)) \geq V(U(y))$ if and only if $U(x) \geq U(y)$. Cardinal properties are not necessarily preserved when one function is transformed into another by an increasing transformation.[4]

So for the remainder of this chapter I shall assume that all of the utility functions I mention are ordinal and noncomparable. (In fact, all of the results I am going to discuss hold also when the utility functions are cardinal

---

[3] For a discussion highlighting the pitfalls of not regimenting one's use of "utility," see Broome (1999a).

[4] As noted in section 2.2, cardinal properties of a function are preserved only by positive affine transformations.

and noncomparable.) This means that anything that *looks* like a social choice social welfare function in this chapter will have to be understood in some other way. My task is to explain what that other way is.

3.5 Aggregating Utilities in a General Equilibrium Framework

Suppose that we have a set of N consumers, which might include consumers who are not yet alive. And suppose that each of these individuals has (or will have) a preference ordering that is defined over a set of possible alternatives (e.g., possible lifetime consumption bundles). Let each of these orderings be representable by an ordinal utility function. As we have just seen, each of these utility functions can be transformed into a different utility function that represents the same ordering just as well. But let us suppose that we have picked one utility function for each individual from the infinite number of functions that represent their preferences.

Here is a fairly trivial implication of these assumptions: If an outcome a gives rise to the vector of ordinal utilities $(U_1^a, U_2^a, ..., U_N^a)$, and if this vector maximizes the following function

$$W = \sum_{i=1}^{N} U_i \qquad (3.2)$$

then this outcome is Pareto efficient. The proof is simple. Suppose for the sake of argument that the outcome were not Pareto efficient. Then it would be possible to move to a different outcome b that nobody disprefers to a, and that at least one consumer strictly prefers to a. But if there were such an outcome, the vector of utilities associated with it, $(U_1^b, U_2^b, ..., U_N^b)$, would be such that $U_i^b \geq U_i^a$ for all consumers, and $U_i^b > U_i^a$ for at least one consumer. But if that were true, then $(U_1^b, U_2^b, ..., U_N^b)$ would be the vector that maximizes (3.2), not the vector $(U_1^a, U_2^a, ..., U_N^a)$. So if the vector associated with outcome a really is the vector that maximizes (3.2), then a is Pareto efficient.

Now consider this question: If an outcome is Pareto efficient, is there some function that it maximizes? It turns out that if we make all the assumptions necessary for the Second Fundamental Theorem of Welfare Economics, plus one additional assumption that is always made in general equilibrium climate change economics, the answer is yes.[5] Granted those assumptions, here is the form of the functions that are maximized by Pareto efficient allocations:

$$W = \sum_{i=1}^{N} \alpha_i U_i \qquad (3.3)$$

The α_i's in (3.3) are called *Pareto weights*, and (given our assumptions) every Pareto efficient allocation maximizes a function of this form. In each of these functions at least some Pareto weights will be positive, and all will be non-negative (Kreps 2013, p. 178; Mas-Colell et al. 1995, p. 560).

I cannot stress enough that the functions whose form is given by (3.3) are *not* social choice social welfare functions. Remember, for a function of (3.3)'s form to be suitable for representing a *ranking* of vectors of U_i values, those values must stem from cardinal and interpersonally comparable functions. But this is not something that must be true of the utility functions that (3.3) uses solely to *characterize* Pareto efficient allocations (Kreps 2013, p. 184). In the interest of brevity, and to mark the important distinction between social choice social welfare functions and these different functions that arise within the general equilibrium framework, I shall call the latter *character functions*.

3.6 Pareto Weights

General equilibrium character functions have a further neat property that falls out of the mathematics underlying them. To explain this property, I first need to say a bit more about the prices that prevail in any given competitive equilibrium. Recall that the Second Fundamental Theorem says that every Pareto efficient outcome is a competitive equilibrium for some distribution of wealth. In the general equilibrium framework, a consumer's wealth in a given competitive equilibrium is a function of (1) the goods she owns in that equilibrium and (2) those goods' prices. We know that each good has such a price, for a competitive equilibrium is in part defined by a vector specifying a price for each marketed good. It is these prices that consumers use to determine which consumption bundles they can afford, and that producers use to

---

[5] The additional assumption is that all utility functions are concave.

determine which production plan will maximize their profits. So if Claire is endowed with three apples and four oranges in a given competitive equilibrium, her wealth is

$$(3 \cdot p_A) + (4 \cdot p_O)$$

where p_A and p_O are the equilibrium prices of apples and oranges, respectively.

In a general equilibrium framework, prices can be determined only in *relative* terms; there are no absolute prices. Standard assumptions entail that for any given price vector **p** that prevails in a given competitive equilibrium, a different vector in which every price in **p** is multiplied by a positive constant would work just as well. For when we increase every price by applying that positive constant, we simultaneously increase consumers' wealth by the same proportion. This price change will have no effect on consumers' (or producers') economic behavior.

Suppose now that the equilibrium price of oranges is twice the price of apples. It follows that, in the equilibrium, each consumer is indifferent between consuming two apples and one orange. To see this, imagine that one consumer were *not* indifferent. Suppose, for example, that someone who owns positive amounts of both apples and oranges prefers having two apples to one orange. Then she would sell one of her oranges to acquire two more apples. But then she would continue making this kind of trade until it *were* true that she is indifferent between one orange and two apples. Thus it is only when one's *marginal rate of substitution* of oranges for apples equals their price ratio that one consumes the bundle of goods that one most prefers out of the bundles one can afford at the prevailing set of prices. And as we have seen, this is what all consumers do at a competitive equilibrium in the private ownership economy we have been discussing.

I stated this last point in terms of individuals' consuming their most preferred affordable bundles of goods. Yet having already introduced utility functions, I could instead have referred to consumers' *maximizing utility* at equilibrium prices. After all, maximizing one's utility is nothing over and above consuming one's most preferred affordable bundle of goods. But when we have utility functions to work with, we gain some useful mathematical tools. For example, even with purely ordinal utility functions we can speak of a given good's *marginal utility* for a consumer who is already consuming a given bundle of goods. Good *g*'s marginal utility for consumer *i* at a given competitive equilibrium outcome a is the difference between i's utility in a and what i's utility would be if he consumed one more unit of g than he consumes in a (holding his consumption of all other goods and services fixed). Of course, since we are supposing that i's utility function is ordinal, the absolute magnitude of this numerical difference lacks any significance beyond its relation to the underlying preference ordering. But if, for example, an extra unit of a different good, j, has a marginal utility for i that is greater than that of g, it follows that i prefers the bundle that has the extra unit of j to the bundle that has the extra unit of g (assuming i does not have to give anything up to get either g or j). It also follows that at a competitive equilibrium, every consumer is such that the following holds for any pair of marketed goods j and g:

$$\frac{MU^i_j}{MU^i_g} = \frac{p_j}{p_g} \qquad (3.4)$$

where MU^i_j and MU^i_g denote j's and g's marginal utility for individual i; and p_j and p_g denote j's and g's equilibrium prices in their respective competitive markets. Equation (3.4) says that for every consumer at any competitive equilibrium in our private ownership economy, the ratio of their marginal utilities of any two goods—their marginal rate of substitution— equals the ratio of those goods' market prices. Note that since any increasing transformation of an ordinal utility function represents exactly the same preference ordering, the equality in (3.4) tells us that the *ratios* of marginal utilities do not change when any consumer's utility function is transformed into another by an increasing transformation. And it is these equilibrium ratios that equal the corresponding ratios of equilibrium prices.[6]

Recall now the form of each general equilibrium character function, which is given by (3.3). And recall that each Pareto efficient outcome in our private ownership model maximizes a function of this form for some vector of Pareto weights. I can now explain the neat property of these weights that I referred to at the start of this section. To begin, observe that by rearranging (3.4) we obtain

---

[6] This invariance of ratios of marginal utilities to increasing transformations of ordinal utility functions is distinct from the invariance of the *ratio of utility differences* to positive affine transformations of cardinal utility functions.

$$\frac{MU^i_j}{p_j} = \frac{MU^i_g}{p_g} \tag{3.5}$$

for any consumer i. Both the right-hand and left-hand side of (3.5) gives what is known as i's *marginal utility of unit of account*. A general equilibrium model's unit of account is whatever unit the prices p_j and p_g are denominated in. It is standard to normalize prices so that the price of one good—apples, say—is set to 1, with other goods' prices rescaled accordingly. In that case, we say that apples are the model's unit of account, or *numeraire*. Then if the price of an orange is 2, it means that one must give up two apples to obtain one orange. What (3.5) says is that with the expenditure of every marginal unit of the numeraire good at a competitive equilibrium, every consumer achieves the same increase in his (ordinal and noncomparable) utility. If this were not true, then at least one consumer could better satisfy his preferences by shifting his expenditures around somewhat. But that would contradict the assumption that the economy is at a competitive equilibrium, since one thing that defines a competitive equilibrium in our economy is that all consumers are maximizing their utility subject to their budgets and the economy's prices.

Now let us select an arbitrary Pareto efficient outcome in our private goods economy, and find the set of Pareto weights, $(\alpha_1, \alpha_2, \ldots, \alpha_N)$, such that the Pareto efficient outcome maximizes a character function that is outfitted with this set of weights. The neat property that I referred to is that each consumer i's Pareto weight in this character function is equal to the reciprocal of i's marginal utility of unit of account in the maximizing Pareto efficient outcome:

$$\alpha_i = \frac{1}{MU^i_j/p_j} = \frac{1}{MU^i_g/p_g} \tag{3.6}$$

for any goods j and g (Bewley 2009, pp. 195–209).

In economic models that ascribe strictly concave utility functions to each consumer (as general equilibrium climate change policy optimization models uniformly do), an upshot of this mathematical property of Pareto weights is that consumers who enjoy high consumption in a given competitive equilibrium will have a low marginal utility, and thus a large Pareto weight. The reverse will be true of consumers who have very low consumption. This makes intuitive sense: if a character function gives one agent a lot of weight by applying a relatively large Pareto weight to her utility function, then the Pareto efficient allocation that the function characterizes will prioritize her interests commensurately, and her marginal utility of unit of account in that allocation will end up being lower than it would be if she enjoyed less consumption (Varian 1992, p. 335).

You might wonder what will happen to the Pareto weights when a given (ordinal) utility function is transformed, using an increasing transformation, into a different function that represents the same preference ordering. The answer is that since the weights are reciprocals of marginal utilities of the unit of account, and since the marginal utilities associated with different changes in consumption are in part a function of the utility functions used to measure them, the weights may have to change when the utility functions change.[7]

3.7 Negishi's Method

Takashi Negishi was the first to study character functions and the relation between their respective Pareto weights and each i's marginal utility of unit of account in the competitive equilibrium that maximizes a character function having those weights (Negishi 1960). He did so in the context of an effort to prove that for a given set of initial endowments among consumers, a competitive equilibrium exists for the private ownership economy we have been discussing. To say that a competitive equilibrium with respect to a given set of endowments "exists" is to say that there is an allocation of consumption, a set of production plans, and a vector of equilibrium prices such that (1) supply equals demand in all markets, (2) all consumers maximize utility subject to the budget constraints imposed by their initial endowments, (3) all productive firms are maximizing profits, and (4) the government does not redistribute endowments among consumers.

---

[7] This is further confirmation that general equilibrium character functions differ from social choice social welfare functions in not representing orderings of social states. As we saw in section 2.2, a weighted utilitarian social welfare function, using the very same weights, represents the very same ordering when well-being functions are subjected to informationally admissible transformations. In an ordinal general equilibrium framework, any arbitrary set of individual-specific increasing transformations is an informationally admissible set of transformations. But when the utility functions change, so too might the weights and thus so too might the character function itself.

To prove the existence of a competitive equilibrium with respect to a given set of initial endowments, Negishi formulated an abstract character function whose Pareto weights would be varied iteratively. Since we know that all competitive equilibria are Pareto efficient, and that each Pareto efficient outcome maximizes a character function for some vector of Pareto weights, one can scan the full set of competitive equilibria by varying the weights. The trick is then to use the mathematical techniques of constrained optimization to compute the equilibrium prices that are associated with each character function, which amounts to computing equilibrium prices for each Pareto efficient outcome.[8] Next, one uses these prices to determine the market value of each consumer's equilibrium consumption bundle in each Pareto efficient outcome. One then compares this value to the market value, at those same prices, of each consumer's initial set of endowments, subject to the condition that this set is not supplemented or diminished by redistributive transfers. When one finds a set of weights that yields equilibrium prices that make these two market values equal for each consumer, one has found the competitive equilibrium that corresponds to the given initial set of endowments. This particular set of weights is referred to as *Negishi weights*. In theory, the competitive equilibrium that maximizes a "Negishi-weighted character function" is an equilibrium that could be reached by firms and consumers who engage in production and trade in complete competitive markets.[9]

Sometimes economists say that this is a proof of Adam Smith's famous parable of the "invisible hand," for it indicates how a Pareto efficient outcome can be reached by a decentralized process whose underlying psychological motivations are consumers' self-interested preference (or utility) maximization and producers' single-minded pursuit of profit maximization.

---

[8] Here's an important detail: if one requires that all Pareto weights be positive, then every character function that is created by varying the weights will be such that there is a Pareto efficient allocation that maximizes it in constrained optimization. But some Pareto efficient allocations may be the solution to character functions some of whose Pareto weights are equal to zero. Moreover, some Pareto *in*efficient allocations will maximize character functions in which some Pareto weights equal zero. So when the weights are allowed to be zero, one cannot identify all and only Pareto efficient allocations simply by varying the weights and then maximizing the resulting character function (Kreps 2013, pp. 182–183). This problem is evaded in general equilibrium climate economics by assuming that all Pareto weights are positive.

[9] I am greatly indebted to Scott Ashworth for very helpful discussions about Negishi weights.

3.8 Public Goods

To foreshadow a bit, we are on our way to seeing how economists can use the mathematical tools I have been describing in this chapter to compute the pollution taxes—including carbon taxes—needed to achieve Pareto efficiency in an economy in which consumption or production creates harmful external effects. We will eventually see how these tools and this goal lead to a social cost of carbon concept that differs conceptually from those described in chapter 2, even though the mathematics used in the respective derivations looks identical. To get to that point, however, I must first introduce some departures from the standard private ownership economy. This is because the sort of external harm engendered by "dirty" consumption or production is not part of the landscape I have described to this point.

Recall that we have been assuming that all goods and services in the economy are private goods, in the sense that if one person consumes a good, it is not available for another person to consume. (I added that no private consumption imposed external effects on others except for the effects that are mediated by the price system.) Let us now relax that private-goods assumption. Thus suppose that there is a *pure public good* in the economy. A pure public good (which I will just call a *public good*) is a good that, if consumed by *anyone* in a certain amount, is also consumed by *everyone* in that same amount. In standard terminology, a public good is both *nonrivalrous* and *nonexcludable*. It is nonrivalrous by being consumable by multiple people at the same time, without any one person's consumption diminishing the consumption possibilities of anyone else. And it is *nonexcludable* by virtue of its being impossible to prevent one person from consuming it whenever it is available for anyone else to consume. A system of national defense is often cited as an example of a public good. If such a system exists, then one citizen's benefiting from it does not preclude or diminish another person's benefiting. True, it is possible to raise questions about national defense's claim to being a *pure* public good, by thinking of how exclusion might be engineered. It used to be that economics textbooks cited radio or television signals as examples of pure public goods, but then devices such as scramblers and cable boxes introduced the distinction between *receiving* radio or TV signals and actually *consuming* the broadcasts they carry. Nevertheless, some goods, like clean air or a climate with fewer heatwaves, continue to be plausible examples of pure public goods.

Public goods are typically excluded from the picture when economics textbooks discuss the two Fundamental Theorems of Welfare Economics.

This is because when public goods are present, there is no guarantee that an economy's equilibrium outcome will be Pareto efficient. One way to see this is to suppose that a new private producer enters the economy and offers for sale a certain public good, G, that had not previously been available to purchase. This producer is now willing to sell units of G to any consumer who is willing to pay the producer's per-unit price. Suppose that since G has not hitherto been available, many people strongly want to consume it. We might even imagine that most consumers would be willing to pay quite a lot to consume each of several initial units of G. But on the other hand, each consumer prefers to consume G without having to pay for it at all. And this they can do, if only some other consumers do choose to pay for it. Since G is a public good, there is therefore an incentive for consumers to "free-ride" on one another's purchases. But of course if everyone attempts to free-ride, no one will step up and purchase the good, even though everyone could be made be better off if each person voluntarily paid some (possibly quite small) fraction of the cost of the first unit of G. These incentives can lead to an outcome that is not Pareto efficient.

A Pareto inefficient outcome can also arise when at least some consumers do *not* act as free-riders. Suppose that one such consumer, i, decides he wants the first initial units of G so much that he is willing to pay their entire cost himself. This could involve trading some amount of the economy's numeraire good to the firm that produces G. (If his holdings of that numeraire good get too low for his tastes, he can sell some of his other goods for more units of the numeraire.) Suppose that i continues to purchase more and more units of G right up to the point at which his marginal utility of G, divided by G's price, equals his marginal utility of any other good divided by its price. When that condition obtains, he is maximizing his utility subject to the constraints of affordability. Now since G is a public good, other consumers may also benefit from i's purchases. And by the time i buys his final unit of G, it may well be that each of the other consumers finds that their own utility would be *diminished* if they took over and purchased the next unit. Since they now enjoy the benefits of the units i has purchased, perhaps none of the others is willing to pay the price that G's producer must charge to stay in business. That is to say, for each of these others, their marginal utilities of G divided by G's price may be *less* than their marginal utility per unit of account of some other good or service in the economy. But again, this can be so even when it is also true that everyone could be made better off by paying for more units of G, if only they could *jointly* finance the next unit of by each paying some *fraction* of its price.

As you no doubt already see, it would be very hard for a private producer of a public good to arrange for the joint purchases of its product, especially in light of consumers' incentive to wait and see if other people agree to purchase additional units of G. This predicament has led economists, beginning with Erik Lindahl, to imagine a scenario in which the government becomes the producer of a public good and charges each consumer a *personalized* price for it in the form of a legally required tax payment (Lindahl 1958). The idea is to have the government identify (1) a level of provision of the public good (i.e., a number of units) and (2) a set of personalized prices for the public good such that, if the public good *were* a rivalrous and excludable private good like all the other goods in the economy, each consumer's utility-maximizing choice would involve purchasing that number of private units of G at that personalized price. The government would then supply that same number of units to all, while levying personalized taxes that are computed by multiplying that number of units by each consumer's personalized price for G. The tax revenue would of course be used to pay for provision of that amount of G. It is only via the use of personalized prices that we could achieve a Pareto efficient outcome in which each consumer i's marginal utility of G, divided by i's personalized price, is equal to i's marginal utility per unit of account for every other good he consumes.

In a general equilibrium analysis of public goods, a *Lindahl equilibrium* is (in part) defined in terms of an allocation of goods among consumers, a set of firms' production plans, a vector of "anonymous" market prices for all of the economy's private goods, and vectors of personalized prices for each public good. To be a genuine *equilibrium*, such a description of the economy must meet the conditions that every consumer's consumption bundle maximizes her utility; every firm's production plan maximizes its profits; and supply equals demand in all markets, including the government-created markets for public goods. As I have already indicated, at a Lindahl equilibrium each consumer's marginal utility per unit of account will be the same for each good, including for each public good. A second necessary condition, known as the *Samuelson condition*, holds that in an economy with public goods, Pareto efficiency requires that the numeraire-denominated cost of producing a marginal unit of a public good equal the *sum* of consumers' marginal rates of substitution of the public good for the numeraire good (Samuelson 1954). That is, we determine how much of the numeraire good each consumer would be willing to give up to secure that final unit of the public good G, and we sum those amounts. This sum represents consumers' aggregate willingness to pay for that final unit of G. The Samuelson condition says that at a Pareto efficient outcome in an economy with a public good, this sum must equal the cost of producing that last unit of G. This cost is also denominated in terms of the numeraire good: it represents the amount of that good a producer is willing to accept in exchange for providing a marginal unit of a public good. If the producer is the government, as we have been imagining, the costs of production amount to the total amount of the numeraire good that the government must supply to (e.g.) the employees and contractors whose combined efforts produce the public good. This total cost is known as the public good's *marginal rate of transformation*.

It can be proved that all Lindahl equilibria are Pareto efficient (Foley 1970). This is the counterpart to the First Fundamental Theorem for an economy with public goods. Moreover, a counterpart of the Second Fundamental Theorem can also be proved: if a feasible allocation with public goods is Pareto efficient, then there is a vector of anonymous prices for private goods and a vector of personalized prices for each public good such that the efficient allocation can be decentralized by first redistributing initial endowments and then letting the economy's agents pursue utility- and profit-maximization while facing those prices (Myles 1995, p. 276). Of course, for reasons related to nonexcludability, the government would need to pursue decentralization by working out the relevant Pareto efficient level of each public good and then imposing the appropriate personalized taxes for each consumer.

3.9 Externalities

Although the concept of a Lindahl equilibrium has most commonly been used to explain how Pareto efficiency can be achieved in an economy with public goods, it can also be used to address externalities, including negative externalities like those associated with climate change. A negative externality occurs when an agent makes an economic choice that imposes costs on other, uninvolved agents. That is exactly what happens with greenhouse gas emissions: when I drive one hundred miles, I must pay for the gas this requires and for the routine maintenance my car needs. But I do not pay for the harms that my car's emissions cause, whether in the form of the global climate damages they make more likely, or in the form of the localized air pollution that people in my city are forced to breathe when they go outside.

It is a standard lesson of economics that when people or firms can make choices without having to consider their external costs, the resulting outcome will be Pareto inefficient (Foley 2009; Broome 2012, ch. 3). If I can ignore the harm that my car's emissions cause, then in deciding whether to take a trip, I will compare the trip's benefit *to me* with its costs *to me*. After making many such decisions, however, my emissions may be causing others a lot of harm—indeed so much harm that they might prefer a situation in which *they* pay *me* to drive less.

Of course, this victim-bribes-perpetrator arrangement may seem ethically perverse. But this is a good reminder that right now we are focused on Pareto efficiency, and that Pareto efficiency is a very limited normative notion. For now, let us suppose that redistributing endowments is off the table. Thus we shall maintain our example's assumption that it is currently legal to emit harmful pollution. For in an economic model involving externalities, the legal landscape—who is permitted to do what—becomes part of what is specified when one specifies the initial set of endowments. (This is no different from a setup involving private goods only: when one's endowment of private consumption goods includes a kite, there must be some—perhaps implicit—stipulation concerning what a consumer is permitted to do with a kite.)

We can examine externalities through the lens of Lindahl equilibria by conceiving of private pollution abatement as a privately produced public good. When I drive my car less, I help to make the entire world a less dangerous place, if only marginally. And even if my actions improve the world more for some than for others, this is consistent with viewing my actions as creating a public good. We already know that Pareto efficiency in the context of public goods allows for different people to have different marginal rates of substitution of the public good for the numeraire good. That is why the Pareto efficiency of a Lindahl equilibrium requires personalized prices. Personalized prices will also be needed in the context of externalities. But now, instead of one government that produces each public good for many consumers, we have myriad producers of myriad public goods, each of which will require a vector of personalized prices if we hope to find a Pareto efficient allocation in which the aggregate amount of pollution abatement supplied by private producers equals the total amount of abatement demanded by its beneficiaries.

In fact, it can be shown that personalized prices for externalities and privately produced public goods can work this trick (Hammond 1998; Kreps

2013, pp. 380–383). They also do the job when the setup is altered so that those who would be harmed by emissions—call them the "receivers"—are now endowed with the legal right to forbid emissions. In this new case, we imagine that emitters must pay fees to those who would be harmed by their emissions. When emitters have to pay what receivers demand to be paid, it is easy to see that each polluting action will carry two costs, the market cost of engaging in that behavior (e.g., the cost of the gas required to drive a polluting car) and the price the receivers demand in compensation for tolerating the harms they will suffer. At a Pareto efficient equilibrium, emitters will engage in a set of behaviors whose marginal private benefit *to them* exactly equals the sum of the market costs of those behaviors and the marginal payments they must make to receivers. If emitters emitted *less* than this amount, then the private benefit they would gain by emitting a bit more will be larger, from the point of view of their own preferences (and thus from the point of view of their utility function), than the marginal cost of emitting a bit more. Likewise, receivers will sell emitters rights to emit right up until the payments they receive exactly compensate them for the harm done to them by those emissions. If emitters emitted less than this, then receivers would actually benefit from selling a few more pollution rights to emitters, as the marginal harm from pollution would be less than the marginal benefit of what emitters are willing to pay for the right to emit one more unit.

Here again it can be proved that in a private ownership model with externalities, Lindahl equilibria exist, are Pareto efficient, and can be supported as competitive equilibria given suitable price vectors and a suitable initial distribution of endowments (Hammond 1998). As was the case in the context of public goods, each Lindahl equilibrium is associated with a vector of personalized prices for each public good, including the privately produced public goods that arise when externalities enter the picture. If emitters begin with the right to emit, then the personalized prices are what each receiver is willing to pay to induce emitters to dial back their polluting behavior; if receivers begin with the rights to be free of pollution, the personalized prices give the size of the compensation payments each receiver would accept in exchange for transferring the right to emitters and tolerating the ensuing pollution. Finally, at every Lindahl equilibrium, and regardless of how rights are allocated, the following condition always obtains: for each emitter, the private benefit of emitting (denominated in the numeraire good) is equal to the sum of (1) the market cost of emitting (e.g., the cost of gasoline) and

(2) the sum of receivers' personalized prices (which is also denominated in the numeraire).

Thus when an emitter has the right to emit, their marginal private benefit of emitting at a Lindahl equilibrium will be equal to the sum of the marginal market costs of the emitting behavior and the total of all the bribes offered to them by receivers to reduce their emissions (Sandmo 2000, pp. 29–30). This latter total is categorized as a *cost* because it is a benefit the emitter *forgoes* when he chooses to emit rather than accept receivers' bribes. It is what economists call an *opportunity cost* of emitting. Alternatively, if each receiver is endowed with a right to a pollution-free atmosphere, then an emitter's cost of pollution-generating behavior is the sum of the market cost of that behavior and the total of personalized compensation payments the emitter must pay to receivers. It is easier to see in this case why, at a Lindahl equilibrium, the total of receivers' personalized prices is a cost that each emitter must pay over and above the market cost of the emitting behavior. But this total is also properly categorized as a cost when emitters are endowed with rights to pollute.

Because counterparts of the two Fundamental Theorems can be proved for economies with public goods and externalities, we know that the prices that characterize any given Lindahl equilibrium are such that the allocation and production plans that partially define the equilibrium are utility- and profit-maximizing for each and every economic agent. This means that it is the allocation or plan that each agent would choose, given those prices, if each externality-causing behavior (and its reduction) were just another private good that agents could purchase in competitive markets. Of course we already know that externality-generating behaviors are *not* just any other private good, and that free markets cannot be relied upon to deliver Pareto efficient amounts of them. The problems related to nonexcludability arise here, just as they did in the context of pure public goods. Yet here too, government-assessed taxes can help overcome these problems, as the next section explains.

3.10 The Lindahl-Pigou Pricing Scheme

The version of the Second Fundamental Theorem that applies to Lindahl equilibria entails that every such equilibrium with pollution externalities can be supported with a set of pollution taxes—one for each form of externality-generating behavior—that are set at the total of receivers' personalized prices in the equilibrium. This might seem puzzling at first. For I have noted that some Lindahl equilibria can be thought of as the hypothetical result of well-functioning markets for the externalities in contexts in which emitters are endowed with rights to emit. But if they begin with rights to emit, how can the specific Pareto efficient outcome that would result from emitters' voluntarily selling those rights be achieved instead by imposing a tax on emitters?

Here is how. First, use an economic model to determine the prices, allocations, and production plans that characterize the imaginary Lindahl equilibrium that would arise given an initial set of endowments that grants emitters rights to emit. That is, imagine—contrary to fact—that markets for externalities worked just like markets for any other private good. Then, the result of market trading would be a Lindahl equilibrium in which every emitter's marginal private benefit equals the sum of the market costs of emitting and receivers' personalized prices. Now, once we know this equilibrium allocation—an allocation that specifies all the goods and services that each consumer enjoys once trading has ceased—the second welfare theorem ensures that this very same allocation can be supported as a competitive equilibrium in which (1) it is *receivers* who have rights over the atmosphere; (2) emitters pay a tax for each unit of pollution that is equal to the sum of receivers' personalized prices for that pollution in the Lindahl equilibrium; (3) the tax revenue is paid out to receivers in amounts commensurate with their respective personalized prices; and (4) initial endowments are redistributed in such a way that utility- and profit-maximizing behavior leaves the economy in exactly the same Lindahl equilibrium that we imagined at the start. Thus instead of having emitters decide how many of their rights to emit they are willing to sell to receivers, they now decide how many such rights they are willing to buy from receivers.

This is what Peter Hammond calls a Lindahl-Pigou pricing scheme, because it combines Lindahl's insights concerning public goods and personalized prices with the famous claim, ascribed to the economist Arthur C. Pigou, that the way to harmonize externality-creating behavior with Pareto efficiency is to levy a tax equal to the external harm the behavior causes (Pigou 1932, pp. 183–184; Hammond 1998). The transfers of endowments referred to in step (4), the ones required to ensure that consumers reach the levels of utility they would reach in the imaginary economy without a tax, in effect replace the bribes that emitters are paid by receivers in the imaginary economy in which emitters are endowed with rights to emit. In the imaginary setup, emitters begin with a set of endowments and, in light of prices associated with the given Lindahl equilibrium, decide to accept a bribe if and only if doing so is part of a process that converts their endowment into a new bundle of goods and services they prefer. When instead we engineer this outcome using the Lindahl-Pigou pricing scheme, emitters no longer contemplate accepting bribes for each unit of pollution they can *abate*; they instead contemplate paying a Pigouvian tax for each unit of pollution they *generate*. So when they see that the newly imposed tax is larger than their marginal private benefit of emitting, they will reduce their emissions, but they will no longer receive payments from receivers for doing so. Thus while it is rational for emitters to abate in order to avoid the new tax, doing so leaves them with a consumption bundle they *disprefer* to their starting bundle, rather than with one they prefer. This shows that if the Lindahl-Pigou pricing scheme is to be used to mimic the outcome of free and functional markets for externalities in which emitters have rights to emit, some initial redistribution will have to take place.

This sort of redistribution acts as a kind of compensation: in the case we have been discussing, it compensates emitters for having their right to emit replaced by a requirement to pay a tax. When combined with suitable Lindahl-Pigou prices, the transfers create the initial conditions needed for utility- and profit-maximizing behavior to bring the economy to the same Pareto efficient outcome that arises in our imaginary economy in which emitters were endowed with rights to emit, and where externalities were traded in well-functioning markets as if they were typical private goods. And this shows how the Lindahl-Pigou pricing scheme can be used to decentralize Pareto efficient allocations involving externalities, including allocations we might have been interested in as the result of a thought experiment that makes no reference whatsoever to pollution taxes.

It is important to stress that not all transfers of initial endowments are compensatory in the sense just described. Some transfers are purely redistributive. Purely redistributive transfers are known as *lump-sum transfers*. We can define them as follows. Select (1) any (possibly Pareto inefficient) distribution of initial endowments among consumers and (2) any (Pareto efficient) Lindahl equilibrium. Now, given those choices, find the market value of each consumer's initial endowment using the prices associated with the selected Lindahl equilibrium; next, using those same prices find the market value of each consumer's final consumption bundle in the Lindahl equilibrium.[10] Any difference between these two values is a lump-sum transfer. (Thus such transfers must be defined with respect to a pair of allocations, one initial and one final.) Moreover, the sum of all such transfers will equal zero. Taking our selected set of initial endowments as the baseline, the identified set of lump-sum transfers is what must be combined with the selected Lindahl equilibrium's price vectors if that equilibrium is to be the result of utility- and profit-maximizing behavior by the consumers and firms. But now we return to the point from the previous paragraph: lump-sum transfers are not the only sort of transfers that might be needed to support a given Lindahl equilibrium with a Lindahl-Pigou pricing scheme. In some cases, distinctly compensatory transfers will be needed.

3.11 Negishi's Method and Pareto-Improving Climate Policy

As we have seen, when emitters of pollution do not take into account the effect they have on third parties—when, that is, emitters face neither Pigouvian taxes nor opportunity costs in terms of real bribes offered by receivers—then the outcome will be Pareto inefficient. By contrast, Lindahl equilibria are Pareto efficient and any Lindahl equilibrium can be brought about by suitable pricing and redistribution. This does not mean, however, that any given Lindahl equilibrium will be Pareto-*improving* when compared with any given set of initial endowments. A move from one allocation to a second allocation is Pareto-improving if and only if no consumer prefers the first and at least one consumer prefers the second. Let us now ask: Is there a way to identify the Lindahl equilibria that *are* Pareto-improving with respect to a given inefficient baseline allocation?

Yes, there is, and it uses the method of Negishi's that I described in section 3.7. Granted the requisite assumptions (which are uniformly embedded in general equilibrium climate change policy optimization models), each Pareto efficient Lindahl equilibrium will be the solution to a character function, for some set of Pareto weights, just as was true of each Pareto efficient

---

[10] By a consumption bundle's "market value," I here mean its numeraire-denominated value at the prices given by the price vectors that partially define the relevant Lindahl equilibrium. Since public goods and externalities will not actually be traded in markets, this use of "market value" may be misleading. But it is less cumbersome than the alternatives I could think of.

allocation in the economy Negishi studied (Ginsburgh and Keyzer 2002, pp. 325–332).[11] When this economy is extended to include public goods, the utility functions to which the Pareto weights are applied will include the public goods as arguments. In the case of externalities, the utility functions may or may not feature the externality-generating behavior as an argument, for the concept of a Lindahl equilibrium is still relevant when consumers fundamentally care only about their consumption of private goods and services.[12]

Thus each Lindahl equilibrium can be modeled as the solution to a character function for some set of Pareto weights. Moreover, Negishi's method for proving the existence of competitive equilibria can be used to identify the Lindahl equilibria that are Pareto-improving with respect to a given baseline set of endowments. Here is how.

First, construct a schematic character function appropriate to a given economy. (Here is where it matters what consumers' utility functions are actually like, because these are the functions that, along with the Pareto weights, compose the relevant character functions.) Next, select an arbitrary vector of Pareto weights and maximize the character function they define in a constrained optimization exercise. The results of this exercise give the price vectors and the allocation of goods associated with the Lindahl equilibrium that maximizes that character function. Then, by iteratively varying the Pareto weights, one can identify the full set of Lindahl equilibria and their respective allocations and prices. Finally, one can use these sets of prices to identify the subset of Lindahl equilibria at which the market value of every consumer's final consumption bundle is equal to the market value of their endowment income. This is equivalent to finding the set of Lindahl equilibria in which every consumer's lump-sum transfer is exactly zero.

---

[11] Here I, like many policy optimization modelers, am ignoring an important problem known as the "problem of fundamental nonconvexities." For more on this, see Starrett (1972), Dasgupta (1982, pp. 55–60), and Hammond (1998, pp. 250–253).

[12] If, for example, another consumer's polluting behavior damages the goods I own and wish to consume, then I will certainly be concerned about her behavior, and either willing to pay her to modulate it, or else insistent that she pay to compensate me. But that concern can be entirely derivative, a function of my ultimate concern with the goods she damages. If so, there is no need to include her behavior directly in my utility function; it is enough to keep track (in an economic model, say) of how her behavior affects those things that do belong in my utility function, and what sorts of externality-relevant agreements we are willing to enter into. Still, the framework works just as well if one person's behavior *is* an argument in another's utility function.

When a Lindahl equilibrium meets these criteria, it follows that no consumer is worse off with their final consumption bundle than they were with their endowment. We know this because the absence of lump-sum transfers means that no one's purchasing power was altered in moving from their endowment to their final consumption bundle. We therefore know that their initial endowment and their final consumption bundle are both affordable for them at the Lindahl equilibrium's prices. And since all Lindahl equilibria exhibit utility-maximization by consumers, we know that if a consumer's endowment differs from his final consumption bundle, then he is either indifferent between the two, or he prefers the final bundle. Since the modeler already possesses each consumer's utility function, she can actually just check to see which of these two possibilities holds for each consumer. If the initial set of endowments was Pareto inefficient, as it will be if one aims to model a real-world economy with unpriced externalities, its corresponding *Lindahl-equilibria-with-no-lump-sum-transfers* will undoubtedly be Pareto-improving. And granted the technical assumptions uniformly embedded into climate change policy optimization IAMs, there will always be one unique Lindahl equilibrium for any given set of initial endowments.[13] In line with the terminology in section 3.7, the Pareto weights that appear in the character function that is maximized by an allocation's Lindahl-equilibrium-with-no-lump-sum-transfers are that allocation's Negishi weights.

A Lindahl equilibrium with respect to some Pareto inefficient baseline—which I also just called a Lindahl-equilibrium-with-no-lump-sum-transfers—is therefore Pareto-improving relative to that baseline (Foley 1970). Since by this point the modeler has obtained the price vectors associated with the equilibrium, she can work out the Lindahl-Pigou pricing scheme that can support this equilibrium as a decentralized competitive equilibrium. Remember that although this scheme involves no *lump-sum* transfers, implementing the Lindahl-Pigou policy may require other tax-financed transfers that mimic the payments that, for example, receivers would be willing to make to emitters in exchange for emitters' not exercising their rights to emit. At the end of section 3.10 I called these sorts of transfers compensatory transfers.

---

[13] The relevant technical assumption here is that the constrained optimization problem to be solved is what is known as a strictly concave maximization problem. See Kehoe et al. (1992, p. 44).

3.12 Optimal General Equilibrium SCCs

I have explained that at a Lindahl equilibrium, each emitter's marginal private benefit of a polluting activity is equal to the market price of the emitting activity plus the sum of receivers' personalized Lindahl prices. And we have seen that the sum of receivers' personalized prices also gives the Pigouvian tax that must be imposed if the Lindahl equilibrium is to be supported as a decentralized competitive equilibrium using the Lindahl-Pigou pricing scheme.

Now, I have been discussing a *static* general equilibrium economic framework, one that lacks the dimension of time. But everything I have explained about Lindahl equilibria applies also to a dynamic setting in which economies exist through time. In this context, a consumer's utility function must reflect their preferences concerning the distribution of consumption across their lifetime. As was true in the social choice framework, consumption of the same good at different times must be treated by the model as consumption of an entirely different good. That is, a loaf of the sort of bread that I like and consume today must be distinguished from a qualitatively identical loaf next year. This is because the model must be able to assign different prices to the same sort of bread depending on when in time it would be consumed. Let us refer to a quantity of a specific *dated good* using $x_{2,0}$, which denotes a certain quantity of good-2-at-time-0. Since I will never need to refer to more than a few types of goods, I will omit the comma in these subscripts; so x_{10} and x_{21} will refer, respectively, to quantities of good-1-at-time-0 and good-2-at-time-1, and not to undated quantities of good 10 and good 21.

In a dynamic general equilibrium model, we can use a character function associated with a given Lindahl equilibrium to compute *optimal general equilibrium social costs of carbon* (GE-OPT SCCs) for each time at that equilibrium. Of course, these will not be indicators of a *normatively* optimal allocation with public goods and externalities, because that result requires a social choice SWF and I have stipulated that our character functions feature ordinal and interpersonally noncomparable utility functions. However, it is a further neat thing about the mathematics underlying character functions that when we use them to compute GE-OPT SCC figures for each time at a Lindahl equilibrium, these SCC figures turn out to equal the Pigouvian taxes that must be imposed at those times in order to support that Lindahl equilibrium as a decentralized competitive equilibrium with a Lindahl-Pigou pricing scheme. Let me explain how this result arises.

Recall from section 2.7 the formula for optimal social choice SCCs:

$$SCC_{t,OPT} = \frac{\Delta V/\Delta e_t}{\Delta V/\Delta c_t}\bigg|_{OPT} \qquad (3.7)$$

To signal that we are no longer working with an SWF within the social choice framework, I am going to use W (rather than V) to denote a character function. Let us also replace "*OPT*" on the right side of the bar, to indicate that the small changes we are interested in are the changes we would see if we added an extra unit of emissions at time t—denoted by Δe_t—at the intertemporal Lindahl equilibrium that maximizes W. Refer to this Lindahl equilibrium as LE_W. Finally, let us suppose we are concerned to compute the GE-OPT SCC for period 0, and that instead of normalizing the numerator by expressing it in terms of the difference made on the character function by a period 0 unit of generalized consumption, we normalize it in terms of the difference made by a period 0 unit of a more specific numeraire good. Let that good be good-1-at-time-0. With these changes, (3.7) becomes:

$$SCC_{0,LE_W} = \frac{\Delta W/\Delta e_0}{\Delta W/\Delta_{10}}\bigg|_{LE_W} \qquad (3.8)$$

We focus first on the numerator of this formula. To begin, suppose the effects of a marginal unit of emissions at time $t = 0$ in our arbitrary Lindahl equilibrium can be mapped to a set of damages at each future time τ. And suppose that these damages can, in turn, be expressed in terms of how much of good 1-at-τ each receiver who is alive at τ would have to be given then to be fully compensated for the damage she suffers then. We shall express this period-τ willingness to accept by $MRS^i_{e_0,1\tau}$, which is individual i's marginal rate of substitution of emissions in period 0 for good-1-at-time-τ.

Now, since we are supposing W is a character function that our selected Lindahl equilibrium maximizes, we know that each consumer i has a utility function U_i that is in part a function of i's consumption of dated goods. Let quantities of these goods be denoted by x^i_{10}, x^i_{11}, . . ., x^i_{20}, x^i_{21}, . . ., and so on. We also know that at the Lindahl equilibrium each i will have an allocation of goods to which U_i assigns a real number. Moreover, we can use U_i to derive i's marginal utility of any good at that allocation, including the marginal utility of good-1-at-time-τ, which I shall denote by $MU^i_{1\tau}$.[14] Thus at our selected Lindahl equilibrium, a given consumer i's utility would increase by $MU^i_{1\tau} \cdot MRS^i_{e_0,1\tau}$ in period τ if an emitter magnanimously reduced his first-period emissions by one unit. Conversely, that is the amount i's utility would decrease were the emitter to emit one additional unit in the first period. In this way we can use each consumer's utility function to translate marginal damages into sequences of changes in marginal utility, one sequence for each consumer who is affected.

Since it is a weighted utilitarian function, we know that W aggregates changes in consumer's utilities by weighting the changes and summing them. So the next step in fleshing out the numerator of (3.8) is to weight the marginal changes in consumers' utilities by their respective Pareto weights that feature in the character function W. Recall that these weights are equal to the inverse of each consumer's marginal utility of unit account at the Lindahl equilibrium LE_W that maximizes W. We have already set our unit of account—our numeraire—as good-1-at-time-0. So to determine each consumer i's Pareto weight, we just have to find the inverse of their marginal utility of good-1-at-time-0. If they are alive at time 0, we can find this by calculating MU^i_{10} and taking the inverse. If they are not alive at time 0, we can instead imagine investing a single unit of good-1-at-time-0 until a future period in which the consumer does live. Imagine such a future period τ, and suppose for simplicity that invested units of good-1-at-time-0 grow at a constant rate of MRT_1. ("MRT" for *marginal rate of transformation* of good 1, a notion introduced in section 3.8.) Thus by period τ, a single invested unit of good-1-at-time-0 will have grown into $1 \cdot (1 + MRT_1)^\tau$ units of good-1-at-time-τ. Now we can compute i's marginal utility of unit of account by calculating $MU^i_{1\tau} \cdot [1 \cdot (1 + MRT_1)^\tau]$. We then take the inverse to find i's Pareto weight.[15]

---

[14] More precisely, we can derive marginal utilities if U_i is differentiable, which it is always assumed to be in climate change policy optimization IAMs.

[15] General equilibrium economists might more commonly compute a future consumer j's marginal utility of unit of account by dividing j's marginal utility of that future unit of good-1-at-τ by its numeraire-denominated price, in line with the definition of marginal utility of unit of account given in section 3.6's equation (3.5). The numeraire-denominated price of good-1-at-τ is just the amount of good-1-at-time-0 that would grow into a single unit of good-1-at-τ if it were invested in period

We can now state the expression that gives us (3.8)'s numerator, $\Delta W/\Delta e_0$:

$$\frac{\Delta W}{\Delta e_0} = \sum_{t=1}^{T}\sum_{i=1}^{N} MRS^i_{e_0,1t} \cdot MU^i_{1t} \cdot \frac{1}{MU^i_{1t} \cdot (1+MRT_1)^t} \qquad (3.9)$$

The right-hand side of this expression begins by taking each time, one by one. Focusing for now on the first time period in which damages occur, $t = 1$, the expression multiplies each consumer i's marginal rate of substitution of emissions-in-period-0 for good-1-in-period-t by i's marginal utility of that good. It then weights this utility change by i's Pareto weight, which as we have just seen can be expressed in terms of this same marginal utility. Equation (3.9) then sums the resulting figures for each i who experiences damages in period 1, and then moves to the next period. It performs this Pareto-weighted summation for each time, and then adds up these sums across times. Since we can eliminate the two MU^i_{1t} expressions in (3.9), it simplifies to:

$$\frac{\Delta W}{\Delta e_0} = \sum_{t=1}^{T}\sum_{i=1}^{N} \frac{MRS^i_{e_0,1t}}{(1+MRT_1)^t} \qquad (3.10)$$

Thus, the numerator of the formula for an optimal general equilibrium SCC (GE-OPT SCC) is a discounted sum of marginal rates of substitution of initial-period emissions for period-specific goods, which we know to be a discounted sum of receivers' period-specific personalized prices. And since the discount rates in (3.10) equal the marginal rates of transformation between units of good 1 in adjacent time periods, (3.10) tells us that $\Delta W/\Delta e_0$ from (3.8) equals the sum of all receivers' marginal willingnesses-to-accept compensation, with these willingnesses-to-accept being expressed in terms

---

0 at the marginal rates of transformation that prevail at the intertemporal Lindahl equilibrium. Assuming (again for simplicity) that good 1's marginal rate of transformation is a constant denoted by MRT_1, this amount of good-1-at-time-0 is found by multiplying that future unit of good-1-at-τ by the discount factor $\frac{1}{(1+MRT_1)^\tau}$. This in turn makes j's marginal utility of unit of account equal to $\frac{MU^j_{1\tau}}{1/(1+MRT_1)^\tau}$. We can simplify this expression by multiplying its numerator by the reciprocal of its denominator to get $MU^j_{1\tau} \cdot \frac{(1+MRT_1)^\tau}{1}$, which of course equals $MU^j_{1\tau} \cdot (1+MRT_1)^\tau$. j's Pareto weight is then the inverse of this, which yields precisely the formula given in the text. I thank Truman Bewley for very helpful discussion on the topic of Pareto weights.

of the numeraire good. It is therefore expressed in terms of the amount of good-1-at-time-0 that an emitter at time 0 would have to pay to fully compensate receivers for the harm inflicted by marginal emissions. For receivers who exist far in the future—at some arbitrary time τ, say—emitters at t could invest the appropriate amount of good-1-at-time-t and let it grow at the interest rate MRT_1 for τ periods until it grows into the exact amount of good-1-at-τ that is needed to compensate those future receivers.

That is how one computes the numerator of (3.8), $\Delta W/\Delta e_0$. What about its denominator, $\Delta W/\Delta_{10}$? The answer is that since the denominator concerns the impact that a marginal unit of the numeraire good makes on the character function, the denominator's value is always equal to 1. I will write the expression first, and then explain it:

$$\frac{\Delta W}{\Delta_{10}} = MU_{10}^i \cdot \frac{1}{MU_{10}^i} \tag{3.11}$$

For any consumer i who might be alive at time 0 and who might consume an extra unit of good-1-at-time-0, her change in utility will be equal to MU_{10}^i. Then, to express this change in terms of the change it makes on the character function W, we must weight it by i's Pareto weight in that function. This weight is the inverse of i's marginal utility of unit of account. But since the unit of account just is good-1-in-time-0, its marginal utility for i is $MU_{10}^i \cdot [1 \cdot (1 + MRT_1)^0] = MU_{10}^i$. Thus we have two MU_{10}^i terms in (3.11), and they cancel each other out. The result is that for any consumer i whose consumption in period 0 at the Lindahl equilibrium changes by a single unit of good-1-at-time-0, the impact of this change on W is equal to the magnitude of that change in good-1-at-time-0. It is therefore equal to 1. Hence the value of equation (3.8)'s denominator is always 1, which makes the value of the whole equation equal to its numerator, which again is given by (3.10).

We therefore have the result that an optimal general equilibrium SCC is the discounted sum of receivers' period-specific marginal willingnesses-to-accept compensation at the Lindahl equilibrium, with the discount rates being the marginal rates of transformation that prevail at that equilibrium. And this is exactly the formula for the present period's Pigouvian tax that can (along with the requisite transfers) support as a competitive equilibrium the Lindahl equilibrium whose character function was used to derive that optimal SCC. It is the sum of all receivers' marginal willingnesses-to-accept, expressed in terms of the amount of good-1-in-the-present-period that would need to be invested in the present period to fully compensate receivers for the harm they would suffer from an extra unit of CO_2 emitted today.

This discussion reveals a connection with the Ramsey rule, which I discussed in section 2.7 in the context of social choice climate economics. The general principle behind this rule was that at an allocation that maximizes a social choice SWF, no net effect on the social welfare function's value should be engendered by shifting a marginal unit of consumption around in time, or by changing who consumes it. For example, if a social planner reduced one agent's consumption of good-1-at-time-0 by one unit and invested it instead so that a different agent could consume the investment's yield in some future period, the social welfare function should assign the same value to the original consumption path as it assigns to the new one. If this were not so, the social planner could use such investments to move the world onto a higher-ranked path; but then that would contradict our assumption that the first path really does maximize the social welfare function at issue. Thus if that first path does maximize the social welfare function, then the principle underlying the Ramsey rule holds. The Ramsey rule, stated as equation (2.16) in section 2.7, is the specific version of that principle that is entailed by discounted utilitarian SWFs. The general version says that at an intertemporal allocation that maximizes a social welfare function, the discount rates that apply to any consumption good must equal the economy's marginal rates of intertemporal transformation for that same type of good. And because of their mathematical isomorphism, this principle applies whether one is concerned to maximize a discounted utilitarian character function in a general equilibrium context or a discounted utilitarian social welfare function in a social choice context. It is therefore unsurprising that the discount rates to be used in computing an optimal general equilibrium SCC are equal to the marginal rates of transformation that prevail at the relevant Lindahl equilibrium.

There are, however, two key differences between the contexts that it is important to underscore. First, the discount rates relevant to computing optimal social choice SCCs are dictated by the ranking of allocations that is determined by the underlying social welfare function. By contrast, the discount rates to be used in constructing Pigouvian taxes depend on the Lindahl equilibrium one begins with, which in turn determines the character function one must work with.

Second, while a Lindahl equilibrium's SCCs are perforce indicators of aggregate willingness-to-pay for marginal abatement, this is *not* necessarily true of an optimal social choice SCC. If the individual-specific functions that compose a social welfare function are paternalistic to any degree, then the individuals' well-being-related marginal rates of substitution will not necessarily be indicators of their actual marginal willingnesses-to-pay or -accept. Should we nevertheless treat an optimal social choice SCC value as an indicator of *social* willingness to pay? Not as a rule, no, because a normative social welfare function may well represent a normative ordering of consumption paths that differs from any society's or lawmaking body's actual preference ordering of them. So should we instead interpret an optimal social choice SCC as an indicator of what a society *should* be willing to pay for marginal abatement? That is a difficult question, and it is actually the central topic of Part II. My answer will be no, we should not view optimal social choice SCCs in that way.

3.13 The Ramsey-Koopmans-Cass Model

We are now in a position to understand the general equilibrium foundations of one of the leading policy optimization models in climate change economics. It is a model whose character function is formally identical to the social choice social welfare function used in the *Stern Review*, and whose name derives in part from Ramsey's famous paper on intertemporal social choice. Sometimes it is called the Ramsey-Cass-Koopmans optimal growth model, which is ironic because the relevant papers written by Ramsey, Cass, and Koopmans were explicitly concerned with what Cass calls "prescriptive growth" theory (Spear and Wright 1998, p. 538), in which the task is for "the central planning board ... to choose the *optimum* feasible growth path with respect to the criterion of maximizing social welfare" (Cass 1965, p. 234, emphasis in original). That is to say, Ramsey, Cass, and Koopmans were concerned with applied social choice theory. In contrast, the Ramsey-Cass-Koopmans optimal growth model is the model Nordhaus refers to when he claims that optimization can be used "descriptively," with the sole non-normative purpose of "simulating ... the behavior of a system of interacting competitive markets" and for "estimating the equilibrium of a market

GENERAL EQUILIBRIUM CLIMATE ECONOMICS 67

economy" (Nordhaus 2013, pp. 1110–1111).[16] These are not tasks for social choice theory, but for general equilibrium theory, as I have described it in this chapter.

Much confusion among both philosophers and economists stems from the fact that the very same functional form has been used, in two radically different contexts, to construct policy optimization IAMs for studying quite different dimensions of the climate change problem. I shall discuss how the social choice version of the Ramsey-Cass-Koopmans functional form can be derived from axiomatic foundations in chapter 4. In this section and the next, I show how it can arise within two different general equilibrium models.

We already have some familiarity with the general equilibrium Ramsey-Cass-Koopmans model from my description of its social choice counterpart in chapter 2. I explained in section 2.1 what it means for individual well-being at one time to be a one-argument function of "generalized consumption," $w(c_t)$. I shall retain this focus on generalized consumption in what follows.

Imagine a global economy populated by h households of identical size. Members of each household live for just one time period, at the end of which they have children who will live in just the next period, and so on. Let each household grow at the same constant rate into an infinite future, as the Ramsey-Cass-Koopmans (RCK) model is typically articulated in terms of an infinite time horizon.

Now suppose that aggregate household consumption is always divided equally among household members, and that all households in the initial period share the following two-period utility function:

$$U_{ht} = N_{ht} \cdot u\left(\frac{C_{ht}}{N_{ht}}\right) + U_{ht+1} \cdot \frac{1}{(1+\theta)} \quad (3.12)$$

where h is an index of households, C_{ht} is the aggregate consumption of household h at time t, N_{ht} is the size of h at t, U_{ht+1} is the household's two-period utility function at $t+1$, and $\frac{1}{(1+\theta)}$ is a discount factor on the household's two-period utility at $t+1$. Thus while the presently living members of each household have preferences concerning their

---

[16] For a textbook treatment, see Romer (2012, ch. 2, part A).

consumption, they also have preferences concerning the consumption of their descendants. If the utility discount rate θ is positive, then a household's living members care relatively more about their own preference satisfaction than they do for their descendants'. In the social choice context, I referred to parameters like θ as *pure time discount rates*. There, a positive rate implied that a future unit well-being was not as valuable, from the point of view of a normative social welfare function, as a present unit of well-being. In the general equilibrium context, where a positive θ means that a given agent *cares less* about future preference satisfaction, I shall refer to it as a rate of *pure time preference*.

If each successive generation within a household shares the same two-period utility function, then the present generation also cares about generations far in the future, since there is a chain of concern that connects the situation of future generations to the preferences of the present one. This chain of concern exists even though the generations themselves do not overlap in time; members of each new generation are born at the exact same time members of the previous generation die.

Because of the structure of these chains of concern, the utility function of each of the households that exist at a time t can be written like this:

$$U_{ht} = \sum_{t=0}^{\infty} N_{ht} \cdot u(c_{ht}) \cdot \frac{1}{(1+\theta)^t} \quad (3.13)$$

where $c_{ht} = (C_{ht}/N_{ht})$. (3.13) is often referred to as a "dynastic utility function" (Ginsburgh and Keyzer 2002, pp. 268–269). Since household sizes are identical, each time's N_{ht} value will be identical across households and will be a function of the common household size in the initial period and the rate of household population growth, which is often assumed to be a constant.

RCK models in macroeconomics standardly adopt all the technical assumptions required to characterize all Pareto efficient allocations in the modeled economy as the solution to a weighted sum of h dynastic utility functions. Thus the RCK model's character functions take the following form:

$$W = \sum_{h} \alpha_h \left(\sum_{t=0}^{\infty} N_{ht} \cdot u(c_{ht}) \cdot \frac{1}{(1+\theta)^t} \right) \quad (3.14)$$

This is not the canonical RCK character function, however. For it is standard to assume further that the real-world economy can be modeled as the outcome of economic interaction between dynastic households that begin with an equal share of global resources and that will at no time face lump-sum redistribution (Acemoglu 2009, p. 174n9). This is equivalent to the assumption that (3.14)'s Pareto weights are identical and might as well each be set equal to 1. Given these assumptions, we therefore end up with:

$$W = \sum_{t=0}^{\infty} N_t \cdot u(c_t) \cdot \frac{1}{(1+\theta)^t} \qquad (3.15)$$

where N_t denotes global population at t, and c_t denotes average global consumption at t. While equation (3.15) is the canonical RCK model's character function, both in climate change economics and in macroeconomics more generally, versions of equation (3.14) have also been used in "regionally disaggregated" general equilibrium policy optimization models in climate economics, with h serving as an index of large regions of the world, which are assumed to have their own "dynastic" intertemporal utility functions (Nordhaus and Yang 1996; Digas et al. 2014; Manne and Richels 2005).[17] In that disaggregated version of the model, the Pareto weights are taken to be unequal, and a central applied task is to compute Negishi weights, which, you will recall, are the Pareto weights associated with an allocation's Lindahl-equilibrium-with-no-lump-sum-transfers (see sections 3.7 and 3.11). These are the weights an analyst can use to derive the Lindahl-Pigou prices (including pollution prices), as well as the compensatory transfers, that are needed to support a Pareto efficient and Pareto-*improving* Lindahl-equilibrium-with-no-lump-sum-transfers in a decentralized fashion. As Nordhaus puts it:

> The calculations of the potential improvements in world welfare from efficient climate change policies examine potential improvements within the context of the existing distribution of income and investments across space and time. There may be other improvements—in environmental

---

[17] Nordhaus and Yang allow Pareto weights to vary by time rather than by region and for that reason their character function looks rather different from (3.14). For strong criticism of time-varying Pareto weights, see Dennig and Emmerling (2017).

policies, in military policies, in tax or transfer programs, or in international aid programs—[that] would improve the human condition, and might improve it even more than the policies we consider, but these are outside the scope of this analysis. (Nordhaus 2013, p. 1082)

I said my primary aim was not exegetical. But I will say this: as I read Nordhaus, he is principally concerned to compute the carbon taxes associated with the Lindahl equilibrium with respect to the prevailing inefficient baseline growth path. Still, he never reports the transfers that would be required to support this Lindahl equilibrium as a competitive equilibrium. This exclusive focus on Pareto efficient *taxes* is unfortunately common in environmental economics.[18] Without the corresponding transfers, implementing the taxes will (at best) leave the economy at a different Pareto efficient allocation from the Lindahl equilibrium with respect to the prevailing inefficient baseline. And there will be no reason to think this allocation will Pareto dominate the baseline. The only rationale for targeting this different efficient allocation over any other will then simply be that this is what environmental economists tend to recommend.

3.14 An Overlapping Generations Model

The RCK model is one of two main types of model taught in advanced macroeconomics courses. The second is known as the *overlapping generations model* (OLG). In climate economics, OLG models have been much less common than the RCK model. This is partly because solving an OLG model can be computationally demanding, and climate economics was established in an era of limited computational capacity.

Alan Manne once said that the RCK and OLG models "represent two polar opposite viewpoints on intergenerational altruism" (Manne 1999, p. 111). This is because the canonical OLG model is populated by individuals who live for multiple time periods and who reproduce, but who consume all their resources while they are alive and leave nothing in the form of bequests for their children. Individuals in the OLG model overlap in time with their

---

[18] For an exception, see von Below et al. (2016, pp. 26, 28).

children (and with other people's children), but members of successive generations are left to consume whatever they earn with their labor in youth, receive in dividends in old age, and are otherwise allocated in the form of transfers by the government (Romer 2012, pp. 77–100). In contrast, while the RCK model's generations do not overlap, members of one generation do choose to leave bequests to their offspring in the next generation, because the satisfaction of the next generation's preferences is an explicit argument in the previous generation's utility function. It is in this sense that the RCK model, but not the OLG model, reflects the phenomenon of intergenerational altruism.

Consider the following OLG model components.[19] At each date t, a new generation of individuals is born. Let n_t be that generation's population size. Each individual in this generation lives for $L+1$ periods and enjoys the annual consumption levels $(c_{t,t}, c_{t,t+1}, c_{t,t+2}, \ldots, c_{t,t+L})$. Here $c_{t,t+i}$ is the consumption level at $t+i$ of any individual born at t. Now let each of these individuals' *intertemporal* or *lifetime* utility function be given by

$$U_t = \sum_{i=0}^{L} u(c_{t,t+i}) \cdot \frac{1}{(1+\varepsilon)^i} \qquad (3.16)$$

where ε is the individual's rate of pure time preference.

An OLG model is further specified by defining the economy's initial conditions (e.g., who is alive and how much in total each person has to consume or invest), individuals' labor market behavior (e.g., how much time to allocate to work versus leisure), and the production side of the economy (e.g., how the investments that individuals make in firms in one period translate into specific returns in future periods).

Once again, so long as the requisite technical assumptions are made, we can give the form of the character function whose solutions comprise the set of Pareto efficient allocations in the OLG model:

$$W = \sum_{t=0}^{\infty} n_t \cdot \alpha_t \cdot U_t \qquad (3.17)$$

---

[19] In what follows I draw heavily on an OLG model developed by Richard B. Howarth. See Howarth (1996, 1998).

While the mathematics underlying Pareto weights permits them to vary by individual, (3.17) simplifies by assigning every individual who is born in the same time period t the same Pareto weight, α_t. If U_t is then given by (3.16), we can expand (3.17) as follows (Howarth 1996, p. 104):

$$W = \sum_{t=0}^{\infty}\sum_{i=0}^{L} n_{t-i} \cdot \alpha_{t-i} \cdot u(c_{t-i,t}) \cdot \frac{1}{(1+\varepsilon)^i} \qquad (3.18)$$

This character function first finds the sum of the weighted utility of all who exist at time $t = 0$. It does this by summing the weighted utility of those who are born in period 0, and then combining it with the weighted utility of those who were born one period earlier in $t-1$, and also with those who were born in $t-2$, and so on until it has added in the weighted utility of those who were born in $t-L$ who are in their last period of life. The character function then does this for each time in the analysis, and then sums across times.

Now, take any completely specified Pareto efficient intertemporal consumption path, and also select a lifetime utility function for each individual of the form given by (3.16). (Recall that any increasing function of (3.16) would represent a consumer's preferences just as well. I am asking us to select (3.16)'s form for the purposes of constructing the OLG model's character functions.) Now express the selected consumption path as a vector of lifetime utilities, one for each individual. Next, find the vector of α_t values such that the path maximizes (3.18) subject to the model's constraints. Label that vector α. Now abbreviate the chosen consumption path as an *aggregate path* of the form

$$C = (C_1, N_1, C_2, N_2, ..., C_\tau, N_\tau, ...)$$

where C_τ is aggregate consumption at τ and N_τ is total global population at τ. Howarth (1996, p. 106) then shows that C maximizes

$$W = \sum_{t=0}^{\infty} N_t \cdot u\left(\frac{C_t}{N_t}\right) \cdot \beta_t \qquad (3.19)$$

where the β_t values are given by

$$\beta_t = \frac{1}{N_t} \sum_{i=0}^{L} \alpha_{t-i} \cdot n_{t-i} \cdot \frac{1}{(1+\varepsilon)^i} \qquad (3.20)$$

Although one must start with a given vector of Pareto weights α in order to compute (3.19)'s β_t values, the result in (3.19) shows that one can also derive something very similar to the RCK model's functional form from within an OLG model. The only difference is that the β_t weights in (3.19) are not simple exponential utility discount factors, as they are in the RCK character function given by equation (3.15). Bewley (2009, pp. 464–465), however, shows that all Pareto efficient allocations in this OLG model will also maximize character functions having the following form:

$$W = \sum_{t=0}^{\infty} v(C_t) \cdot \frac{1}{(1+\varepsilon)^t} \qquad (3.21)$$

where ε is the individual rate of pure time preference from (3.16) and $v(C_t)$ is the maximum amount of Pareto-weighted utility that can be created by dividing C_t among the N_t individuals who are alive at t.

What this and the previous section show is that there are two quite different ways within the general equilibrium framework to derive character functions that mathematically mirror the discounted utilitarian social welfare function used by Stern and others in social choice climate economics. As I have explained, a general equilibrium character function can be used to compute the Pigouvian taxes that are required to support, in a decentralized fashion, any preselected Pareto efficient allocation. Whether a given intertemporal schedule of Pigouvian taxes really could engender a Pareto efficient level of emissions in the real world depends in part on whether the character function's utility functions are accurate representations of real people's preference orderings. That is why character functions should be parameterized "descriptively," as Nordhaus has stressed (Nordhaus 2013, p. 1114). In contrast, it is perfectly coherent to parameterize social choice social welfare functions "prescriptively," as Stern does (Stern 2008). This is because Stern's social welfare function is constructed with an eye toward generating a normative ordering of consumption paths, and not with an eye to merely characterizing some predetermined Pareto efficient allocation.

If (as I have suggested) Nordhaus is working within the general equilibrium framework and is concerned to identify an objective function whose solution is the Lindahl-equilibrium-with-no-lump-sum-transfers, then Nordhaus and Stern are simply concerned with different analytical questions. This shows the danger of drawing quick inferences from the fact that Nordhaus and Stern "use the same basic data and analytical structure" (Nordhaus 2008, p. 165). Since that structure can arise in quite different ways from within radically different analytical frameworks, one cannot conclude that Nordhaus and Stern disagree with one another when they adopt radically different parameter values within identical functional forms.

3.15 Baseline General Equilibrium SCCs

Here again is the character function in the canonical Ramsey-Cass-Koopmans general equilibrium optimal growth model:

$$W = \sum_{t=0}^{\infty} N_t \cdot u(c_t) \cdot \frac{1}{(1+\theta)^t} \qquad (3.22)$$

As explained in section 3.13, any consumption path that maximizes this equation, subject to the model's technological feasibility constraints, is Pareto efficient. Recall that these paths are not the only possible Pareto efficient solutions in the model, however, because (3.22) implicitly narrows the analytical focus to Pareto efficient solutions in which each "dynastic family" is initially endowed with the same level of consumption. That is why (3.22) omits any explicit reference to Pareto weights: it implicitly takes them all to equal 1. If the Pareto weights are permitted to vary, other Pareto efficient solutions are possible in the model.

Suppose there is reason to think that the real-world intertemporal global economy can indeed be modeled using a general equilibrium model whose character function is of the standard RCK form given by (3.22). Assume further, as is standard in macroeconomics, that (3.22)'s utility function has the form:

$$u = \frac{c_t^{1-\sigma}}{1-\sigma} \qquad (3.23)$$

Observe that this utility function has the same form as the well-being function given by (2.9) in section 2.4. As noted there, to be used in discounted utilitarian social choice aggregation, (2.9) must be cardinal and interpersonally comparable. By contrast, here we require only that (3.23) faithfully represent each consumer's preferences *ordinally*.[20]

Given these assumptions, we know that the Ramsey rule obtains along any consumption path that maximizes (3.22). Once again, the Ramsey rule says that along a consumption path that maximizes an intertemporal objective function, the consumption discount rate for any time t must equal the real rate of return on an investment in consumption that is made at t. For a model whose objective function has the mathematical form of (3.22), and whose utility function has the form of (3.23), we know from section 2.7 that the Ramsey rule takes the following form:

$$r_t = \theta + \sigma \cdot g_t \tag{3.24}$$

where r_t is the real interest rate at t; θ is the rate of pure time preference that appears in (3.22) and that stemmed originally from the pure time preference exhibited by dynastic households (see equation (3.12)); and σ is the same parameter that appears in consumers' common utility function (given by equation (3.23)).

A standard way to choose values for θ and σ in applied uses of the Ramsey-Cass-Koopmans growth model is to suppose that the inefficient baseline path is a *specially constrained* solution to the very same character function whose solution is the Lindahl equilibrium with respect to *that same* inefficient baseline path. The special constraints are added to the model's core feasibility constraints so that when maximization is undertaken subject to the new, larger constraint set, the solution becomes the inefficient baseline path, rather than its associated Pareto efficient Lindahl equilibrium.

This assumption—that certain inefficient and efficient outcomes can be expressed as solutions to the very same character function—is partially supported by a result in general equilibrium theory established by Kehoe et al. (1992). Kehoe, Levine, and Romer demonstrate that inefficient outcomes caused by the presence of externalities also can be expressed as solutions to weighted character functions, so long as the constraints to which the optimization is subjected are supplemented to reflect the presence of an

---

[20] Or, if one wishes to assume that (3.23) is cardinal, it is enough for my purposes that we not assume it is interpersonally comparable.

uncorrected externality. Kehoe and colleagues do not, however, describe the conditions under which inefficient and efficient outcomes will maximize the very *same* character function when subject to different constraint sets. So far as I know, no published result along those lines exists in the literature.[21]

This result from Kehoe and colleagues appears to be the theoretical basis for Nordhaus's use of the Ramsey rule to calibrate θ and σ in his DICE model.[22] For he assumes that the prevailing Pareto inefficient baseline also maximizes the character function that is maximized by his target Pareto efficient allocation, with the baseline path maximizing this function subject to the additional constraint that no greenhouse gas mitigation is undertaken along that path.[23] Having made this assumption, it follows that the Ramsey rule is satisfied along the inefficient baseline path. Call the present time period $t+1$, and place on the left-hand side of the Ramsey rule the Pareto inefficient real interest rate on investments that were made in t and that paid a return in the present period, $t+1$. This is the interest rate that is in principle observable along the actual Pareto inefficient path. Next, calibrate g_t on the right-hand side of (3.24) by observing the real growth in per capita consumption from t to $t+1$ along the prevailing inefficient path. Of course, even if these two variables in (3.24) can be calibrated empirically and with certainty, this still leaves one with infinitely many *pairs* of θ and σ that are consistent with those choices of r_t and g_t. But if one then believes it is possible to calibrate one of the two remaining parameters empirically, one can use that calibration to infer the other parameter's value.

And this is what Nordhaus does, although the details of his approach have changed over time: in Nordhaus (1994, pp. 10–12), he adopted $\sigma=1$ and then computed the corresponding value of θ; whereas in Nordhaus (2008, p. 50), he adopts $\theta=0.015$ and computes the corresponding value of σ. Either way, with values for θ and σ now in hand from this use of the Ramsey rule, Nordhaus uses them to parameterize the RCK character function that he then uses to compute *both* the inefficient baseline path—where the maximization is subject to the no-abatement constraint—as well as the

---

[21] I thank Timothy Kehoe for helpful discussion on this last issue.
[22] I introduced and briefly discussed the DICE model in chapter 1.
[23] Rezai (2011, p. 892) writes: "While Nordhaus (2008) lists the equations of DICE-07, specific assumptions about the parameters and the exogenous time profiles are only presented in the computer code of the publicly available model. In this section, I provide a compact guide for the GAMS-illiterate . . ." Rezai confirms that Nordhaus computes his baseline path by maximizing his chosen objective function subject to the exogenous constraint that mitigation is held to zero for hundreds of years.

full Pareto efficient path along which the greenhouse gas externality has been corrected (Nordhaus 2008, pp. 60–69; Rezai 2011). (Since Nordhaus is using optimization to construct empirical projections, we now see that sometimes chapter 1's distinction between "what-if" IAMs and "policy optimization" IAMs dissolves.)

Suppose one used this method to compute the present inefficient baseline consumption path and the time series of real interest rates associated with it. And suppose one used the method of section 3.12 to compute the initial period's general equilibrium SCC along this baseline path. The result would be an indicator of aggregate willingness to pay for marginal abatement along this inefficient path. It would be a sort of hybrid SCC—a cross between a baseline social choice SCC, on the one hand, and an optimal general equilibrium SCC, on the other: like social choice baseline SCCs (SC-BASE SCCs), this new SCC figure would reflect an aggregation of marginal damages along a non-optimal baseline path; but like optimal general equilibrium SCCs (GE-OPT SCCs), these marginal damages would be discounted back to a single present value using a time series of real interest rates, rather than a series of normative consumption discount rates derived from a social choice social welfare function.

We know from chapter 2 that normative discount rates are to be used in the service of a cost-benefit analysis whose question is, "Will this abatement project move the world onto a normatively higher-ranked consumption path?" But that cannot be the question that this new type of SCC helps to answer, for we have been assuming that the RCK objective function that underlies this new type of SCC is a not a social welfare function, but a general equilibrium character function. Nor can this new type of SCC be a Pigouvian tax, for Pigouvian taxes are equivalent to GE-OPT SCCs, which are SCCs that prevail along Pareto efficient consumption paths. In contrast, this new type of SCC aggregates damages along the *inefficient* baseline path. So let us ask: Is this new type of SCC—a type I shall call *baseline general equilibrium SCCs* (GE-BASE SCCs)—policy relevant?

Some climate economists believe so. They claim that instead of drawing on a ranked ordering of all feasible paths, policy analysts can invoke what is known as the *compensation principle* (Boadway and Bruce 1984, pp. 96–102). This principle says that path B is better than path A if the move from A to B would be a *potential Pareto improvement*, in the sense that it would be feasible in B to rearrange endowments so that everyone is at least as well off as they were in A, and at least one person is better off than they were in A.

The standard procedure for determining whether a greenhouse gas abatement project satisfies the compensation principle is to treat GE-BASE SCCs as an indicator of the total willingness to pay for marginal abatement, so that it can be compared with the present cost of that abatement. Let me stress, however, that it is *not* standard to derive these aggregate willingness to pay indicators from a character function that the prevailing baseline path maximizes subject to the constraint that nations undertake no greenhouse gas abatement. Instead, those who compute SCC figures with the compensation principle in mind typically use other methods to project baseline marginal willingnesses-to-pay and the time path of baseline real interest rates needed to discount them. They then claim that if the resulting SCC is greater than present abatement costs, then it follows that the future "winners" from abatement can fully compensate the present "losers" who would pay the abatement costs today (Goulder and Williams 2012). Let me explain this more fully.

Suppose we express future climate damages in monetary terms as the amount of consumption future victims of climate change would be willing to pay present emitters to refrain from emitting. That is, damages can be expressed as the maximum amount that future victims of damage would be willing to pay to prevent the cause of the damage. For example, if you knew you were going to suffer $100 of damage in period τ and could pay some amount of money in τ to prevent it, you should be willing to pay up to $100 to do so; if the cost of prevention is less than $100, then your payment enables you to improve upon the status quo. However, we must be careful with the notion of a future person's willingness to pay to prevent climate damage. This is because $100 in the future is not the same as $100 today. If, for instance, the interest rate on savings is 3 percent, then if I offered you $100 in ten years or $100 today, you should choose $100 today. For with $100 today, you could invest that amount and end up with $100 \cdot (1+0.03)^{10} = 134.39$ dollars in ten years—or you could spend the $100 today. So whether you prefer to consume today or in ten years, $100 today is more valuable to you than $100 ten years in the future.

Now consider Charlie, who will suffer $100 in climate damages in ten years. And suppose that because we are interested in the compensation principle, we want to know what he would be willing to pay people today to reduce their harmful emissions. Since we know that future dollars are worth less than present dollars, we cannot simply treat his willingness to pay as $100. We should instead discount Charlie's future-dollar-denominated willingness to pay at the real interest rates that prevail within the real-world baseline scenario. Thus if (for the sake of argument) the interest rate will be a constant 3 percent between now and then, then the *present value* of Charlie's future willingness to pay is $100 \cdot (1.03)^{-10} = \$74.41$. According to the compensation principle, then, an abatement project that prevents \$100 of damages in 10 years is a good thing if its present cost is less than \$74.41. In that case (the argument goes), future people will be better off because they experience less damage, and it would in principle be possible to fully compensate present abaters for their mitigation efforts. For example, if Denise is the present abater and it costs her \$50 per ton to abate, the government could require Denise's contemporary Emily to pay her \$50 in compensation, and then later require Charlie to pay Emily $50 \cdot (1.03)^{10} = \$67.20$ in ten years. Since Emily (like everyone else) already adjusts her consumption and investment behavior to the prevailing interest rates, she (like everyone else) will be indifferent between \$50 worth of consumption today and \$67.20 worth of consumption in ten years.[24] In this way (so the argument continues), the "loser" from a government-mandated abatement project (in this case, Denise) can be fully compensated by the winner (Charlie) even if Denise and Charlie will never live at the same time. So long as Emily's life overlaps with each, or so long as we can find a succession of people whose lives form an overlapping chain, the future winners from abatement can compensate the present losers. And the compensation principle says that an abatement project is a good thing just so long as compensation is possible.

The compensation principle was devised to address the skeptical worry that it is impossible to make interpersonal comparisons of well-being, and thus impossible to construct benefit measures suitable for a social choice cost-benefit analysis. As chapter 2 explains, social choice cost-benefit analysis requires a cardinally measurable and interpersonally comparable notion of well-being. If one cannot say that a project actually increases the sum of well-being, what is left to say about the project from the standpoint of normative welfare economics? Nicholas Kaldor and John Hicks, who first promulgated compensation principles, believed that one thing you could say is that a project offering a potential Pareto improvement increases society's capacity to satisfy preferences (Kaldor 1939; Hicks 1939). A project that increases this capacity is now said to promote *Kaldor-Hicks efficiency* or *potential Pareto efficiency*.

---

[24] This assumes that Emily is not so poor that she must spend the \$50 today on necessities.

There are two categories of objection to the compensation principle as a criterion for project evaluation. The first category is ethical, the second technical. The ethical objection is simple: there is no good reason to care about merely *potential* Pareto improvements. If compensation actually takes place and the beneficiaries of the project are still better off, then the project (plus compensation) results in an *actual* Pareto improvement. And if actual compensation is going to occur, one need not invoke the compensation principle; it is enough to invoke the concept of Pareto improvements. But if compensation will not occur, there is no ethical merit in the mere fact that the project's winners *could* compensate its losers and still be better off. If, for example, those who benefit are rich and those who are harmed are poor, it is not as if the poor will be mollified by the fact that it is *feasible* to compensate them fully. Feasible compensation is not the same thing as actual compensation, and the compensation principle is concerned solely with the former. Indeed, that is supposed to be one of its virtues: the economist doing the analysis can focus solely on "potential Pareto efficiency," leaving things like fairness or justice to the policymakers who have the authority to require (or to forgo) compensation. Yet it is one thing for an economist to *report* that a policy, plus compensation, would generate a Pareto improvement. It is quite another to deem the project a good thing even in the absence of Pareto-improving compensation from its beneficiaries. But the compensation principle does the latter.

Suppose, for example, that Policy A would give each of ten poor people $100 more in income, and would reduce each of ten rich people's income by $101. Such a project may very well increase the net total of human well-being, but it would clearly not be possible for the poor to benefit if they were also required to fully compensate the rich. Now suppose that Policy B would increase the incomes of each of ten rich people by some amount greater than $100 while reducing the income of ten poor people by $100 each. And suppose it were feasible to combine Policy B with income-redistribution that would fully compensate the poor. Lawrence Goulder and Roberton Williams claim, "[M]ost people would agree that satisfying the Kaldor–Hicks criterion gives a policy option greater appeal, other things equal" (Goulder and Williams 2012, p. 1250024–9). One who agrees with Goulder and Williams might hold that Policy B has "greater appeal" than Policy A on account of the fact that only Project B can be combined with redistribution to engender a Pareto improvement. But note that this purported merit of Project B vanishes if Policy B will not *in fact* be combined with the compensatory transfers. Yet, again, the compensation principle is entirely insensitive to what will in fact happen, since it is exclusively concerned with what is possible.

Sometimes the compensation principle is defended on the grounds that if it "is consistently used to select policies offering the largest net [monetary] benefits and there are no consistent losers, then it is likely that overall everyone will actually be made better off" (Weimer 2008, p. 2). I am not aware of any systematic, evidence-based defense that there are or would be no consistent losers if the compensation principle were consistently used in project and policy selection. Indeed, it seems clear that the compensation principle advantages projects that disproportionately benefit the rich, since the rich will often be willing to pay more for their preferred projects simply because they are able to pay more.

Moreover, this defense seems particularly difficult to sustain for intergenerational issues like climate change. If the current generation will have to pay the costs for investment projects that pay returns far in the future, then those who pay the costs will not be around to enjoy the fruits of a portfolio of projects each of which imposes uncompensated costs. One might argue in response that those who are alive today have already benefited from portfolios of compensation principle–approved projects that were undertaken in the past. But whether that is so is again an empirical matter whose truth is very much up for debate. In any case, this defense of the compensation principle is again not really a defense of that principle at all, but instead a defense of the view that public policy should strive to be actually Pareto-improving; the defense then just adds the claim that what matters is whether a temporally extended portfolio of policies is Pareto-improving, rather than single policies taken one by one.

The second category of objection to the compensation principle is technical. Three such objections have been particularly influential in the literature.[25] The first is due to Scitovsky (1941), who showed that when a new project would alter the economy's set of production possibilities, it is possible for the compensation principle to prefer the project over the status quo, and also to prefer moving back to this status quo once the project is undertaken. This is sometimes called the "reversal paradox." Scitovsky then

---

[25] Here I draw heavily on Boadway and Bruce (1984, pp. 98–102, 267–271).

considered a "double criterion" whereby a project would pass the (new) compensation test only if it is not subject to the sort of reversal he identified. Later, Gorman (1955) showed that even this stronger compensation principle allows for intransitivities where the principle prefers one project to a second, the second to a third, but the third to the first.[26]

The third technical problem with compensation principles is that the standard test for determining when they are satisfied is flawed. This problem is known as the "Boadway paradox." Robin Boadway (1974) showed that since relative prices can change when post-project compensation is actually paid, a project can pass the compensation principle's cost-benefit test even when the project does not in fact make Pareto improvements possible. Recall that the relevant cost-benefit test here is whether a project's winners are willing to pay more for it than its losers would need to be paid to fully compensate them. In my example above involving Denise and Charlie, I presented the test as whether the (discounted) monetary value of the climate damages Charlie would suffer was larger than the amount Denise would need to receive to fully offset the mitigation costs that the project would require her to pay. For the purposes of the compensation principle's cost-benefit test, the damages to Charlie are the mitigation project's benefits (since the project would prevent this amount of damage), and the price Denise must pay to fund the project (or the monetary value of the damages she suffers as a result of the project) are its costs. As indicated when I first described the case, the standard way to quantify these benefits and costs are to ask Charlie how much he would be willing to pay to secure the project, and to ask Denise how much she must be compensated to feel as well off as she would be without it. The problem is that these questions are typically asked relative to the post-project outcome in which compensation is *not* paid. What Boadway showed is that the amounts can change depending on whether or not compensation is paid. This is because the prices consumers will face after compensation is paid can differ from the prices they would face before it is paid.

This makes it possible for a project to pass a Kaldor-Hicks-based cost-benefit test when post-project-but-pre-compensation prices are used, but to fail such a test when the prices reflect post-project compensation. Yet in applied settings, the relevant willingnesses-to-pay and willingnesses-to-accept are virtually never evaluated at the prices that would prevail if compensation

---

[26] Samuelson (1950) had articulated yet another compensation principle that ruled out such reversals and intransitivities, but his principle's conditions of application were very restrictive and difficult to identify in practice (Boadway and Bruce 1984, p. 100; Jones 2005, pp. 13–16).

were paid. The result is a test that may count a project as enhancing "potential Pareto efficiency" even though its "winners," if forced to pay compensation, would actually prefer the pre-project status quo to the post-project, post-compensation outcome (Boadway and Bruce 1984, p. 271; Johansson 1991, p. 55; Blackorby and Donaldson 1990).

Both separately and together, the two categories of objection to compensation principles raise serious doubts about the analytical relevance of general equilibrium baseline SCC figures in welfare economics generally, and in climate change economics more specifically. They are very likely the objections that led the authors of the chapter on discounting and intergenerational equity in the Intergovernmental Panel on Climate Change's (IPCC's) Second Assessment Report to declare flatly—in 1996—that the compensation principle "is no longer accepted" (Arrow et al. 1996, p. 142n18). Clearly these authors were mistaken as to the principle's popularity. The authors of the chapter on ethics and economics in the IPCC's Fifth Assessment Report were more accurate. Citing Scitovsky, Gorman, and Boadway and Bruce, these authors swiftly dismissed the Kaldor-Hicks compensation principle for being "subject to severe objections" (Kolstad et al. 2014, p. 225).

My own conclusion is that baseline general equilibrium SCC figures are, for all these reasons, positively irrelevant, and should never be used in climate change policy evaluation. I know that many economists, especially environmental economists who do applied work, will not like this conclusion. And as we shall see in chapter 8, it conflicts with the cost-benefit analysis methodology used by federal agencies in the United States. But in light of the problems I have canvassed here, I do not see how this conclusion can be avoided. Accordingly, a main goal of this book is to nudge economists toward the view that the only baseline SCC concept that genuinely bears on climate policy analysis is the baseline social choice SCC.

***

Despite the policy-irrelevance of baseline general equilibrium SCCs, there is a very important notion that we can extract from the way that they are used in policy analysis. As I explained above, the compensation principle is commonly interpreted as being concerned with a type of efficiency. The idea is supposed to be that projects satisfying the compensation principle enhance the world in one respect, namely in the respect of society's capacity to satisfy preferences, even if they do not make the world better in all respects. And while I have argued that the compensation principle is ethically misguided, this notion—the notion that an evaluative dimension can be important even when it captures only part of a larger evaluative story—*is* very important. Call it *normative abridgement*: a normative criterion (or a ranking that is predicated upon a normative criterion) is *normatively abridged* if the criterion fails to reflect or embody all of the normative values and principles that responsible public policy should attend to.

Much of Part II will be concerned with the idea of normative abridgement. But even with just this quick definition I can use the idea to further explain this book's subtitle. General equilibrium climate economics is intrinsically normatively abridged—and to that extent analytically limited—in virtue of being predicated solely upon the thin normative notion of Pareto efficiency. The general equilibrium framework, as I have defined it, does not itself furnish the evaluative criteria needed to place allocations into a normative, policy-relevant ranking. Yet a great deal of general equilibrium climate economics is focused on computing the taxes associated with a single Lindahl equilibrium, which I have called a Lindahl-equilibrium-with-no-lump-sum-transfers. But without supplementing the general equilibrium framework with normative values and principles that are external to it, this Lindahl equilibrium is just one of a vast array of Pareto efficient allocations whose merits and drawbacks the general equilibrium framework cannot evaluate. Even Pareto efficiency itself needs to be ratified normatively, given that at least two leading social welfare functions are inconsistent with it (as I shall explain in chapter 6).

None of this implies that general equilibrium climate economics is a misguided enterprise. I have, for example, explained how it can be used to formulate Pareto-improving climate policy, and it may turn out, after a full normative accounting, that climate policy ought to be Pareto-improving. But, again, one must go beyond the general equilibrium framework to fully evaluate this—or any other—climate policy proposal. (I shall return briefly to the topic of Pareto-improving climate policy in chapter 8.)

You might be getting the impression that I am setting up the social choice framework to emerge as the hero in this drama. For I have argued (1) that baseline general equilibrium SCCs are flatly policy-*irrelevant* (because of the ethical and technical problems with the compensation principle) and (2) that any optimal general equilibrium SCC's policy-relevance is uncertain until its associated Pareto efficient allocation has been ratified by a more complete normative appraisal. Moreover, I have just called into question the normative importance of Pareto efficiency itself, noting that it conflicts with multiple leading social choice SWFs.

But in fact I will not be arguing that a social choice SWF can save the day. Instead, Part II argues that the most defensible SWF is also likely to be radically normatively abridged. If that is correct, then climate change economics is doubly limited and all the more in need of supplementing by values and principles that policy optimization frameworks ignore or ought to ignore. After arguing for this abridgement thesis in Part II, I shall try in Part III to describe and defend the use of certain SCC concepts in climate change policy analysis.

Before moving to Part II, I want to stress that I have chosen to focus on discounted utilitarian objective functions in this part because of their prominence in real-world social choice and general equilibrium climate economics. The important theoretical differences between these two frameworks would remain if one or both moved away from discounted utilitarianism in favor of alternative functional forms. At the end of chapter 1 I suggested that one could coherently reject discounted utilitarian SWFs while still embracing or remaining agnostic on the use of discounted utilitarian character functions.[27] I hope it is now clear why this stance is perfectly consistent. Moreover, its availability is very important dialectically, since philosophers like me typically have no expertise in what general equilibrium character functions should look like. This is why Part II explores the theory underlying social choice SWFs and their use in climate policy analysis, and why Part III's discussion of character functions is conducted in rather general terms and without reference to any specific formalism. I shall have nothing further to say about the proper functional form of character functions.

---

[27] One can also coherently reject discounted utilitarian character functions, if we distinguish the general *weighted* utilitarian functional form that all character functions take (exhibited by equation (3.3)) from a more specific *discounted* utilitarian character function whose derivation depends on particular assumptions concerning the form of individuals' intertemporal utility functions (as equations (3.15) and (3.21) do).

PART II
PHILOSOPHY

4
A Foundation for (Discounted) Utilitarian Social Welfare Functions

In chapter 2 I used a discounted utilitarian function as the main example of a social choice social welfare function (SWF). This was because of that function's prominence in climate change economics. As I explained there, the job of a social choice SWF is to numerically represent a normative ordering. In climate economics, the ordering at issue is standardly an ordering of intertemporal consumption paths. When an integrated assessment model's objective function is a social choice SWF, SCC figures become indicators that can be used in the normative evaluation of climate policy, as explained in sections 2.3 and 2.7.

Chapter 2 also stated the specific discounted utilitarian SWF used in the *Stern Review*:[1]

$$V = \sum_{t=0}^{\infty} N_t \cdot w(c_t) \cdot \frac{1}{(1+\delta)^t} \tag{4.1}$$

I noted that this SWF is standard in part because of the pioneering work of Frank Ramsey (Ramsey 1928). (Ramsey insisted that the pure time discount rate in (4.1), δ, be set to zero. I return later in this chapter to this issue and to Ramsey's views on it.) Ramsey clearly believed that utilitarianism was a reasonable default social choice framework for intertemporal welfare economics, but he made no attempt to justify it from first principles.

It was not until the work of Tjalling Koopmans in the 1960s that someone provided axiomatic foundations for an SWF suitable for the infinite-time-horizon framework that Ramsey adopted. Meanwhile, in the 1950s, John Harsanyi had formulated an axiomatic defense of a weighted utilitarianism

---

[1] I have converted the *Stern Review*'s formalism from continuous to discrete time and used "w" to clarify that Stern's analysis takes place within a social choice SWF framework that aggregates well-being across individuals.

that (1) cannot accommodate an infinite time horizon but that (2) offers a general framework within which both discounted and undiscounted utilitarianism can be defended as special cases. In this chapter I describe these two efforts to put (discounted) utilitarianism on secure axiomatic footing. As will become clear, I am more optimistic about a Harsanyian route, despite the many assumptions that must be made—and eventually defended—along the way. (When I refer to a framework's broad potential for justifying either discounted or undiscounted utilitarianism, I will sometimes use the unspecific term "(discounted) utilitarianism.")

4.1 Koopmans's Axiomatic Utilitarianism

Like Ramsey before him, Koopmans began from the simplifying assumptions that population size would be held constant across an infinite time span, and that there would be no intratemporal consumption inequality. Thus Koopmans sought to derive a function that can represent an ordering of infinite paths of per capita consumption of the form:

$$(c_0, c_1, c_2, \ldots, c_t, \ldots)$$

Koopmans proved that if one adopts a certain set of axioms that must be obeyed by an ordering defined over a set of infinite paths of this sort, then the only functions able to represent such an ordering will be of the form:

$$V = \sum_{t=0}^{\infty} w(c_t) \cdot \frac{1}{(1+\delta)^t}, \quad \text{with } \delta > 0 \qquad (4.2)$$

Observe that in (4.2) the pure time discount rate, δ, is stipulated to be positive.

Koopmans's axiomatization of discounted utilitarianism has been very influential in intertemporal welfare economics broadly, and in climate change economics more specifically. It is, for example, the only theoretical basis mentioned in the *Stern Review* and by Richard Tol in his leading textbook on climate economics (Stern 2007, p. 662; Tol 2019, p. 149).[2] Many economists

---

[2] For further indications of Koopmans's influence, see also Heal (1998), Dasgupta (2005, 2012, 2019).

believe that Koopmans proved that a positive pure time discount rate cannot reasonably be avoided. As we shall soon see, Koopmans did not necessarily agree with this assessment.

One of the axioms underlying Koopmans's derivation of (4.2) is that the ordering to be represented by this SWF be a *complete* ordering. This means that for every pair of infinite consumption paths, either one is ranked strictly higher than the other, or they are level in the ordering.

But what if one seeks only a *partial* ordering? This, in fact, was Ramsey's solution to the problem raised by the need to sum an infinite number of well-being indicators. First, he posited a maximum possible achievable level of well-being, which he termed *Bliss*, or B. He then reinterpreted the utilitarian criterion: instead of being concerned to maximize the sum of every generation's (per capita) level of well-being, he proposed the criterion of minimizing the sum of generational *shortfalls* from B (Ramsey 1928, p. 545).

Next, Ramsey assumed that the set of feasible consumption paths can be partitioned into two subsets: first, those paths along which generational well-being levels steadily approach B over time; and second, those that do not steadily approach B. Ramsey claimed that each member of the subset of paths along which well-being steadily approaches B is "infinitely more desirable" than any path along which this does not happen, for there will be an infinite number of times at which well-being along the first path is strictly higher than well-being at the same time along the second path (Ramsey 1928, p. 545). In effect, therefore, Ramsey argues that it is sufficient for his SWF to yield an ordering of only the subset of paths that steadily approach B and that are, thereby, amenable to the trick of ranking paths by the degree to which they minimize the sum of shortfalls from B. This allows for the use of an *un*discounted utilitarian SWF within the context of an infinite time horizon, which is what Ramsey was after: he wished not to "discount later enjoyments in comparison with earlier ones, a practice which is ethically indefensible and arises merely from the weakness of the imagination" (Ramsey 1928, p. 543).

One obvious hurdle for this approach is selecting a Bliss level. I suspect this is a main reason why virtually no contemporary analysis follows Ramsey in invoking Bliss to solve the problem of summing an infinite number of well-being indicators. A second problem is this: while one may be able to identify a single best feasible consumption path in Ramsey's framework, it may be impossible to compare certain suboptimal paths with one another. Consider the set of paths that do not indefinitely approach Bliss. For these, the sums of shortfalls from Bliss themselves may not converge, which leaves them unranked by Ramsey's SWF. For this reason, Ramsey's framework might not be able to compute baseline social choice SCC figures, which are tools for comparing the existing suboptimal path with similar suboptimal paths.

Like Ramsey before him, Koopmans "admit[s] to an ethical preference for neutrality as between the welfare of different generations" (Koopmans 1965, p. 239). But instead of invoking the notion of Bliss to combine temporal impartiality with an infinite time horizon, Koopmans experimented with combining an undiscounted utilitarian SWF with the so-called *overtaking criterion* introduced by von Weizsäcker (von Weizsäcker 1965). This criterion holds that consumption path *a* overtakes path *b* if and only if there is a time T^* such that for every $T \geq T^*$:

$$\sum_{t=0}^{T} w(c_t^a) > \sum_{t=0}^{T} w(c_t^b) \qquad (4.3)$$

where c_t^a denotes the per capita consumption level at time t along path *a*. Note that since the consumption paths at issue are infinite, the overtaking criterion can be thought of as first ranking such paths by their limiting well-being value. If one infinite path's limiting value is greater than another's, then eventually the first will overtake the second.[3] But if two paths share a limit, the overtaking criterion can still rank them with respect to one another by determining whether there is in fact a time T^* such that, for every $T \geq T^*$, all of the non-infinite sums of well-being associated with one path are larger than those associated with the other. Koopmans found that while one cannot achieve a *complete* ordering of consumption paths by combining undiscounted utilitarianism with the overtaking criterion, one *can* identify a unique optimal path in the stylized economy that Ramsey studied (Koopmans 1967, p. 5).[4] In this respect, Koopmans used the overtaking criterion to achieve what Ramsey sought to achieve with the notion of Bliss.[5]

Unfortunately, the overtaking criterion cannot be used to compute SCC values. For although this approach incorporates an undiscounted utilitarian

---

[3] For a proof, see Heal (1998, p. 67).
[4] For a visual example that proves the overtaking criterion's incompleteness, see Heal (1998, pp. 65–66).
[5] While the overtaking criterion is often defined as embedding an undiscounted utilitarian SWF, that is a mistake. For example, the criterion's key notion of overtaking can just as well be combined with a prioritarian SWF. See Adler (2008, pp. 1516–1517). I will introduce prioritarianism in section 4.3 and discuss it further in chapter 6.

UTILITARIAN SOCIAL WELFARE FUNCTIONS 93

criterion, it does not ultimately rank consumption paths using that criterion alone. Rather, we have just seen that the overtaking criterion's procedure for ranking two paths against one another is *lexicographic*: it involves applying one test, and if that test is passed equally well by both paths, it applies a second, tie-breaking test. Yet it is well-known that lexicographic orderings cannot be represented by any real-valued mathematical function (Sen 2017, pp. 81–82; Heal 1998, p. 67). This undermines any attempt to use the overtaking criterion to derive social choice SCC values.

Koopmans notes a further problem with combining the overtaking criterion with undiscounted utilitarianism. To explain it, it helps to switch for a moment to a continuous time formulation of the discounted utilitarian SWF he worked with:

$$V = \int_0^\infty w(c(t))e^{-\delta t} dt \qquad (4.4)$$

Suppose (4.4) can be derived from Koopmans's axioms just as well as (4.2) can.[6] Now suppose that, instead of confining ourselves to Ramsey's framework in which population size is held constant over time, we let the population grow at an exogenous rate n. If we then normalize first-period population by setting it equal to 1, we get the following discounted utilitarian SWF:

$$V = \int_0^\infty e^{nt} w(c(t))e^{-\delta t} dt \qquad (4.5)$$

which is equivalent to:

$$V = \int_0^\infty w(c(t))e^{-(\delta-n)t} dt \qquad (4.6)$$

Recall now that Koopmans was able to relax his original requirement that the pure time discount rate be positive by combining an undiscounted utilitarian SWF with the overtaking criterion. This yielded only a partial ordering of consumption paths, yes, but it showed how one might preserve impartiality with respect to the timing of well-being. Koopmans notes, however, that this approach still requires that the pure time discount rate in (4.4)

---

[6] Koopmans (1972, p. 80) suggests that this should be possible but he did not supply a proof.

be nonnegative. If it is negative, then no optimal consumption path exists. (To see this, suppose we have identified the path with the highest feasible limiting well-being level. Then this is the path that overtakes all others. And yet with negative pure time discounting, this path will be less desirable than a path that is virtually identical to it, but which moves one unit of well-being from one time to any later time. But if this can always be done—as it can in many of the models studied by economists—then one faces what Koopmans labels "the paradox of the indefinitely postponed splurge," because "the moment when that maneuver pays off best ... never arrives!" (Koopmans 1967, pp. 6–8). This is problematic: it is one thing to embrace an evaluative criterion that cannot rank or compare very suboptimal paths; it is quite another to be unable to perform *any* useful evaluative task.) Yet the mathematics that forbids $\delta < 0$ when combining the overtaking criterion with (4.4) also forbids $\delta - n < 0$ when using (4.6) instead. The upshot is that if the rate of population growth n is positive, then even when using the overtaking criterion one must adopt a positive pure time discount rate if one hopes to identify a top-ranked path. But this is an odd *ethical* conclusion to be forced to accept simply as a result of choosing to work with an economic model characterized by (1) a growing population, (2) the ability to move well-being around through time, and (3) an infinite time horizon.

Finally, despite employing an undiscounted utilitarian function, it turns out that the overtaking criterion violates temporal impartiality. Heal gives the following example inspired by an example in Lauwers (1993). Consider the following well-being paths:

$$(1,1,1,1,\ldots)$$
$$(0,1,1,1,1,\ldots)$$
$$(0,0,1,1,1,1,\ldots)$$
$$(0,0,0,1,1,1,1,\ldots)$$

Each of these has the same total well-being, "and [they] differ only in that this is postponed further and further into the future" (Heal 2005, p. 1114).[7] Yet the first path overtakes the second, which overtakes the third, and so on.

---

[7] Heal's example uses paths of consumption, but the point remains when paths of well-being are at issue.

The ranking of paths given by the overtaking criterion therefore exhibits temporal partiality by demoting paths whose well-being is simply moved into the future.

John Broome notes that a similar sort of temporal partiality characterizes the axiom of Koopmans's that may seem the most innocuous. To this point I have mentioned only Koopmans's completeness axiom, choosing primarily to focus on the (discounted) utilitarian functional form that his axioms together entail. Broome examines Koopmans's axiom of continuity, which holds that "two programmes [e.g., two well-being paths] that are close to each other should occupy nearby positions in the ordering" (Broome 1992, p. 104). Broome explains that the continuity condition "has to be filled out by specifying when programmes are to be counted as close to each other. We need a concept of 'distance' between programmes" (Broome 1992, p. 104). Koopmans's notion of distance relies on the "sup norm," which states that the distance between two paths is the maximum difference between corresponding temporal well-beings along the paths. That is, for any two vectors of per capita well-being, $(w_1, w_2, \ldots, w_t, \ldots)$ and $(w'_1, w'_2, \ldots, w'_t, \ldots)$, the sup norm distance between them is the maximum difference between any two w_t and w'_t values. Now consider a new set of four distinct well-being paths:

$$(1, 0, 0, 0, \ldots)$$
$$\left(\frac{1}{2}, \frac{1}{2}, 0, 0, \ldots\right)$$
$$\left(\frac{1}{3}, \frac{1}{3}, \frac{1}{3}, 0, 0, \ldots\right)$$
$$\left(\frac{1}{4}, \frac{1}{4}, \frac{1}{4}, \frac{1}{4}, 0, 0, \ldots\right)$$

Broome remarks:

> An impartial valuation would insist that each member of this sequence is equally good, however far down the line we go. Certainly, each is better than the programme $\left(\frac{1}{2}, 0, 0, 0, \ldots\right)$. However, as we go down the line the members of this sequence of programmes gets closer and closer to $(0, 0, 0, \ldots)$, according to the ["sup norm"] distance measure I specified.

Consequently, if the ordering is continuous, later members of the sequence will have to be close to $(0,0,0,\ldots)$ in the ordering. But $(0,0,0,\ldots)$ must be below $\left(\frac{1}{2},0,0,\ldots\right)$. So later members of the sequence must be below $\left(\frac{1}{2},0,0,\ldots\right)$. That is required by continuity. Impartiality, however, requires them to be above $\left(\frac{1}{2},0,0,\ldots\right)$. Impartiality and continuity are therefore inconsistent. (Broome 1992, p. 105)

Broome shows that when Koopmans's continuity condition is imposed on orderings of infinite well-being paths, the effect is a systematic bias against future well-being. The sup norm notion of distance looks only at the maximum difference between any two corresponding locations along two paths. It therefore cares only that the maximum distance between any two corresponding locations in $\left(\frac{1}{2},0,0,\ldots\right)$ and $(0,0,0,\ldots)$ is greater than the maximum distance between any two corresponding locations in $\left(\frac{1}{4},\frac{1}{4},\frac{1}{4},\frac{1}{4},0,0,\ldots\right)$ and $(0,0,0,\ldots)$. So although the path $\left(\frac{1}{4},\frac{1}{4},\frac{1}{4},\frac{1}{4},0,0,\ldots\right)$ contains more aggregate well-being, the sup norm continuity condition places that path between $\left(\frac{1}{2},0,0,\ldots\right)$ and $(0,0,0,\ldots)$, rather than above both. A function that represents a continuity-compliant ordering of the above well-being paths will therefore favor paths in which well-being is moved earlier in time. Koopmans was therefore mistaken to claim that the sup norm conception of distance "treats all future periods alike, and, if anything, has a bias toward neutrality with regard to the timing of satisfaction" (Koopmans 1960, p. 290).

Broome's example shows that by assuming the sup norm notion of continuity, Koopmans restricts from the beginning the set of orderings his analysis is concerned with. This is not a problem for the formal mathematical result that Koopmans proved: it remains true that, concerning the orderings Koopmans focused on, those orderings can be represented only by functions of the form of equation (4.2). But *pace* Partha Dasgupta, Koopmans's argument does not show that sup norm continuity is one of the "moral conditions that a concerned citizen would wish to respect" when seeking to place infinite consumption or well-being paths into a morally defensible ranking

UTILITARIAN SOCIAL WELFARE FUNCTIONS 97

(Dasgupta 2012, p. 105). Instead, one needs an independent normative argument in favor of adopting sup norm continuity in the first place, and I know of no attempt by an economist to supply it.

4.2 The Trouble with Infinite Paths

I certainly do not mean to asperse Koopmans for his choice of axioms. As it happens, it is extremely difficult to respect seemingly plausible axioms while working with infinite paths of the sort he studied. The axiom I have been calling "temporal impartiality" is a version of an axiom commonly articulated in terms of "anonymity." As Matthew Adler puts it, anonymity is a sort of "permutation" axiom: "Given some outcome x, if the arrangement of well-being levels in y is simply a permutation of the well-being levels in x, then y and x are equally morally good" (Adler 2012, p. 52).

It is the infinite character of well-being paths that conflicts with this anonymity criterion. Suppose once again that the paths we wish to rank are infinite paths of per capita well-being. Now consider the so-called strong Pareto condition. An ordering of infinite paths of per capita well-being satisfies strong Pareto just in case one path is always ranked higher than a second if, at every time, per capita well-being in the first is at least as high as it is in the second, and if there is at least one time at which well-being is higher in the first path than in the second. Now consider an example from Asheim, which he draws from work by Van Liedekerke and Lauwers (Asheim 2012; Van Liedekerke and Lauwers 1997). Asheim asks us to consider two infinite time paths of well-being (shown in Table 4.1). If the sole condition imposed on orderings of well-being paths were anonymity, then these two paths would be level in all compliant orderings. For it is possible to produce Path Two merely by rearranging occurrences in Path One—that is, "by moving location 2 to location 1, all other even locations two periods backwards, and all odd locations two periods forwards" (Asheim 2012, p. 135). Of course, this

Table 4.1 Two Infinite Paths of Well-being

Path One:	1	0	1	0	1	0	...	1	0	...
Path Two:	0	0	1	0	1	0	...	1	0	...

trick is possible only because the paths are infinite. But now note that according to strong Pareto, Path One *dominates* Path Two, since well-being at all times is at least as high in Path One as it is in Path Two, and there is one time at which well-being is higher in Path One than in Path Two. But that means the strong Pareto axiom conflicts with the anonymity axiom (Asheim 2012, p. 135).[8]

Because the strong Pareto and anonymity axioms both seem independently plausible, it is not immediately clear how to choose between them. But before one concludes that one must do so, it is worth questioning the assumption that we should be focusing on infinite paths in the first place. Some economists may wish to order infinite paths because of a belief that the world (or at least the existence of humans in the universe) will never end. But Geoffrey Heal explains that it more commonly reflects "a reluctance to specify a date beyond which nothing matters, as one does when one chooses a terminal date T that is finite" (Heal 2005, p. 1108). I am sympathetic to this reason for adopting infinite time horizons in intertemporal welfare economics, even when we know that assumption is false. One should wish to avoid analyses that give outsized influence to an arbitrarily selected final date T. But rejecting anonymity or strong Pareto is a high price to pay to do this.

One rationale for adopting what looks like a positive pure time discount rate, and which would let us choose strong Pareto over anonymity, relates to the chances that we (and other sentient creatures) will become extinct in the future. The nineteenth-century utilitarian philosopher Henry Sidgwick wrote:

> [I]t may be asked, How far we are to consider the interests of posterity when they seem to conflict with those of existing human beings? It seems, however, clear that the time at which a man exists cannot affect the value of his happiness from a universal point of view; and that the interests of posterity must concern a Utilitarian as much as those of his contemporaries, except in so far as the effect of his actions on posterity—and even the existence of human beings to be affected—must necessarily be more uncertain. (Sidgwick 1907, p. 414)

---

[8] The anonymity condition here is strong anonymity, which "entails indifference to any permutation of utilities of an infinite number of generations" (Asheim 2010, p. 60). Weak anonymity, by contrast, concerns permutations "of two (or a finite number of) generations" (p. 4).

Within intertemporal welfare economics the prospect of extinction has been used as a basis for adopting what formally resembles positive pure time discounting in the context of an infinite time horizon, but which is really discounting for risk in a world that will certainly end at some point. Indeed, this was the basis invoked by the *Stern Review* when adopting a pure time discount rate of 0.001 (Stern 2007, p. 53). The idea behind this approach is to posit a constant conditional exogenous risk ε of humanity's ending in any given future year. That is, conditional upon humanity's surviving until some future year t, the risk that humanity will become extinct in t is ε. By making this assumption, a social choice model with a known finite time horizon but random extinction date can be formally transformed into a model with an infinite time horizon and a constant "pure time discount rate" equal to ε.[9]

Is the assumption of a constant conditional risk of extinction plausible? Probably not. But even if there were a constant *exogenous* risk of extinction, there are clearly additional *endogenous* risks of extinction that stem from humanity's policy choices. Climate change is itself one such risk. We should want a framework that can account for the *total* risk of extinction, which will vary from one set of public policies to another. But such a framework would not allow an exogenous extinction risk to serve as a pure time discount rate while accounting for endogenous risks in some other way. Both risks should be handled systematically and together, which undercuts Stern's rationale for using a positive pure time discount rate.

4.3 Harsanyi's Axiomatic Utilitarianism

Five years before Koopmans published his axiomatic derivation of discounted utilitarianism, John Harsanyi published a distinct theorem that can, when used twice and supplemented with several further premises, underwrite a (discounted) utilitarian SWF so long as the analysis does not seek to order infinite consumption or well-being paths. The analytical context must not involve an infinite time horizon or an infinite population, that is to say. Like the extinction-risk rationale for pure time discounting, considerations of risk play a crucial role in Harsanyi's framework. But Harsanyi's framework

---

[9] For the formal basis of the transformation, see Acemoglu (2009, p. 156). The argument goes back at least to Yaari (1965). See also Dasgupta (2001, pp. 101–103).

requires that exogenous and endogenous risks to well-being be treated similarly. That is a virtue.

This route to discounted utilitarianism is rarely discussed in climate economics. That is perhaps because economists wish to work with infinite paths, which Harsanyi's approach again cannot accommodate. Yet even when more theoretically inclined environmental economists do mention Harsanyi's work as a possible foundation for a discounted utilitarian SWF, they often point to an argument of Harsanyi's that invokes the idea of reasoning behind what John Rawls later called a "veil of ignorance" (see Dasgupta and Heal 1979, pp. 269–275; Dasgupta 2012, pp. 107–108; Heal 2005, p. 1114; Harsanyi 1953). But it is a later, independent theorem of Harsanyi's that offers the sort of axiomatic route to discounted utilitarianism that Koopmans sought to provide, and it is this second theorem that I will focus on here (Harsanyi 1955). (I will return to the veil of ignorance argument in chapter 5.)

The specific Harsanyian line of argument I shall explicate is due to John Broome. Broome is a leading moral philosopher, and the leading moral philosopher writing on climate change economics. He was an advisor to the *Stern Review* and lead author of the Working Group 3 chapter in the IPCC's Fifth Assessment Report, "Social, Economic, and Ethical Concepts and Methods" (Kolstad et al. 2014). For more than three decades Broome has been exploring the promise and limitations of using Harsanyi's so-called "aggregation theorem" to underpin normative economic evaluations. But few climate economists seem to know this work. In what follows I draw heavily on Broome's writings, especially Broome (1991, 2004, 2015). I share his view that if there is a cogent route to either a discounted or undiscounted utilitarian social choice SWF, it runs through Harsanyi's aggregation theorem.

4.3.1 Harsanyi's Aggregation Theorem

Like Koopmans's theorem, Harsanyi's result is a representation theorem: it says that if an ordering satisfies a certain set of axioms, then it can be represented by function having a certain form. Harsanyi himself believed that his proof establishes an "axiomatic justification of utilitarian theory" (Harsanyi 1977, p. 636). But he was mistaken about this, for his result is perfectly compatible with a rival to utilitarianism called prioritarianism. Prioritarianism holds that before they are summed, individuals' well-being indicators should be transformed by a strictly concave function. To explain the premises needed to arrive at (a finite version of) the standard discounted utilitarian SWF using Harsanyi's aggregation theorem, I will first explain how it can be used to derive a form of prioritarianism. This will highlight the additional premises needed to rule out prioritarianism in favor of (discounted) utilitarianism. (I shall omit many details—including the actual proof of Harsanyi's theorem—that are set out and discussed in Resnik (1987, pp. 197–204), Peterson (2009, pp. 276–282), and Broome (1991, ch. 10).)

The derivation of Harsanyi's theorem requires premises from an area of decision theory known as expected utility theory. Harsanyi's original proof assumed an early version of expected utility theory that was first articulated by John von Neumann and Oskar Morgenstern in 1947 (von Neumann and Morgenstern 1947) and refined by Jacob Marschak (Marschak 1950). It turns out that Harsanyi's theorem can be proved within several quite different versions of expected utility theory (Broome 1990, p. 477; 2015, p. 250). While most economists are familiar with the von Neumann–Morgenstern framework, some important and subtle philosophical points about its central terms and concepts emerge when examining the relationship between Harsanyi's theorem and prioritarianism.

Let me begin by stating a finite version of the discounted utilitarian SWF used in the *Stern Review*:

$$V = \sum_{t=0}^{T} N_t \cdot w(c_t) \cdot \frac{1}{(1+\delta)^t} \qquad (4.7)$$

This SWF exemplifies what Broome calls a "snapshot route" to aggregating individual well-being for the purposes of constructing a social welfare ordering (Broome 2004, p. 104). That is, first it takes snapshots of each time taken separately. This involves adding together the *temporal well-beings* of each individual who is alive at a chosen time. Then it adds together all these temporal snapshots to arrive at a total intertemporal evaluation. An alternative approach to aggregation is what Broome calls "the people route." The people route first computes the lifetime well-being of each person who will live in a given intertemporal outcome, and then it aggregates these lifetime values across people to arrive at a final social value for that outcome. Equations (4.8) and (4.9) together give an example of the people route to aggregation:

$$w_i = \sum_{j=0}^{L} w(c_{t_i+j}) \cdot \frac{1}{(1+\delta)^j} \qquad (4.8)$$

$$V = \sum_{i=1}^{N} w_i \qquad (4.9)$$

Equation (4.8) expresses the lifetime well-being of individual i as the discounted sum of the temporal well-beings she experiences throughout her life. (4.8) assumes that i will live for $L+1$ time periods, the first of which is denoted by t_i. Next, equation (4.9) adds together the lifetime well-beings of each individual who will live in an outcome. As we will see, this people route can end up at the same place as a snapshot route to discounted utilitarian aggregation given in (4.7), if the functional forms are set just right.

In describing Harsanyi's aggregation theorem and its capacity to justify an SWF like (4.7), I will rely on the people route to aggregation. Thus let us suppose that our task is to order interpersonal vectors of lifetime well-being of the form:

$$W = (w_1, w_2, \ldots, w_N)$$

where w_i denotes the lifetime well-being of individual i. One restriction imposed by this route to (discounted) utilitarianism is that we must assume, at least for now, that all possible vectors report lifetime well-being indicators for the very same set of people. Without further amendments, Harsanyi's theorem has purchase only in settings where the composition of the evaluated population is constant across all possible well-being vectors. So at first I shall assume that feasible well-being vectors differ only in the levels of lifetime well-being they report for this constant set of people. I will relax this assumption in section 4.3.3.

I have referred several times to vectors of well-being like W above as an *outcome*: it expresses a way the world could turn out, with individuals 1 through N enjoying the lifetime well-beings w_1 through w_N. Typically, however, agents are not able to act in ways that will bring about a specific outcome for certain. For example, if I go for a drive, this act carries various risks for me and for others, and different distributions of lifetime well-being will be made more or less likely depending on how fast I choose to drive (and on many other decisions and background variables). I am typically unable to bring about a given outcome with certainty. Instead, my driving at a certain speed will be associated with an uncertain *prospect*, where a prospect is a collection of outcomes each of which is associated with a specific probability of coming about.

Different versions of expected utility theory formalize the general idea of an uncertain prospect in different ways. The version Harsanyi employed, the von Neumann–Morgenstern (vNM) framework, focuses on *lotteries*. A (simple) *lottery* is a set of possible outcomes, each of which is associated with a definite probability. Thus, if there are M different possible outcomes, a lottery L will be a vector, $L = (p_1, p_2, \ldots, p_M)$, that gives the probability of each outcomes's occurring. A *compound lottery* is a lottery of lotteries, such as (p_{L_1}, p_{L_2}) that gives the probabilities that each of two different simple lotteries—L_1 and L_2—accurately describes the chances of different outcomes' occurring. A key feature of the vNM framework is that each compound lottery is to be treated as equivalent to some simple lottery: that is, it is assumed that each uncertain prospect can be articulated as a set of final outcomes and a corresponding set of probabilities of those final outcomes (Kreps 1988, pp. 51–53; Peterson 2009, p. 101).

Let us continue to focus on outcomes expressed as vectors of lifetime well-being. Suppose there are again M possible outcomes of this sort. And suppose that i's *betterness ranking over lotteries*—that is, the ranking of how good the lotteries in fact are for i—is sensitive only to i's own well-being in the possible outcomes.[10] Then, the vNM expected utility framework establishes that if each individual i's betterness ranking of lotteries complies with four key axioms (to be stated below), that ranking can be represented by an *expectational utility function* of the form:

$$V_i(p_1, p_2, \ldots, p_M) = p_1 \cdot v_i(w_{1i}) + p_2 \cdot v_i(w_{2i}) + \ldots + p_M \cdot v_i(w_{Mi}) \quad (4.10)$$

where w_{mi} is i's lifetime well-being in outcome m.

Now, I was careful in Part I to use the term "utility" to refer only to the value of a function that represented preferences. This was the sort of function that featured centrally in the general equilibrium framework described in chapter 3. In the context of social choice climate economics, I spoke of well-being instead of utility, and I left open the possibility that an individual might not prefer that which is actually good for her. It is,

---

[10] This assumption still allows for one's well-being level to be influenced by the conditions of others. See Broome (2015, pp. 257–258).

however, common for both economists and philosophers to use "utility" as a synonym for "well-being." This can be very problematic, especially when there are two different frameworks on the table and when one framework exclusively employs noncomparable utility functions, while the other requires cardinal and unit comparable well-being functions. Obviously it invites confusion when "utility" is used to refer to both. That is why I never used "utility (function)" and "well-being (function)" synonymously in Part I.

The risk of confusion worsens when the theoretical foundations of social choice climate economics make use of expected utility theory. While this name has the term "utility" in it, nothing in the theory requires that it be applied only to preference orderings. As Broome writes, "Expected utility theory was originally intended as a theory of preferences. But it is only a collection of axioms and a proof. It can be applied to any relation that satisfies the axioms" (Broome 1991, p. 121). He then applies it to various betterness relations, such as a betterness ordering of lotteries defined on outcomes expressed in terms of an individual i's well-being in those outcomes. Two paragraphs back I called this i's *betterness ranking*. Since expected utility theory plays a large role in what follows, I will need to refer to the machinery of that theory. But I want to avoid the confusion that could arise if I were to use the standard terminology of "utility" and "utility function" when in Part I I reserved those terms for contexts in which people's actual preference rankings were at issue. To keep these contexts separate, I shall follow Broome (2019a) and use the terms "value function" and "value" when referring to the functions and numerical indicators that arise when the machinery of expected utility theory is applied to betterness orderings in the social choice context.

As it is expressed above in (4.10), neither i's expectational value function V_i, nor the "subvalue" function v_i, is itself a well-being function. Rather, V_i is a function that represents an *ordering of lotteries*, where the outcomes tied to those lotteries are articulated in terms of a prior well-being function w. Furthermore, the shape of the subvalue function v_i is entirely dictated by its role in facilitating V_i's representational purpose. Since we are assuming we can use the prior well-being functions to map outcomes in the world to vectors of lifetime well-being, we should not assume that the (sub)value functions in (4.10) are themselves well-being functions. Let me explain this further with an example.

Take two lotteries concerning an individual i's lifetime well-being, with the first giving i 50 units of well-being for certain, and the second giving her a 50 percent chance of getting 0 units and a 50 percent chance of getting 100 units. i's betterness ordering of lotteries exhibits risk-*neutrality* about lifetime well-being if and only if these two lotteries are level in her ordering—that is, if and only if each lottery receives exactly the same ranking score by i's value function V_i. (We here retain the assumption, made above, that i's betterness ordering is concerned only with her own well-being in the possible outcomes.) But if the first lottery comes higher in the ordering than the second, then the ordering represented by V_i exhibits risk-*aversion* about lifetime well-being. In that case, her ordering of lotteries privileges the achievement of a given well-being level for certain over a risky prospect having that level (in this case 50) as its mathematical expectation. In (4.10), V_i will exhibit risk-aversion just in case the subvalue function v_i is strictly concave.

If V_i represents i's betterness ordering of lotteries, and if in addition it exhibits risk-aversion, then it follows that avoiding risk is better for i than courting it. But—and this is the key point—we should not on that basis say that avoiding risk increases i's well-being itself. For w is already a well-being function, and V_i is a different function from w (as is v_i). Instead, we should say that risk to well-being is *bad* for i when her value function features a strictly concave subvalue function. We have no reason yet to treat this badness as a dimension or component of her well-being. By distinguishing between a person's well-being and the *goodness* for her of various lotteries concerning her well-being, we are able to say things like, "It would be better for i not to maximize her expected well-being, because that would be riskier than an option in which her expectation of well-being is lower."

In the vNM framework, an individual's betterness ordering of lotteries can be represented by a function having (4.10)'s form just in case that ordering satisfies the following axioms (Kreps 1988, pp. 43–50; Peterson 2009, pp. 98–100):

1. *Completeness*: For any two lotteries, A and B, either A is ranked higher than B, B is ranked higher than A, or A and B are level in the ordering.
2. *Transitivity*: For any three lotteries, A, B, and C, if A is ranked higher than B, and B is ranked higher than C, then A is ranked higher than C.
3. *vNM Continuity*: Let the abbreviation ApC stand for a compound lottery in which lottery A obtains with probability p and lottery C obtains

with probability $1-p$. Then an ordering exhibits *vNM Continuity* just in case, for any three lotteries A, B, and C, if A is ranked higher than B, and B is ranked higher than C, then there exist probabilities p and q, each greater than 0 and less than 1, such that the compound lottery ApC is ranked higher than B, and B is ranked higher than AqC.

4. *Independence*: For any three lotteries A, B, and C, lottery A is ranked higher than lottery B if and only if the compound lottery ApC is ranked higher than the compound lottery BpC.

I will not defend these axioms here. I find them reasonable, at least in the context of a betterness ordering. For sympathetic discussions of vNM Continuity, see Kreps (1988, pp. 45–46) and Peterson (2009, p. 100); and for a sophisticated defense of the general idea behind Independence, see Broome (1991, pp. 94–100).

If the vNM axioms are satisfied, then not only will an individual's betterness ordering of lotteries be represented by an expectational value function taking (4.10)'s form, but it will also be represented by any value function that is a positive affine transformation of V_i. I explained what this last part means in section 2.2. I also explained in section 2.2 that when a function is unique up to a positive affine transformation, it is a *cardinal* function. A cardinal value function is one whose ratios between differences are retained when the function is replaced by any positive affine transformation of it. For example, suppose that V_i assigns a value of 4 to lottery A and 8 to lottery B, and a value of 12 to lottery C and 16 to lottery D. Then the ratio of the difference between A and B to the difference between C and D is 1. So if V_i is a cardinal value function, then any function that is a positive affine transformation of it will also yield a ratio of 1 when that member is used to perform the same calculation. This ratio implies that a switch from lottery A to lottery B offers an incremental benefit that is *just as good for i* as a switch from lottery C to lottery D would be.

Let us suppose that each individual in our hypothetical fixed population has a betterness ordering of lotteries that are defined on interpersonal vectors of lifetime well-being, and that each of these orderings satisfies the vNM axioms. And as before, let each individual's ordering be sensitive only to her own well-being level in the different possible outcomes. Thus her value function is expectational and looks like (4.10).

Next, suppose that each individual is risk-averse about their lifetime well-being, in the sense defined above. So each individual i's subvalue function, v_i, is strictly concave. Note that this does not entail that the individuals' value functions are identical, as it is possible that they exhibit risk-aversion to different degrees.

Suppose next that we can define a "general" betterness ordering of lotteries defined on the same interpersonal vectors of lifetime well-being. This general betterness ordering might be interpreted as a "social" ordering—in line with many economic analyses—or it might be interpreted as an ordering constructed "from the point of view of the universe"—a notion that is invoked in the quotation above from Sidgwick and that is in line with the utilitarian tradition in moral philosophy. However it is interpreted, let us for now suppose that this general betterness ordering *also* satisfies the vNM axioms.

Finally, suppose that this general betterness ordering satisfies the *ex ante strong Pareto* axiom. As the name suggests, this axiom is related to the strong Pareto axiom discussed briefly above in section 4.2. It holds that, for any two lotteries A and B, if no individual's betterness ordering ranks B above A and at least one person's ordering ranks A above B, then A comes higher in the general betterness ordering than B.

What Harsanyi proved is that if each individual's betterness ordering of lotteries satisfies the vNM axioms, if the same is true of the general betterness ordering, and if the general betterness ordering also satisfies the ex ante strong Pareto principle, then the general betterness ordering of *outcomes* can be represented by a social welfare function having the following form (Resnik 1987, pp. 197–204; Peterson 2009, pp. 276–282; Broome 1991, ch. 10):

$$V = \sum_{i=1}^{N} a_i \cdot v_i(w_i) \qquad (4.11)$$

Harsanyi's theorem allows each a_i weight to take any value greater than zero.[11]

Harsanyi thought that the only thing needed to get from this aggregation theorem to social choice utilitarianism is to set all the a_i weights equal to 1. But as (4.11) shows, this is not correct: if one applies his theorem

---

[11] Broome notes that published versions of Harsanyi's aggregation theorem invoke a further premise that he says is not absolutely required for the theorem's derivation. Broome calls this premise the *rectangular field assumption* (see Broome 1991, sec. 4.4; 2004, pp. 80–81, 133–134). I will have nothing further to say about this premise.

to orderings of lotteries defined on outcomes expressed as interpersonal vectors of lifetime *well-being*, and if one makes all the further assumptions I have had us make in this section, then Harsanyi's mathematical result does not yield weighted utilitarianism, but rather weighted *prioritarianism* (Broome 2015, p. 256).

Harsanyi's theorem is compatible only with a prioritarianism of a very specific kind, which I will call *Harsanyi-compliant prioritarianism*. On that view, the transformation functions to be applied to lifetime well-being in *interpersonal* aggregation are the very same transformation functions that get applied *intra-personally* when aggregating across different possible outcomes for a given individual. Suppose that all of the individuals in our hypothetical population are risk-averse to the very same degree. If that justified replacing each v_i in (4.11) with a single identical v, then (4.11) would comply with the so-called Pigou-Dalton principle, which holds that a transfer of an increment in well-being from a better-off person to a worse-off person always counts as an improvement from the perspective of the general betterness ordering, so long as the relative standing of the two people is not affected by the transfer (i.e., so long as the person who began better off is still better off after the transfer).[12] The Pigou-Dalton principle is an egalitarian principle insofar as it favors transfers of well-being from better-off individuals to worse-off individuals. The degree of this favoritism is reflected in the curvature of the v function. But we have seen that this curvature is just the curvature that expresses the degree of risk-aversion exhibited by each individual's betterness ordering. If its premises are true, therefore, Harsanyi's aggregation theorem forges a link between intrapersonal risk-aversion and interpersonal inequality-aversion.

Since Harsanyi's theorem is consistent with a brand of prioritarianism, and since prioritarianism must be rejected if one is to ratify a (discounted) utilitarian SWF, we might ask how one can rule out prioritarianism. One way to do this is to adopt what Broome calls

Bernoulli's hypothesis. One [lottery] is better for a person than another if and only if it gives the person a greater expectation of wellbeing than the other. (Broome 2004, p. 89)

---

[12] Strictly speaking, I am referring here to the *Pigou-Dalton-with-respect-to-well-being* principle. It is conceptually possible to reject this principle while accepting a distinct Pigou-Dalton-with-respect-to-consumption principle.

Bernoulli's hypothesis implies that each individual is risk-*neutral* about their lifetime well-being. In the context of the SWF stated as (4.11), Bernoulli's hypothesis would imply that the v_i functions (which come from each individual's version of equation (4.10)) are linear, rather than strictly concave. In that case, they could be omitted without changing the ranking represented by the SWF. This in turn would make the SWF inconsistent with the Pigou-Dalton principle, and therefore inconsistent with prioritarianism. Thus, if individuals were risk-neutral with respect to lifetime well-being, and if all the other premises of Harsanyi's aggregation principle remained true, then the general betterness ordering would be represented by a weighted sum of individuals' lifetime well-beings; and that is just weighted utilitarianism:

$$V = \sum_{i=1}^{N} a_i \cdot w_i \qquad (4.12)$$

So one route back to a utilitarian approach to interpersonal aggregation—at least while retaining the three main premises underlying Harsanyi's theorem—is to embrace Bernoulli's hypothesis by ruling out risk-aversion with respect to lifetime well-being.

To many, Bernoulli's hypothesis seems a tough pill to swallow. And Broome agrees it is a tough pill. But he argues it must be swallowed—not because Bernoulli's hypothesis is intuitively plausible (he agrees it is not) but because he is skeptical we can establish the prior notion of well-being that prioritarianism needs in the first place. Recall that I began this discussion of Harsanyi's aggregation theorem by assuming there was a quantitative notion of well-being we could use to express a given outcome as a vector of lifetime well-beings. For prioritarianism to be a viable option, we need the underlying notion of lifetime well-being to be a quantitative notion; after all, the Pigou-Dalton principle says it is a good thing to reduce a better-off person's well-being if we can increase a worse-off person's well-being by the *same* amount. A precondition of being able to say this is that the notion of well-being at work be quantitative and interpersonally comparable. How could we arrive at such a notion?

Recall that by imposing the vNM axioms on an individual's betterness ordering, the Harsanyi-based approach constructs a cardinal value function representing that ordering. The key to this construction was the idea of having the relevant ordering be one of *lotteries* rather than one of outcomes. When it was an ordering of lotteries defined on interpersonal vectors of lifetime well-being, the shape of the resulting value function represented the degree to which risk to lifetime well-being was bad for the individual. One might therefore wonder if something similar can be done for a notion of well-being. That is, can we use expected utility theory to construct a cardinal notion of well-being, just as we used it to construct a cardinal notion of the goodness of well-being (and of the badness of risks to it)?

The answer is that we can do this, yes; but by doing it we rule out the sort of prioritarianism we were hoping to rescue. To see why, suppose we did not yet have a quantitative notion of well-being. In that case, we could not yet characterize outcomes in terms of vectors of lifetime well-being. If we then wanted to use expected utility theory to construct a quantitative notion of well-being, we would have to define a person's well-being ordering on outcomes characterized in descriptive terms—for example, a full cataloguing of what goods, services, relationships, and so on, individuals enjoy and experience in a given outcome. Let us denote such outcomes with x_m, where the subscripts are the same subscripts we used when we were helping ourselves to a quantitative notion of lifetime well-being. Thus each outcome x_m is related to a given interpersonal vector of well-being.

Given this mapping of descriptive outcomes to well-being vectors, any ordering of such vectors will also be an ordering of outcomes characterized descriptively. Now suppose we assume that the three premises of Harsanyi's aggregation theorem hold in this new setup, where the relevant orderings are defined on the set of lotteries generated from a set of descriptively characterized outcomes. In that case, individuals' orderings would be represented by a value function with the following form:

$$V_i(p_1, p_2, \ldots, p_M) = p_1 \cdot v_i(x_1) + p_2 \cdot v_i(x_2) + \ldots + p_M \cdot v_i(x_M) \qquad (4.13)$$

where p_m is the probability of outcome x_m's occurring. As before, the nature of the v_i subvalue function is determined entirely by the role it plays in ensuring that V_i faithfully represents i's betterness ordering of lotteries defined on descriptive outcomes. Now, since we are exploring whether expected utility theory can furnish a cardinal notion of well-being, we are supposing that the betterness ordering represented by (4.13) is also an ordering of lotteries with respect to their ability to promote i's expected lifetime well-being. Yet in this new context, there is no conceptual room for the subvalue function to reflect risk-aversion about lifetime well-being. When an individual's betterness ordering of lotteries defined on descriptive outcomes is also her well-being ordering, it is always best for her to maximize the expectation of her well-being. And this is just Bernoulli's hypothesis.

Thus, if one wishes to adopt the premises of Harsanyi's aggregation theorem while using expected utility theory to construct individuals' cardinal well-being functions, the general betterness ordering of outcomes will be represented by the following weighted utilitarian SWF:

$$V = \sum_{i=1}^{N} a_i \cdot w_i(x_m) \qquad (4.14)$$

where the w_i functions yield cardinal indicators of lifetime well-being and are identical to the subutility functions that appear in each i's value function of form (4.13). This would rule out prioritarianism.

So while it is tempting to use expected utility theory to produce the quantitative notion of well-being that Harsanyi-compliant prioritarianism requires, that method cannot be used for that purpose, because it is definitive of the notion of value falling out of expected utility theory that maximizing its expectation is always best for a person (Greaves 2015). But Harsanyi-compliant prioritarianism entails that what is best for a person is not maximizing the expectation of lifetime well-being, but rather maximizing the expectation of well-being *that has been transformed by a concave function*. And if one cannot use the expected utility framework to construct a prior quantitative notion of well-being, it is very hard to see where an alternative approach might come from. This is Broome's argument for accepting Bernoulli's hypothesis. As he puts it, risk-neutrality about lifetime well-being is not so much an intuitively compelling idea as it is the result of a tractable approach to cardinalizing well-being in the first place (Broome 2004, pp. 134–135). If Broome is right about this, then Harsanyi-compliant prioritarianism is prevented from helping itself to the quantitative notion of well-being it needs even to get off the ground (Broome 1991, pp. 142–148; 2004, pp. 89–91; 2015, pp. 262–264; Greaves 2015).

4.3.2 Interpersonal Comparisons of Well-being

Earlier I mentioned that Harsanyi's theorem has been proved in very different versions of expected utility theory. This includes versions that—unlike the vNM framework—treat probabilities not as objective and known to all, but as subjective credences or degrees of belief (Broome 1999b, p. 91). In this second sort of framework, differences in individuals' preferences can reflect differences in the subjective probabilities that individuals assign to outcomes.[13] And this raises a major problem for Harsanyi's original argument, which concerned preference orderings. It turns out that for the general betterness ordering to comply both with expected utility theory axioms and with the ex ante strong Pareto axiom, it must be true that all individuals agree about the probability of every outcome (Broome 1991, pp. 152–153). Broome calls this the probability agreement theorem. Since such uniformity of belief is very unlikely to hold in the real world, this raises a significant problem for any attempt to put Harsanyi's theorem to practical use.

What is to be done? If we wish to preserve Harsanyi's result, we certainly cannot permit the general betterness ordering to violate the axioms of whatever expected utility theory framework is being employed. Nor can we completely sever the important link between general betterness and the betterness orderings of individuals that Harsanyi established with the ex ante strong Pareto axiom. What we *can* do is double-down on the fact that the social choice framework seeks *social* evaluations which must inevitably reflect the normative judgments of whomever is performing the evaluation. Moral philosophers routinely work with the distinction between what a person happens to be *interested in*, on the one hand, and what is in fact *in her interest*, on the other. If the general and individual betterness orderings were oriented around this second notion, then the evaluator who is charged with constructing all these orderings could draw on a single set of probabilities, namely the evaluator's own subjective probabilities. Put differently: by recognizing that the social choice framework need not require the same sort of reliance on individuals' actual preferences as the general equilibrium framework, a social evaluator could respect the probability agreement theorem without invoking objective probabilities. She could instead invoke her subjective probabilities alongside her subjective judgments about what in fact conduces to the well-being of the individuals she is concerned with. Of course she should strive to ensure that her subjective judgments about this are intellectually responsible and responsive to thoughtful criticism. But that is the position that *any* social evaluator is in when she engages in the normative evaluation of public policy.

---

[13] Strictly speaking, the issue concerns the probabilities individuals assign to different *states of nature*. I will briefly introduce this notion in section 6.2. For my purposes here, I think little harm is done if I speak about the probabilities individuals assign to outcomes rather than to states of nature.

This response to the probability agreement theorem makes individuals' actual preferences non-decisive in social evaluation. It does not render those preferences irrelevant, however. It remains open to an evaluator to view a person's well-being as a function of both her *attributes* (e.g., her levels of consumption of conventional commodities, labor, and environmental amenities) as well as her actual preferences or tastes (Broome 1999c, p. 38; Adler 2016). For example, it would be perfectly coherent for a social evaluator to maintain that it would be better for a person to be a schoolteacher who wants to be a schoolteacher than a philosophy graduate student who wants to be a schoolteacher, and also better for her to be a schoolteacher who wants to be a schoolteacher than a philosophy graduate student who wants to be a philosophy graduate student. Such judgments might in turn be justified on the basis of what individuals happen to want for themselves *as well as* the respective positions' salaries, job perks, and prospects for career advancement. To be sure, the fact that this set of judgments is *coherent* does not mean it is defensible. I am here stating only the *sort* of preference-sensitive position that is left open by the response to the probability agreement theorem sketched in the previous paragraph. A lot of normative work is still required to construct a defensible betterness ordering for a given individual.

There is a further important idea related to that of defining an individual's betterness ordering on a set of outcomes described in a fine-grained manner so that they specify both attributes and preferences. It is this:

> If I were a financial analyst living the life of a financial analyst, subject to all the causal influences that determine how well off a financial analyst is, then I should be exactly as well off as anyone else would be if she occupied that position. The same is true for the alternative of being an academic in the causal situation of an academic. Therefore, if it is better for me to live the life of an academic, it would be better for anyone. The life of an academic would, simply, be better. (Broome 1999c, p. 38)

In other words: if one life, described in a sufficiently fine-grained way, would be better than another fine-grained life for an individual i, then it would also be better for any other individual. This idea, which seems hard to doubt, provides a basis for interpersonal comparisons of well-being within a social choice context: if an evaluator can construct a suitably fine-grained betterness ordering for one person, it will be just as valid a betterness ordering for any other person. But actually, an evaluator would surely not make the inference in this order; she would not, that is, choose a specific individual, then construct a betterness ordering for him, and then infer that the same betterness ordering applies to everyone else. Rather, she would consider the set of fine-grained alternatives and seek to construct a betterness ordering of them that would apply to all individuals who could conceivably live those sorts of lives (Broome 1999c, p. 43; 2004, pp. 94–97). If she then used the setting of risk to fashion a defensible cardinal well-being function representing an ordering of lotteries defined on a set of fine-grained lives, she could use the same function for everyone else in (discounted) utilitarian social choice aggregation.[14]

In actual applied analyses various shortcuts will be needed. We have already seen, for instance, that instead of focusing on fine-grained outcomes for individuals, mainstream social choice climate economics characterizes outcomes in terms of just a single indicator of non-preference attributes, namely generalized consumption. It then adopts a simple isoelastic cardinal and interpersonally comparable well-being function. Shortcuts like these are inevitable, and I do not have much to say about which ones are reasonable in light of the limitations in data, time, or simply where welfare economics is as a discipline. I shall suggest in Part III that focus groups offer a way for economists to calibrate the curvature of an isoelastic well-being function in a democratic but still deliberative manner.

4.3.3 Same-Number Aggregation

I mentioned in section 4.3.1 that without further assumptions, Harsanyi's aggregation theorem is restricted to orderings in which all outcomes are vectors of lifetime well-beings for the very same group of people. A way to extend this to different populations of the same size is to adopt a principle of impartiality across people (Broome 2004, pp. 135–138). This principle can be expressed formally by setting all a_i weights in (4.14) equal to 1. It is how a philosophical utilitarian would set the a_i weights, too. If, in a context where the population is held constant, the respective identities of the individuals are irrelevant for how their lifetime well-beings should be aggregated, then when the population changes it should also not matter whose well-beings

---

[14] For a detailed framework for making interpersonal comparisons of well-being that has some of these ideas at its center, but goes well beyond them, see Adler (2016).

are at issue. So by adopting a principle of impartiality, we gain license to compare total well-being for same-sized populations, even when those populations are comprised of different individuals. Broome refers to this as extending Harsanyi's framework to the context of "same-number aggregation" (Broome 2004, p. 137).[15]

For now I shall assume that every possible population has the same number of people in it. Later, in chapter 7, I will consider issues that arise when this assumption is relaxed, and thus when the size of the intertemporal population becomes a policy variable.

4.3.4 Same-Lifetime Aggregation

Suppose one uses expected utility theory to construct cardinal indicators of individuals' lifetime well-being. Not only would this entail Bernoulli's hypothesis, but it also delivers the first premise of Harsanyi's aggregation theorem. Suppose these indicators are interpersonally comparable, and also that the other premises of Harsanyi's theorem are true. Finally, suppose we adopt a principle of impartiality that sets all the a_i weights in (4.14) equal to 1. Then the result is unweighted utilitarianism:

$$V = \sum_{i=1}^{N} w_i(x_m) \qquad (4.15)$$

As I indicated when I introduced the "people route" to aggregation, to get from (4.15) to (a finite version of) the standard discounted utilitarian social choice SWF, one could supplement it with a specific version of equation (4.8). That is, one could hold that each individual's lifetime well-being is the exponentially discounted sum of their temporal well-beings. One would then also have to select very carefully the pure time discount factors that weight individuals' temporal well-beings: all temporal well-beings enjoyed at any given time would have to be discounted back to the initial period of the overall analysis using the very same discount factors. This would have to be so regardless of whose well-beings they are, and regardless of where in these individuals' lives those temporal well-beings fall.

---

[15] The impartiality principle at work here is the same principle discussed in the context of anonymity in section 4.2.

Broome has shown how using Harsanyi's theorem a second time can get one most of the way to the same-lifetime aggregation that the people route needs to establish the standard discounted utilitarian SWF (Broome 1991, pp. 224–227; 2004, ch. 15). Suppose that for each of N individuals there is a vNM value function, V_i, that represents individual i's betterness ordering of lotteries generated from descriptive outcomes $x_1, x_2, \ldots, x_M$. And suppose we embrace Bernoulli's hypothesis, so that the subvalues that feature in an individual's value function can be treated as indicators of i's well-being in a given outcome. We can then create a grid associating each outcome with a vector of individuals' lifetime well-beings in that outcome:

$$\begin{array}{cccc} w_1^1 & w_2^1 & w_3^1 & \ldots & w_N^1 \\ w_1^2 & w_2^2 & w_3^2 & \ldots & w_N^2 \\ \vdots & \vdots & \vdots & & \vdots \\ w_1^M & w_2^M & w_3^M & \ldots & w_N^M \end{array}$$

Here w_i^m is individual i's lifetime well-being in outcome m. When one uses it to address the task of *interpersonal* aggregation, Harsanyi's theorem effectively works by imposing two conditions on a general betterness ordering of lotteries generated from the rows of this grid. The first condition is that the general betterness ordering also satisfies the vNM axioms; the second is that the general betterness ordering satisfies the ex ante strong Pareto principle. Thus, so long as a grid like this can be constructed, where the indicators in each row are interpersonally comparable vNM well-beings, and the general betterness ordering of lotteries generated from the rows satisfies those two further conditions, the general betterness ordering of the rows themselves—the ordering of all possible outcomes—can be represented by a function that is the weighted sum of the items in each row. This is the sum given by equation (4.14).

Now suppose that we change the *items* that make up each row in a grid like this while still retaining the *structural* conditions of the ordering of lotteries generated from those rows. In particular, let us shift contexts radically, from the interpersonal aggregation of lifetime well-beings to the *intra*personal aggregation of well-being at different times within a single person's life. In particular, we shall think of each row of a new grid as a vector of *temporal* well-beings that the *same* individual i would enjoy in a given outcome. To justify this, let us assume that for each time in i's life, t, there is a *dated betterness ordering of* lotteries generated from descriptions of the way the world could be for i at t. A dated betterness ordering with respect to i and t is an ordering of lotteries generated from outcomes for i at t that ranks these lotteries in terms of how good they are for i at t. Suppose all of these orderings, one for each time in i's life, satisfy the vNM axioms. Now adopt a temporal version of Bernoulli's hypothesis, so that the subvalue functions that feature in the value functions representing i's dated betterness orderings are also interpretable as as i's temporal well-being functions. Having made these assumptions, we can arrange i's temporal subvalues in a grid analogous to the one above, with the rows of the new grid representing intertemporal paths of temporal well-being for the same person i in a given possible outcome m:

$$\begin{array}{ccccc} w^1_{t_i+0} & w^1_{t_i+1} & w^1_{t_i+2} & \cdots & w^1_{t_i+L} \\ w^2_{t_i+0} & w^2_{t_i+1} & w^2_{t_i+2} & \cdots & w^2_{t_i+L} \\ \vdots & \vdots & \vdots & & \vdots \\ w^M_{t_i+0} & w^M_{t_i+1} & w^M_{t_i+2} & \cdots & w^M_{t_i+L} \end{array}$$

Here t_i and $t_i + L$ denote, respectively, the first and last periods of individual i's life; and $w^m_{t_i+j}$ is individual i's well-being, in outcome m, j periods following the first period in which he lives. Each row therefore captures how i's life would go in a given outcome, expressed as a path of temporal well-beings. I shall assume that each of i's dated value functions incorporates the very same subvalue function, which I have written as w because we have assumed the temporal version of Bernoulli's hypothesis. And here again I assume that all of these temporal well-being functions are interpersonally unit comparable.

Let there now be a *lifetime* betterness ordering for i that is defined on the lotteries generated from the rows of this second grid. And suppose this lifetime ordering also satisfies the vNM axioms. Finally, assume a temporal version of the ex ante strong Pareto principle. This version says that for any two lotteries generated from the rows of the second grid, if both lotteries are at least as good for i at every t, and if one is better for i at some t, then the one that is better for i at some t is better from the point of view of i's lifetime betterness ordering as well.[16]

By adopting all of these assumptions, which are counterparts of the assumptions we made when employing Harsanyi's theorem in interpersonal aggregation, we have imposed the same structural relations on the second grid as we had imposed on the first. This second set of structural relations entails that i's betterness ordering of possible lifetimes—her betterness ordering of the second grid's rows—can be represented by the following function (Broome 2004, p. 218):

$$w_i = \sum_{j=0}^{L} a_{t_i+j} \cdot w_{t_i+j} \qquad (4.16)$$

where again w_i is i's lifetime well-being in a given outcome, w_{t_i+j} is i's temporal well-being j periods after the first period in which he lives in the relevant outcome, and the a_{t_i+j}'s are time-specific weights greater than zero.[17]

If we make the impartial utilitarian assumption that all the a_{t_i+j} weights are properly set equal to 1, then an important implication of this Harsanyian approach to same-lifetime aggregation is that it would not be possible to make a life better (for the person who lives it) by holding fixed its overall amount of well-being while changing its temporal pattern. It could not be made better, for example, by starting low in well-being and ending high, rather than the reverse, or by staying relatively steady, rather than being marked by wild swings from year to year. So long as two possible lives contain the same total amount of well-being, the Harsanyian approach to same-lifetime aggregation will treat them as equally good for a person (Broome 1991, ch. 11; 2004, pp. 220–223). This is a consequence of the temporal version of the ex ante strong Pareto principle. Together with the other structural conditions imposed on the second grid, the temporal ex ante strong Pareto principle entails that times are *separable*, in the sense that the contribution made to a

---

[16] Throughout all of this we also must assume that i's life will stretch over the very same timespan in all possible outcomes. This is the counterpart to an assumption we had to make in the context of interpersonal aggregation in section 4.3.1. By adopting temporal impartiality in the present context of same-lifetime aggregation, we could extend the result to apply to timespans that are equal in duration but that involve the individual's living at different times. This move, which seems reasonable, would undermine the route to *discounted* utilitarianism that I state in the first paragraph of the next section. To extend the evaluation to lives of different length one would need a within-lifetime analog to the analysis of differently sized populations that I give in chapter 7. I will not explicitly return to the within-lifetime issue.

[17] Observe that (4.16) is a more general version of (4.8).

person's overall good by her well-being at a given time never depends on her level of well-being at another time. This is the counterpart of *separability of people* that falls out of the conditions that we imposed orderings of rows in the first grid. There, the ex ante strong Pareto principle, along with the other two structural conditions, entails that when we evaluate an outcome's distribution of well-being across people, the contribution made by one person's well-being to the general (or social) goodness of the outcome never depends on comparisons with another person's level of well-being in the outcome.

It is important to note that these two kinds of separability are not a package deal: it is perfectly coherent to accept one and reject the other. For example, Broome (2004) defends separability of people while remaining highly skeptical about separability of times. While I will return to separability across people at the end of this chapter, I will not say much more about separability of times.[18] Like Broome, I am uneasy with it, because it does seem plain that a life can be improved by having its total amount of well-being rearranged into a more desirable pattern—for example, by avoiding wild swings in the levels of temporal well-being. For Broome's part, he presented the second use of Harsanyi's aggregation theorem because he was looking for "a default position ... which can serve as a starting point for more complicated [theories]" (Broome 2004, p. 223). For my part, I am looking for a theoretical basis for the standard discounted utilitarian SWF, in order to explain how it might be derived and to highlight its key assumptions and philosophical implications.

4.3.5 Complete Aggregation

We can now put all of the pieces together. We have stated a set of theoretical assumptions sufficient to establish a finite version of social choice discounted utilitarianism, which is the dominant SWF in social choice climate economics. Suppose that the only features of any individual's temporal situation that are relevant to her temporal well-being can be expressed as a single temporal indicator of generalized consumption, c_t. Next, suppose that every temporal well-being function of every individual has the following isoelastic form:

$$w = \frac{c_t^{1-\eta}}{1-\eta} \qquad (4.17)$$

---

[18] Broome has more to say in Broome (2004, pp. 223–229).

Our assumptions entail that this function is cardinal, and we also know that we must assume it is interpersonally comparable. Finally, suppose that all the a_i weights used in interpersonal aggregation are set equal to 1 (as they are implicitly in equation (4.15)), and that the a_{t_i+j} weights on times within each individual's life (see (4.16)) are set so that all weights indexed to the same time t are identical and take the form $(1+\delta)^{-t}$. For example, every unit of temporal well-being at time $t = 100$, regardless of whose life contains it or how old they are, shall be weighted by a discount factor of $(1+\delta)^{-100}$. I, like other moral philosophers, find this pure time discounting scheme poorly motivated and ethically problematic in a social choice framework, but let us adopt it temporarily for the sake of argument.[19]

All of these assumptions together entail a finite version of the social choice SWF that was adopted in the *Stern Review*, as expressed in equation (4.7) and restated here:

$$V = \sum_{t=0}^{T} N_t \cdot w(c_t) \cdot \frac{1}{(1+\delta)^t} \qquad (4.18)$$

(4.18) reflects a specific fleshing-out of the "people route" to aggregation. If one rejected the gerrymandered and ethically dubious approach to pure time discounting that underlies (4.18), this version of the people route could support an undiscounted utilitarian SWF. Of course, this SWF cannot be used to rank infinite consumption paths. Nor can one reintroduce pure time discounting by positing an exogenous risk of extinction of the sort discussed in section 4.2. For in the Harsanyian framework, an outcome's chance of occurring is a function of all the factors that bear on that probability; there is no way to include some probabilities as discount rates and others as conventional probabilities of outcomes. The Harsanyian framework treats probabilities systematically, as functions of exogenous and endogenous factors working in concert.

Lastly, by allowing consumption levels to vary across regions of the world, we can use equation (4.18) to re-create equation (2.12) from section 2.5. The latter was a regionally disaggregated discounted utilitarian SWF, and is

---

[19] And remember: it is perfectly consistent to reject exponential pure time discounting in the social choice context while embracing exponential pure time preference in the general equilibrium context.

stated here in its finite form—that is, in a form that avoids reference to an infinite series of times:

$$V = \sum_{r}\sum_{t=0}^{T} N_t^r \cdot w(c_t^r) \cdot \frac{1}{(1+\delta)^t} \tag{4.19}$$

* * *

Because the distinction between social choice and general equilibrium climate economics is not well-recognized, and because it is possible to derive discounted utilitarianism from within each analytical framework, it is impossible to know how many published discounted utilitarian SCC figures are social choice SCC figures. Still, one can confidently say that the vast majority of social choice SCC figures stem from discounted utilitarian SWFs. And Koopmans's axiomatic analysis undoubtedly underlies a significant proportion of these. In this chapter I have described some problems for Koopmans's approach, and I have devoted considerable attention to an alternative axiomatization that gives rise to Harsanyi's aggregation theorem. I have explained this latter theorem's main assumptions, and how they might be defended. But I have not defended them myself, so I cannot conclude that the correct SWF is the finite undiscounted utilitarian SWF. Moreover, each of the assumptions I have discussed is philosophical in nature and thus not amenable to empirical confirmation or disconfirmation. This means that if a climate economist wishes to compute SCC figures but wants to avoid controversial philosophical assumptions, the only SCC figures available to her are general equilibrium SCC figures. Yet since I *have* argued that baseline general equilibrium figures have absolutely no policy relevance, that leaves the philosophy-averse climate economist with only optimal general equilibrium figures, whose policy relevance in turn depends upon normative argumentation concerning the desirability of the corresponding Pareto efficient allocations. Such are the limitations of non-normative climate change economics.

Instead of further defending the assumptions needed to derive a nondiscounted utilitarian SWF from Harsanyi's aggregation theorem, I will spend the rest of this part examining reasons for thinking that sound social choice SCC figures will also be limited in an important sense.

5
Normative Abridgement and Pure Time Discounting

5.1 The Concept and Possibility of Normative Abridgement

Harsanyi concludes his 1977 paper, "Morality and the Theory of Rational Behavior," with this qualification:

> Let me end with a disclaimer. I think the utilitarian theory I have described in principle covers all interpersonal aspects of morality. But I do not think it covers *all* morality. There are some very important moral obligations it fails to cover because they are matters of individual morality and of individual rationality. Perhaps the most important such obligation is that of intellectual honesty, that is, the duty to seek the truth and to accept the truth as far as it can be established—regardless of any possible positive or negative social utility this truth may have. (Harsanyi 1977, pp. 655–656, emphasis in original)

Let us refer to the entire collection of sound considerations that bear on what ultimately ought to be done as the *normative domain*. Harsanyi's view is that the normative domain can be divided into at least the sub-domain of *interpersonal morality* and the sub-domain of "individual morality and individual rationality." And he suggests that while the former sub-domain may sometimes underwrite a normative recommendation to violate strictures of intellectual honesty, the latter sub-domain never will. Thus to decide what one ultimately ought to do—"all things considered," as philosophers put it—one must find a way to adjudicate between the recommendations emanating from different parts of the larger normative domain. According to Harsanyi, therefore, the domain of interpersonal morality is captured by his utilitarian SWF, but that domain is (to coin a term) *normatively abridged*. That is to say, it does not reflect all of the values, principles, and other normatively relevant considerations that properly bear on final choice.

If Harsanyi is correct to divide up the normative domain and to associate his aggregation theorem with only one part of it, it follows that no Harsanyi-compliant ordering, no matter how sound, should be viewed automatically as an all-things-considered ordering that reflects what ought to be done. Indeed, contrary to how I put things in the previous paragraph, it is not clear that any *recommendation* of any kind emanates from a normatively abridged sub-part of the normative domain. For if that part excludes considerations that bear on choice, it should not be interpreted as issuing or underwriting recommendations in the first place. If you wish to buy a new car and I am a tire expert, then I may be able to rank the available cars with respect to the quality of their tires. But if that is all I know about the cars or about your preferences concerning cars, it would be strange if I should recommend a certain car to you solely on the basis of my tire ranking. Likewise, if all subparts of the full normative domain contain considerations that help determine the nature of responsible choice, no subpart should be viewed as issuing recommendations. The most it can do is support responsible choice by illuminating but one normatively relevant set of considerations.

Suppose Harsanyi's theorem, together with Broome's amendments and reinterpretations, was sufficient to justify a utilitarian social choice SWF. But suppose in addition that this Harsanyi-Broome framework was normatively abridged. In that case, the so-called Ramsey rule—stated in section 2.7 as equation (2.16)—would not be a *choice* rule: it would not be a rule that says, "Capital investments ought to be arranged so that the time path of rates of return on such investments is identical to the time path of consumption discount rates." Rather, the Ramsey rule would merely state a condition that an economy *would* achieve *if* it resided on the consumption path ranked highest by the SWF. The Ramsey rule would then be a condition of *optimality*—of a consumption path's being the top-ranked consumption path—but not necessarily a condition of *overall choiceworthiness*. If the Harsanyi-Broome framework was in fact normatively abridged, then the question of whether the economy *ought* to be placed onto the optimal consumption path would be a question the framework itself cannot answer.

Some economists will find the distinction between *optimality* and *overall choiceworthiness* incoherent. It is common for economists to assume that an SWF is ipso facto normatively *un*abridged, and thus that whatever alternative is ranked highest by a sound SWF is ipso facto the most choiceworthy alternative. For example, Lawrence Goulder and Roberton Williams write:

> By definition, the social welfare function offers the most complete measure of impacts of policy on social welfare. In principle, a social welfare function will embrace all relevant normative dimensions (including both efficiency and distributional considerations); this all-encompassing quality gives it great appeal. (Goulder and Williams 2012, p. 1250024-16)

Similarly, concerning the sort of ordering that a social welfare function is intended to represent, Geoffrey Brennan writes:

> Economics also conceptualises the domain of ethics in terms specifically of *actions*. This "action-guiding" ambition has several important implications . . . [including] that the relevant comparisons must be "all-things-considered" ones—involving the appropriate trading off of the potentially many elements that might be ethically relevant. (Brennan 2008, p. 268, emphasis in original)

And here is Dasgupta and Heal:[1]

> As usual, C denotes an infinite consumption sequence. Let Γ denote the set of all feasible consumption sequences. The problem that we are concerned with is the question of ordering the elements of this set in a manner that is ethically defensible. The aim ultimately will be to *choose* that programme which is judged best in terms of this ordering. (Dasgupta and Heal 1979, p. 258, emphasis added)

> The planner is concerned with ranking the set of all feasible consumption sequences, Γ. Suppose for the moment that this welfare ranking . . . can be represented by a function $V(C)$. Following traditional terminology we shall refer to V as a *social welfare function*. (Dasgupta and Heal 1979, p. 260, emphasis in original)

There is nothing in these remarks to suggest that these economists take seriously the idea of a normatively abridged SWF, or the possibility that a correct

---

[1] In the two quotations that follow I have used "C" and "Γ" to replace the characters Dasgupta and Heal employed in their original work.

SWF's optimal consumption path might not be the path that policymakers should aim at.[2]

It may therefore surprise economists to learn that it is quite common for philosophers engaged with social choice welfare economics to defend normatively abridged SWFs, with different philosophers defending different SWFs as well as different types of normative abridgement. Indeed, the concept, ethics, and practice of normative abridgement will be a central thread running through the rest of this book. Later in this chapter I will try to illustrate its importance by using it to analyze the protracted debate over pure time discounting in social choice climate economics. But before I do so, I shall clarify the notion by examining some ways in which leading philosophical treatments of climate economics are self-consciously normatively abridged.

5.2 Examples of Normative Abridgement

We have already seen that Harsanyi took his utilitarian SWF to be normatively abridged: he believed there were important moral considerations that it did not capture. Still, he thought this SWF did capture all choice-relevant considerations of *interpersonal morality*—the domain of morality that T. M. Scanlon refers to as "what we owe to each other" (Scanlon 1998). But according to Harsanyi, interpersonal morality does not encompass all moral considerations, because some moral considerations concern the ethics of personal integrity.

Despite drawing on Harsanyi's aggregation theorem to defend a utilitarian SWF, John Broome combines that SWF with a version of normative abridgement that is very different from Harsanyi's. Broome rejects the view that utilitarianism captures all aspects of interpersonal morality. Broome's view was ultimately incorporated into the IPCC's Fifth Assessment Report's chapter entitled "Social, Economic, and Ethical Concepts and Methods," for which Broome served as lead author. According to the report:

> Ethics may be broadly divided into two branches: justice and value. Justice is concerned with ensuring that people get what is *due* to them. If justice requires that a person should not be treated in a particular way—uprooted

---

[2] For yet another example of this, see Fankhauser et al. (1997, p. 253).

from her home by climate change, for example—then the person has a right not to be treated that way. Justice and rights are correlative concepts. On the other hand, criteria of value are concerned with improving the world: making it a better place. Synonyms for "value" in this context are "good," "goodness" and "benefit." (Kolstad et al. 2014, p. 215, emphasis in original)

Since values constitute only one part of ethics, *if an action will increase value overall it by no means follows that it should be done*. Many actions benefit some people at the cost of harming others. This raises a question of justice even if the benefits in total exceed the costs. (Kolstad et al. 2014, p. 220, emphasis added)

In his book *Climate Matters*, Broome uses the famous *Transplant* thought experiment to illustrate this distinction between justice and value. He observes that while it is intuitively unjust for a doctor to kill a healthy patient to use his organs to save five others, as this would violate the patient's rights, killing the patient might well promote overall aggregate well-being, and thus overall value (Broome 2012, p. 51). Broome concludes that while killing an innocent person might improve the world in terms of the "goodness" contained in the resulting state of affairs, promoting goodness in this way can be morally wrong *all things considered*.

This does not mean that considerations of goodness or value are morally irrelevant, however. Far from it. For it is considerations of goodness that, intuitively, explain why one should save five people rather than one (and rather than flipping a coin) when saving the five people does *not* require using the one person as a mere means to that end. We can see this if we consider a different thought experiment, *Scarce Drug*, in which a physician can either (A) save five patients by giving each of them one-fifth of the life-sustaining medicine she controls, or (B) save one patient by giving him the full amount (since he happens to need five times what each of the others needs). In *Scarce Drug*, it is much more plausible that the morally right choice is to save the five while letting the one die. And surely a main reason for this is that in saving the five, one brings about a state of affairs that contains more goodness in the world than the feasible alternative states of affairs.

In Broome's view, therefore, interpersonal morality is concerned both with moral rights and with value (or goodness). So in embracing a utilitarian SWF that is insensitive to considerations of rights, Broome is committed to a version of normative abridgement in which his SWF is normatively abridged in virtue of being morally abridged (Broome 2008, p. 98; 2012, pp. 99–103). Thus the ranking represented by his SWF does not rank outcomes (or lotteries) with respect to everything that matters to responsible choice, and the reason why it does not is that it does not even rank outcomes (or lotteries) with respect to everything that matters from the perspective of interpersonal morality.

The differences between Harsanyi and Broome illustrate how a given theorist's conception of normative abridgement can be clarified and examined by asking the following two questions:

1. Which normative considerations are embodied in the ranking that is represented by the theorist's preferred SWF?, and
2. Does the theorist believe there are policy-relevant normative considerations to which that ranking is insensitive? If so, which considerations?

As we have seen, Broome and Harsanyi give the same answer to the first question.[3] But their philosophical differences concerning interpersonal morality entail different answers to the second question. Broome believes that utilitarian rankings are insensitive to important considerations of interpersonal morality that Harsanyi does not believe are genuine. Broome is therefore less likely than Harsanyi to infer policy recommendations from an analysis of climate change that is predicated solely upon the utilitarian SWF they both endorse. So long as one can endorse that SWF while remaining committed to truth-telling, Harsanyi seems willing to treat that social welfare function as a *rightness function*, that is, a function that represents a ranking that determines which policies ought to be chosen.

For a final example of normative abridgement in the philosophical literature, consider Matthew Adler in solo-authored work and in work with co-author Nicolas Treich, an economist. Adler defends a version of prioritarianism that is not consistent with Harsanyi's aggregation theorem. (It is therefore not a form of what I called "Harsanyi-compliant prioritarianism" in chapter 4.) Adler agrees with Harsanyi and Broome that responsible public policy must be concerned to promote well-being. But at the same time Adler argues that fairness requires giving individuals who are

---

[3] I am abstracting here from any potential disagreements between Broome and Harsanyi on how to determine individuals' cardinal and interpersonally comparable well-being functions.

worse off in terms of well-being some degree of priority over those who are better off. This concern with fairness leads Adler to endorse a prioritarian SWF that treats a well-being benefit to a worse-off individual as morally more important than an equally sized benefit to a better-off individual.

In their co-authored work on climate change economics, Adler and Treich suggest that the domain of morality is exhausted by the considerations that underly Adler's prioritarianism. They write:

> The great philosopher Sidgwick took the position that a decisionmaker might rationally choose to advance moral aims, or her own interests, or some mix of these considerations. Sidgwick used the term "prudence" to describe what maximizes the decisionmaker's own well-being. On the extreme version of the Sidgwickian view, it would be rational for the present generation either to be fully ethical (maximizing an SWF without discounting), or to be fully prudent (to ignore entirely the interests of future generations), or to do anything "in between." Even if the extreme Sidgwickian position is rejected, it is surely true that an individual or government may rationally depart from the ethical norm of impartiality to some substantial extent . . .
>
> The SWF construct (as we understand it here) offers a framework for fully ethical choice . . . The SWF framework does not purport to guide an individual or government in making rational tradeoffs between ethics and prudence—tradeoffs that anyone except a saint will find herself making . . .
>
> In this Article, we focus on what an impartial, ethical perspective requires of climate policy . . . But we recognize that actual decisionmakers will almost always be motivated by some mixture of ethical and non-ethical considerations, and indeed we believe (along with Sidgwick) that mixed motivations of this sort are quite rational. The recommendations that follow from the SWF construct are, in our view, one input into the climate decisionmaker's rational calculus. (Adler and Treich 2015, p. 285)

The particular "framework for fully ethical choice" that Adler and Treich endorse and explore in their article is Adler's (undiscounted) prioritarianism. But Adler and Treich do not insist that this moral framework captures the only policy-relevant normative considerations. For they assert that it is "quite rational" for policymakers to seek a blend between prioritarian ethics and what they, following Sidgwick, call "prudence." Thus Adler and

Treich agree with Harsanyi (and disagree with Broome) that an SWF can and should capture all dimensions of interpersonal morality. Yet they disagree with both Harsanyi and Broome over which considerations of interpersonal morality are normatively important and policy-relevant. Finally, in defending the normative relevance of prudence while classifying prudence as a "non-ethical consideration," Adler and Treich articulate a new conception of normative abridgement: their prioritarian SWF is normatively abridged because it is insensitive to (what these theorists' believe are) non-ethical yet still policy-relevant normative considerations of legitimate self-interest.

Despite their differences, Harsanyi, Broome, and Adler all endorse SWFs that are welfarist in Amartya Sen's sense of "making no use of any information about the social states [to be ranked] other than that of the personal welfares generated in them" (Sen 1977, p. 1559). Sen contrasts welfarist rankings with ones that are sensitive to the "different sources" of welfare contained in feasible outcomes (Sen 1979, p. 478). As an example of a source-sensitive ranking, consider an evaluative framework that prefers saving the five in *Scarce Drug* to saving the five in *Transplant*. This framework is not welfarist because the two relevant outcomes are alike in having five people alive and one dead. To evaluate these outcomes differently, the evaluative framework must be sensitive to the fact that only *Scarce Drug* involves five lives being saved without the intentional killing of an innocent person. But being sensitive to that fact is to care about the *way* in which the resulting distribution of well-being is brought about. Harsanyi's and Broome's utilitarian SWFs are welfarist because the only information they are sensitive to is the distribution of well-being in an outcome (or lottery). Adler's prioritarian SWF is welfarist for the same reason. Prioritarianism differs from utilitarianism because it applies a concave transformation to well-being levels prior to summing them. This involves an additional operation, yes, but the only information about the world that prioritarianism needs is information about individuals' well-being. It therefore remains welfarist.

In earlier work, Adler, writing with Eric Posner, gave the name *weak welfarism* to a view on which total well-being is always a morally relevant factor in responsible decision-making, but where total well-being might not always be "morally decisive" (Adler and Posner 2006, pp. 52–53). In that work, Adler and Posner defend not just weak welfarism (which is consistent with prioritarianism), but a weak welfarist conception of social choice cost-benefit analysis predicated upon a normatively abridged utilitarian SWF.

Setting aside details concerning the nature of human well-being, this is basically Broome's view. It is also the view I will ultimately endorse in this book.[4]

5.3 Interlude: Harsanyi's Impartial Observer Argument

In chapter 4 I used Harsanyi's aggregation theorem to sketch an axiomatic foundation for (discounted) utilitarianism. I also noted there that economists more commonly mention a different argument that Harsanyi claimed offers a different route to utilitarianism. That different argument is known as Harsanyi's impartial observer argument. Now that I have introduced the distinction between justice and value (or goodness), this is a good time to explain why I will not rely on this other argument of Harsanyi's.

First, I shall explain the argument. Here is Harsanyi:

> If somebody prefers an income distribution more favorable to the poor for the sole reason that he is poor himself, this can hardly be considered as a genuine value judgment on social welfare. But if somebody feels such a preference in spite of being wealthy himself, of if somebody who is in fact poor expresses such a preference, but does it quite independently of the fact of being poor himself, this may well be a value judgment of the required kind.
>
> Now, a value judgment on the distribution of income would show the required impersonality to the highest degree if the person who made this judgment had to choose a particular income distribution in complete ignorance of what his own relative position (and the position of those near to his heart) would be within the system chosen. This would be the case if he had exactly the same chance of obtaining the first position (corresponding to the highest income) or the second or the third, etc., up to the last position (corresponding to the lowest income) available within that scheme. (Harsanyi 1953, pp. 434–435)

---

[4] Adler and Posner claim, "Weak welfarism rejects prioritarianism" (Adler and Posner 2006, p. 56). But I have just said that weak welfarism is consistent with prioritarianism. Who is right? I think I am, and here's why. Prioritarian SWFs exhibit what Adler calls "the Numbers Win property." An SWF exhibits the Numbers Win property if it allows that the world can be improved by imposing a large loss on a badly off person in order to confer very small benefits on a very large number of well-off individuals, so long as the group of better-off individuals is sufficiently large (Adler 2012, p. 369). In this respect, prioritarianism gives some moral weight to total well-being, which makes total well-being morally relevant even if not morally decisive. And that seems to me enough to make it weak welfarist on Adler and Posner's definition. For a possible response, see Adler (2012, pp. 119–124).

Harsanyi therefore claimed that the important ethical value of impartiality is best explored in moral thinking with a thought experiment John Rawls later called the "veil of ignorance" (Rawls 1971). Both individuals and social evaluators should imagine that they do not know who they are or where in society's hierarchy they will find themselves when the hypothetical veil is lifted. If we assume—as both Harsanyi and Rawls do—that the veiled individual is to rank possible social arrangements while motivated by self-interest, it is reasonable to think the individual will rank arrangements with an eye to maximizing her *expected* well-being. And if (as Harsanyi believes) it would be most rational for a veiled individual to assume she has an equal chance of being any member of society when the veil is lifted, then (Harsanyi argues) the ethical requirement of impartiality can be connected to an *average utilitarian* social welfare function:

$$V = \frac{1}{N} \sum_{i=1}^{N} w_i \qquad (5.1)$$

where w_i is an indicator of individual i's well-being in the relevant outcome being evaluated. Harsanyi had a sophisticated theory of interpersonal comparisons of well-being, but I am not going to discuss that here.[5] Nor am I going to ask why Harsanyi neglected to rule out the possibility that his veiled chooser is risk-averse about lifetime well-being, which could have led to an average prioritarian SWF rather than an average utilitarian one. I am simply going to assume that the well-being indicators in (5.1) are cardinal and interpersonally unit comparable, and that we can for now set aside the possibility of prioritarianism.

I want to focus instead on how to interpret the results of Harsanyi's impartial observer's decision-making behind the veil of ignorance. Is Harsanyi's veil of ignorance a device for understanding the requirements of justice? Or does it shed light on how to rank outcomes (and lotteries) in terms of their capacity to "improve the world"—that is, in terms of what Broome and the IPCC call value (or goodness)? In my view, each of these interpretations is problematic.

Let us take the justice interpretation first. Consider again the *Scarce Drug* case from section 5.2. Suppose that all of the people who need the drug are

---

[5] See Harsanyi (1977, pp. 638–644).

the same age and will, if saved, go on to enjoy the very same sequence of temporal well-beings before dying at exactly the same age. Now suppose you are an impartial observer who, behind Harsanyi's veil of ignorance, does not know whether you are the one person who needs the total amount of the only drug that is on hand, or one of the five other people who each needs one-fifth of that available amount. Which option would you choose, *Save the one* or *Save the five*?

Save the five clearly maximizes your expected well-being. It also seems to display the virtues of maximally improving the world and being the intuitively correct option to choose. But now return to the *Transplant* case. Supposing the physician can cause the healthy patient's death without unleashing fears among other users of the health care system, it seems that here too Harsanyi's impartial observer will prefer the option in which five people live and one dies to the option in which one lives and five die. If the observer cares solely about maximizing her expected well-being on the assumption that she could be any of the six patients, she will choose to save the five individuals dying of organ failure, for she has a much greater chance of being one of them.

From the perspective of *justice*, this is a troubling implication of Harsanyi's impartial observer framework. As Frances Kamm puts it in response to a similar argument of Allan Gibbard's:

This implies that, by definition, one *could* not, behind the veil of ignorance, agree to risk being in a *disrespectful* position as a means of maximizing one's prospective average utility. Even being treated as a mere thing could not ... be termed an intrinsically disrespectful position if agreeing to risk being so treated were a concomitant of choosing what would maximize one's prospective average utility. I find this an implausible implication. (Kamm 2008, p. 128, emphasis in original)

Kamm's point is subtle. She claims that if being treated as a "mere thing" by another person is a risk one would accept *behind* the veil of ignorance, then being so treated *beyond* the veil—when it is lifted—would not in fact be a case of disrespectful treatment. This is because the concept of disrespectful treatment is precisely the sort of thing we look to a theory of justice to clarify. But if the correct theory of justice were one predicated upon Harsanyi's impartial observer framework, then being treated as a mere thing (as the healthy patient is in *Transplant*) would not *in fact* be an instance of disrespectful treatment. On the contrary, it would be allowed by the sort of respect that justice consists in.[6]

I find this criticism convincing. This is because I have moral intuitions about what justice requires and allows that are inconsistent with a world in which people can be treated badly as a means to maximizing average well-being. Of course, utilitarian moral philosophers whose utilitarianism is normatively *un*abridged will disagree. This is not the venue in which to evaluate their arguments—or at least I shall not make it such a venue. Instead, I will simply register my view that Harsanyi's impartial observer framework does not seem to me a promising framework for shedding light on the nature of justice.[7]

Might the veil of ignorance framework still shed light on the nature of what Broome and the IPCC call value or goodness? That is to say, might it help us to understand *why* saving the five in both *Scarce Drug* and *Transplant* is, in each scenario, the way to maximally improve the world? If yes, Harsanyi's impartial observer framework could capture what it means to say that an outcome (or a lottery) brings good consequences. In this capacity, there need not be a strong connection between what the framework says and what individuals or policymakers ought, all things considered, to do. As we have seen, a utilitarian conception of the goodness of an outcome can be a normatively abridged conception, one that must be combined with non-utilitarian considerations in order to fully justify an action or policy.

But I do not think this second defense of Harsanyi's impartial observer framework is compelling, either. Note first that in a fixed population context—that is, where the number of individuals who will live is not amenable to influence by policy—the total utilitarian conception of goodness that can emerge from Harsanyi's aggregation theorem is equivalent to the average utilitarianism that emerges from his impartial observer framework. (I am assuming for now that the weights arising out of the aggregation theorem should all be set to 1.) By "equivalent" I mean that they will give rise to the same ranking of outcomes, so long as they are built upon the same mapping of outcomes to vectors of lifetime well-being. Because of this equivalence, one cannot cite the reasonableness of the resulting goodness ranking as a decisive reason to accept the impartial observer framework, because it is equally a reason to accept

---

[6] A similar line of argument was pressed by Scanlon (1982) against both Harsanyi's and Rawls's veil of ignorance–based theories.
[7] For a different objection to Harsanyi's conception of impartiality, see Adler (2019, pp. 117–124).

the utilitarian approach to social choice evaluation that invokes the aggregation theorem. (Moreover, I shall argue in chapter 7 that average utilitarianism is philosophically hopeless when population size can vary.)

Here is a more important reason for doubting the impartial observer framework's ability to justify a sound conception of goodness: it is unclear why a ranking of outcomes (and lotteries) in terms of the impartial goodness of their consequences should be conceptually tied to the perspective of an individual. Consider a thought experiment I shall call *Transplant 2*. Suppose one person, Edward, needs a kidney transplant to live. And suppose Edward's sister, Fran, is a match and is willing to donate one of her two healthy kidneys to Edward. Yet after removing the kidney from Fran but before placing it in Edward, tests are run on the organ and doctors learn that it produces a very rare enzyme which, if introduced to 100,000 people with end-stage renal disease, will save their lives. Unfortunately, using the kidney in this second way would make it impossible to use it to save Edward's life. Now let us ask: If Fran would still like her kidney to go to Edward, may the public health ministry intervene and seize the kidney before it is implanted into him?

We do not need to answer this question fully to see the point I now wish to make. It is this: when weighing the impartial goodness of preventing 100,000 deaths against the goodness of preventing Edward's death, it is more natural to compare these directly—"from the point of view of the universe," as Sidgwick put it. And this is precisely the perspective that is encouraged by Harsanyi's aggregation theorem. For that theorem presumes that the evaluator's aim is to construct a general, social betterness ordering of outcomes that is conceptually distinct from any individual's betterness ordering. Moreover, the aggregation theorem presumes that the connection between the general ordering and the individual orderings is established by a principle—ex ante strong Pareto—which says that whenever two outcomes exhibit identical distributions of well-being except for some individuals' being even better off in one of the outcomes, then that outcome is the socially better outcome. This latter judgment is also not one driven by self-interest (whether veiled or unveiled), but rather one that is concerned with the disinterested evaluation of the general goodness of the outcome. In contrast, it is much less natural and much more contrived to assess an outcome's impartial goodness by adopting the point of view of a hypothetical individual who dons Harsanyi's veil and then asks which policy maximizes her own expected well-being.

For these reasons, I do not believe that Harsanyi's impartial observer argument should be a basis for the social choice welfare economics that underlies SCC calculations.

5.4 Normative Abridgement and Pure Time Discounting

As I have mentioned, all major integrated assessment optimization models use a discounted utilitarian objective function. Sometimes this is because these objective functions are what in chapter 3 I called general equilibrium character functions, which I distinguished conceptually from social choice social welfare functions. If we focus solely on the latter, a question arises about how climate change economists conceive of their discounted utilitarianisms. Do they consider these frameworks to be normatively abridged or unabridged? Earlier I gave examples of economists assuming from the start that the orderings represented by social choice social welfare functions are ipso facto unabridged. It turns out that this tendency can shed very useful light on the protracted debate over pure time discounting in social choice climate economics.

Let me give some examples of climate economists who appear to adopt normatively *un*abridged versions of discounted utilitarianism. Take first William Cline, who argues that the decision about the pure time discount rate in a social choice SWF must be responsive to the intuitive asymmetry between the ethics of harming and the ethics of not-aiding. Cline criticizes Thomas Schelling for likening climate change mitigation projects to foreign aid projects. Schelling had observed that since rich countries appear to discount the distant suffering they could prevent with increased foreign aid, it is not surprising they would also discount the future suffering they could prevent with stricter climate change mitigation policies (Schelling 1995, p. 397). Cline responds by claiming that even if rich countries are right to discount the foreign suffering they could prevent with aid now, there is a key ethical difference in the case of climate change. He claims that Schelling makes

> the mistake of equating greenhouse gas mitigation decisions to the bestowal of a benefit, whether to Bangladesh today or our own unknown descendants in the future. Instead, the issue is the imposition of a damage. Surely there is an ethical difference between refraining from conveying a gift, on the one hand, and imposing a damage, on the other. Americans

might feel no compelling obligation to increase aid to Bangladesh today, but surely they would be loath to despoil Bangladesh today (for example, by holding nuclear tests close by offshore). (Cline 1998, p. 100)

Here Cline invokes considerations that Broome and his IPCC co-authors associated with the branch of morality concerned with justice. And because of these considerations, Cline's economic analysis of climate change was among the first to argue for a pure time discount rate of zero (Cline 1992). As he puts it, "morally there is greater responsibility to avoid imposing harm on others than there is to make sure they can enjoy an extra benefit at a cheap cost. Call it an intergenerational Hippocratic Oath" (Cline 2012, p. 7). Thus while Cline clearly agrees with Broome that considerations of justice are valid and policy-relevant, he appears to disagree with Broome about whether justice considerations should be abridged from the SWF used in climate economics. Broome says yes, Cline says no. So although Cline and Broome both endorse a pure time discount rate equal to zero within a social choice SWF, they must do so for very different reasons: while Cline offers reasons of justice, Broome cannot, because Broome excludes justice from the set of considerations that shapes his preferred SWF. On Broome's view, which is the view shared by most philosophers who have written about discounting, future well-being should go undiscounted because, other things equal, a future unit of well-being contributes to the *goodness* of an intertemporal outcome just as much as a present unit.

Consider next an argument that is very common among economists who endorse a positive pure time discount rate in the context of a social choice SWF. Here is Kenneth Arrow's version of the argument (although he attributes its main idea to Koopmans):

[I]magine that an investment opportunity occurs, available only to the first generation. For each unit sacrificed by them, a perpetual stream of α per unit time is generated. If there were no time preference [i.e., no positive pure time discount rate], what would the optimal solution be? Each unit sacrificed would yield a finite utility loss to the first generation, but to compensate, there would be a gain, however small, to each of an infinity of generations. Thus, *any* sacrifice by the first generation is good. Strictly speaking, we cannot say that the first generation should sacrifice everything, if marginal utility approaches infinity as consumption approaches zero. But, we can say that given any investment, short of the entire income, a still greater investment would be preferred. (Arrow 1999, p. 14, emphasis in the original)

In response, Arrow says:

I find this to be an incredible and unacceptable strain on the present generation ... I therefore conclude that the strong ethical requirement that all generations be treated alike, itself reasonable, contradicts a very strong intuition that it is not morally acceptable to demand excessively high savings rates of any one generation, or even of every generation. (Arrow 1999, p. 16)[8]

Arrow concludes that we must acknowledge "a principle of self-regard, of the individual as an end and not merely a means to the welfare of others," which in turn grants each generation the moral right to "maximize a weighted sum of its own utility and the sum of utility of all future generations, with less weight on the latter" (Arrow 1999, p. 16).[9] The "weighted sum" here is a clear reference to an SWF that involves a positive pure time discount rate. Elsewhere, after setting out the same argument, Arrow says, "Very tentatively, it would seem that the rate of pure time preference should be about 1%" (Arrow 1995, p. 17).

In finding it reasonable for considerations of self-interest to shape the pure time discount rate, Arrow clearly disagrees with Adler and Treich's view that considerations of prudence or rational self-interest should be abridged from social choice SWFs. Moreover, Arrow's discussion suggests he thinks these considerations are themselves ethical, or at least that the room for self-concern that people are entitled to stems from a moral right they possess. Here, then, we have an economist invoking justice-based considerations to defend a *positive* pure time discount rate. This not only contrasts with Cline, who invokes justice considerations to *reject* pure time discounting. It also contrasts with the standard philosophical stance that the rationale underlying social choice SWFs ought to exclude considerations like the injustice of harm-infliction or people's moral rights to self-concern.

---

[8] Arrow's argument here invokes as a key premise what Broome (1994, p. 139) calls the "fertility of technology," or the claim that "commodities in general this year can be converted into a greater quantity of commodities next year" through productive investment.

[9] See also Beckerman and Hepburn (2007).

Once one knows (1) that moral philosophers have often sought normatively abridged SWFs that rank outcomes and lotteries from an impartial perspective concerned with their capacity to promote goodness, and (2) that economists have often sought normatively *un*abridged SWFs that rank policies in terms of all policy-relevant considerations, it becomes easier to understand long-standing disagreements between these two camps. Consider for example the following remarks from Derek Parfit:

> Suppose that, if we aim for the greatest net sum of [well-being] benefits over time, this would require a very unequal distribution between different generations ... We may then wish to avoid the conclusion that there ought to be such an unequal distribution. And we can avoid this conclusion, in some cases, if we discount later benefits. But, as Rawls points out, this is the wrong way to avoid this conclusion. If we do not believe that there ought to be such inequality, we should not simply aim for the greatest net sum of benefits. We should have a second moral aim: that the benefits are fairly shared between different generations. To our principle of utility we should add a principle about fair distribution. This more accurately states our real view. And it removes our reason for discounting later benefits. (Parfit 1984, pp. 484–485)

To an economist like Arrow or Cline, that last sentence might sound bizarre. Here we have Parfit admitting that impartial utilitarian rankings may have moral shortcomings, and that discounting future well-being within the context of an otherwise utilitarian SWF can help to engineer a more plausible ranking of policies. And yet Parfit concludes that when the reason for discounting comes from a moral aim that is external to utilitarianism, this "removes our reason for discounting." If you are Arrow or Cline, you are wondering why a reason for discounting becomes a non-reason for discounting when it stems from "a second moral aim" that is distinct from the aim of maximizing the total amount of human well-being. Why should an ethical reason to discount future well-being lose its status as a reason whenever it is grounded in a distinct moral aim? What is Parfit getting at?

Parfit is making two points. First, he is stressing that when we wish to relieve ourselves of a duty to promote well-being far into the future—either because future people will be better off in terms of well-being, or because such a duty would be unreasonably demanding—then "[a]ll these different reasons need to be stated and judged separately, on their merits. If we bundle them together in a Social Discount Rate, we make ourselves morally blind" (Parfit 1984, p. 486). So that is one reason why Parfit rejects a positive pure *time* discount rate: if our concern is not essentially about time, we should not speak as if it is.

Parfit's second point is that even if those other morally relevant features roughly correlate with time, they do not *perfectly* correlate with time. Parfit offers this example:

> Suppose that, at the *same* cost to ourselves now, we could prevent either a minor catastrophe in the nearer future, or a major catastrophe in the further future. Since preventing the major catastrophe would involve no extra cost, the Argument from Excessive Sacrifice fails to apply. But if we take that argument to justify a Discount Rate, we shall be led to conclude that the greater catastrophe is less worth preventing. (Parfit 1984, p. 485, emphasis in original)

Parfit concludes that if we wish to capture principles like "Prevent excessive sacrifice" by adopting a positive pure time discount rate in a social choice SWF, we risk muddling our thinking about why (and when) the future has a claim on our attention, and we risk drawing morally mistaken conclusions about which future-oriented policies have the strongest claim on that attention.

One can easily see how Parfit's arguments might be used to motivate a normatively abridged utilitarian or prioritarian SWF. One could say that it is always morally important to promote well-being in the world, perhaps with some degree of priority for those who enjoy less of it. Then one could add that it is also reasonable to have other moral aims and concerns, including the aim of enforcing rights against harm and protecting individuals from having to make intuitively unreasonable sacrifices on behalf of others. Finally one can argue that the SWF device is best suited for capturing that first aim, namely the aim of improving the world by promoting (priority-adjusted) well-being within it. This is equivalent to saying that we should adopt an impartial, non-discounted utilitarian or prioritarian SWF, but that we should also treat this SWF as normatively abridged. If this view is correct, policy analysts and policymakers should formulate policies by taking into account *both* the ranking represented by the abridged SWF *and* other important moral factors that are not reflected in that ranking. This is more or less the view that has been adopted by most moral philosophers who have written on climate change economics.

It is rare for debates over pure time discounting to stress the concept of normative abridgement; Parfit is a noteworthy exception.[10] It is even rarer for debates to acknowledge the important distinction between a general equilibrium character function and a social choice social welfare function. It is therefore unsurprising that disagreement reigns between philosophers and economists (and among economists themselves) on the issue of pure time discounting. I suspect that if an economist were forced to operate within the normative social choice framework, were aware of the concept of a normatively abridged SWF, and were forbidden from letting considerations related to moral rights or legitimate self-interest shape her SWF, she might find it easy to accept a pure time discount rate of zero.[11] Subject to those constraints, she might find it quite natural to rank outcomes (and lotteries) in terms of a temporally impartial welfarist SWF. She would then know what it is like to be a moral philosopher writing on climate change economics.

5.5 Should SWFs Be Temporally Impartial and Normatively Abridged?

Parfit's concern about the imperfect correlation between time and other morally relevant features is, I think, reasonable. We should avoid diminishing the importance of future people's well-being more than is actually warranted by the features of the world that we would cite in a full accounting of our normative reasons. This does not automatically rule out pure time discounting in a social choice SWF. Perhaps a case can be made for it. But two other related worries can be added to Parfit's to further support the view that SWFs should be normatively abridged and temporally impartial.

The first other worry is that if we allow non-welfarist information to shape the SWF, different theorists will argue that different sets of non-welfarist considerations are germane to this task. And even where theorists agree on the *set* of non-welfarist considerations they would like to include, there will often be disagreement concerning their interpretation and the proper balance between them. This would make the social choice SWF a less reliable device in the policy analysis toolbox. True, a normatively abridged impartial

---

[10] In Kelleher (2017b) I argue that Rawls (1971) invokes this concept as well.
[11] Here I am setting aside any case for pure time discounting based on an infinite dimension of analysis (e.g., an infinite time horizon).

utilitarian (or prioritarian) SWF cannot alone tell us what ought to be done. But if its job is to assess the important moral consideration of overall well-being, it will convey at least some morally useful information. We cannot say the same for SWFs that are less abridged and therefore less likely to win a wide consensus as legitimate tools for policy analysis. This is not to say that policy analysis can or should always avoid relying on contestable theoretical frameworks. It is simply to say that there is merit in having analytical tools that most can agree are relevant to the task at hand.

The second (and related) worry about letting non-welfarist considerations shape the SWF is that the moral force of many such moral considerations is often context-specific. This means that if we do not abridge non-welfarist considerations, the SWF itself may have to change depending on the circumstances, and different theorists or analysts will have different views about when circumstances warrant the selection of this or that value for a key parameter. To illustrate, consider an argument of Dasgupta's that concerns not the pure time discount rate but the curvature of the well-being function in a (discounted) utilitarian SWF. That is, it concerns η rather than δ in the Ramsey formula for consumption discount rates.[12] I reproduce that equation here:

$$\rho_t = \delta + \eta \cdot g_t \qquad (5.2)$$

To explain Dasgupta's approach to η, it is first necessary to note that he conceives of η as a *compound* inequality aversion parameter. That is, for Dasgupta, η can be used to reflect *both* the diminishing marginal well-being of consumption *and* the diminishing marginal *social value* of *well-being*. In other words, Dasgupta is willing to let η reflect both an individual phenomenon—the declining degree to which an individual converts consumption into well-being—and a social phenomenon—the degree to which social value should be prioritarian by applying an implicit concave transformation to each individual's well-being indicator.[13] In a (discounted) utilitarian social choice framework, each of these entails a form of social inequality aversion: the diminishing marginal well-being of consumption entails an aversion to inequalities *in consumption*, while prioritarianism

---

[12] See equation (2.10) from section 2.4.
[13] See Stern (1977, p. 242) and especially Kaplow and Weisbach (2011) for useful discussions of this maneuver.

entails social aversion to inequalities in well-being. (We encountered prioritarianism in section 4.3 and I will return to it in chapter 6.)

The interesting thing about Dasgupta's calibration of his compound inequality-aversion parameter, η, is that while he rejects the prioritarian rationale that might justify setting η as high as 2 or 3 in *intra*-generational economic analyses, he argues that intra-generational policy analysis should, nevertheless, *use* a value of η in that range.[14] Why? His answer is that while mere differences in well-being are not as morally important as prioritarians think, it *is* important *how* those differences arose. And according to Dasgupta, whereas today's rich world is *not* primarily responsible for the poverty found in today's poor world,

> [w]e should be anxious over the plight of future generations caused by climate change *because we are collectively responsible* for amplifying that change; the rich world especially so. If future generations inherit a hugely damaged Earth, it is *we* who would be in part responsible. (Dasgupta 2008, p. 159, emphasis added).

For this reason, Dasgupta maintains that we in today's rich countries may have stronger obligations to those who will be richer than us in the future than we do to those who are poorer than we are now. And this is because today's rich countries have been actively harming future people, but not (he maintains) today's poor. Dasgupta is therefore invoking non-welfarist factors that I have been saying are largely abridged from the SWFs advocated for by moral philosophers writing on climate economics.

Here is Dasgupta's conclusion: although today's rich do not *owe* much to today's poor, *helping* today's poor may be the best way to discharge distinct duties to the *future* people that today's rich people have been harming. For example, we might be morally obligated to help improve the current economy in today's poor nations, so that over time the benefits of economic growth can be enjoyed by those future people to whom we have strong harm-based obligations. As he puts it, one way to improve "tomorrow's people in today's poor world" is simply to improve today's poor world; this is not because we have obligations to those "others today," but rather because we have

---

[14] When η equals 2, Dasgupta's SWF would treat a 50 percent decrease in the annual income of a person who makes $36,000 as equivalent to a 1 percent decrease for a contemporary who makes $360 (Dasgupta 2008, pp. 151–152).

obligations to "tomorrow's they" (Dasgupta 2012, p. 121). A morally reasonable degree of redistribution can be achieved, Dasgupta suggests, if we use an η between 2 and 3 in a normatively unabridged SWF.

With this line of argument of Dasgupta's on the table, recall the second worry I stated concerning unabridged SWFs: they will be highly context-dependent. We can see this from the views of Cline and Dasgupta. Cline says that the pure time discount rate should be zero in a discounted utilitarian SWF because we must not discount the interests of the future people we are harming with our greenhouse gas emissions. But it is possible to combine that stance with one on which a positive pure time discount rate would be warranted in contexts where a candidate project would *merely bestow a benefit* upon future people, rather than prevent a harm we are imposing. On a complex view like that, we will not know which SWF to use until we know whether a project prevents harm or merely bestows a benefit. The same predicament arises in the context of Dasgupta's arguments concerning η: if it turns out that greenhouse gas mitigation is not best classified as the prevention of harm, then Dasgupta's arguments are consistent with a (discounted) utilitarian SWF whose η value is set somewhat below 2.[15]

Moreover, if greenhouse gases do inflict harm and there is also a second environmental policy context in which we are not harming future people but could still benefit them by bearing the costs today, then on the complex Cline- and Dasgupta-like views we are considering, it could turn out that different SWFs should be used to analyze these different contexts. If we thought it was already hard to settle disputes about social choice SWFs and their parameters, it would become all the more difficult if we had to use different SWFs in different policy contexts. That would be a guaranteed recipe for protracted disagreement among the economists who formulate SWFs for use in their analyses, and for confusion among the regulators and legislators whom these analyses are intended to assist.[16] It is these and related reasons that lie behind Adler and Treich's remark, "Non-welfarist ethical approaches—for example, 'deontological' views—are not well captured by the SWF framework" (Adler and Treich 2015, p. 282).

To be sure, even if a normatively abridged SWF enables one to avoid troublesome disagreements and problematic (or simply confusing)

---

[15] For a compelling philosophical reason for thinking that climate change will *not* harm distant future generations even if it brings many bad things to them, see Broome (2012, ch. 4).

[16] For a further problem caused by context-relative SWFs, see Broome (2012, pp. 150–152).

context-dependence, the underlying sources of the troubles will still have to be grappled with by policymakers (and the staff they rely upon for analysis and advice). That is, even if it is desirable to exclude non-welfarist considerations from SWF-based economic analysis, responsible policymaking must still be responsive to all normatively relevant factors. Yet there may be very good reasons to observe a division of labor, with the SWF (and its discount rates) capturing only the welfarist value of outcomes (and lotteries). This would leave it to the broader policy-evaluation process to combine SWF-based analysis with all the other normative considerations that rightly bear on responsible governance. But at least then it will be clear to all parties what features of the world an SWF aims to reflect, and what further normative analysis must be carried out by the policymakers and regulators who are ultimately responsible for selecting and implementing public policies.

The upshot is this: even if one embraces some of the non-welfarist ethical values and principles that have led economists like Cline, Arrow, and Dasgupta to adjust their discounting parameters, one can coherently resist such adjustments by also embracing normative abridgement. Moreover, there are good philosophical and practical reasons to accept a version of normative abridgement that excludes precisely those non-welfarist considerations from the ambit of social choice climate economics. If these reasons are as strong as I think they are, they leave us with no good reason to accept pure time discounting within a social choice SWF (assuming that we are setting aside reasons related to an infinite time horizon). This frees the SWF to serve the role it is best suited to play, namely the role of facilitating welfarist evaluations of outcomes and lotteries.

5.6 Normative Abridgement and Evaluative Humility

Earlier I pushed back against economists Lawrence Goulder and Roberton Williams for claiming that a social welfare function is "by definition" normatively *un*abridged. Although that claim is mistaken, they are correct to say that it can be very hard to shoehorn all relevant normative considerations into one SWF. They are also correct to say that the Kaldor-Hicks compensation principle is itself normatively abridged:

> In principle, a social welfare function will embrace all relevant normative dimensions (including both efficiency and distributional considerations);

this all-encompassing quality gives it great appeal. At the same time, the appropriate blending or weighting of these various dimensions is subjective and leads to disagreements as to the appropriate form and parameters of the social welfare function. For this reason, some analysts prefer to focus on the narrower Kaldor–Hicks criterion ... Although this criterion focuses only on one normative dimension (namely, the potential for a Pareto improvement), it can be more tractable. (Goulder and Williams 2012, p. 1250024–16)

I explained in section 3.15 why the Kaldor-Hicks criterion is normatively flawed, and why the standard test that economists use to identify potential Pareto improvements is theoretically flawed. Nevertheless, it is important to see that normatively abridged evaluations are often presented by economists as helpful despite that abridgement. It shows that these economists are not inherently hostile to abridged evaluations.

While I have argued against the Kaldor-Hicks-based notion of potential Pareto efficiency, I have in effect argued that normatively abridged welfarist SWFs capture a type of efficiency that really does matter to public policy—namely the relative ability of alternative policies to promote impartially valuable distributions of well-being in the world. Call this type of efficiency *well-being efficiency*.

A famous argument for the Kaldor-Hicks principle is undercut by this picture in which SWFs are abridged tools for evaluating policies' relative well-being efficiency. In an article criticizing the use of SWFs in applied welfare economics, Arnold C. Harberger argues that the virtues of modesty and humility support a focus on potential Pareto efficiency. Instead of directly criticizing SWFs, Harberger criticizes "distributional weighting schemes." But the distributive weights he has in mind are precisely the welfare weights that I discussed in section 2.5 and that always implicate an underlying SWF.

Harberger's argument against the use of welfare weights, which he in turn takes to be an argument for "the traditional criterion of efficiency" based on "the Hicks-Kaldor principle" (Harberger 1978, pp. S119, S115), proceeds as follows. First, he observes that often, in contexts of interpersonal relationships and public policy, our judgments about proper conduct and moral responsibility do not coincide with the rankings that would be produced by a welfarist SWF. He uses the example of a set of adult siblings whose sharing of resources cannot be "explained in terms of distributional weighting schemes," which would result in "systematic transfers taking place" to even out income differences between them. Instead, we observe adult siblings helping one another more when they suffer "major negative windfalls than ... positive ones" (Harberger 1978, p. S118). Harberger claims to observe a similar tendency in public policy, where social support is often "'in kind' and oriented toward meeting a certain minimum," rather than determined by a welfarist SWF and its implicit welfare weights. He concludes:

> Might it not be that there is a message here for economists trying to grapple with distributional questions? I believe so, and the message really tells us to be more modest and humble, less ready to arrogate to our profession and discipline the solution of all of society's problems ...
> In the end, then, we cannot condemn as crass or unfeeling the idea [of] our profession's possibly moving toward a "consensus" based on the traditional criterion of [potential Pareto] efficiency. On the contrary, such a result might well reflect a greater and more sensitive understanding of the value systems of our citizens and our societies, as well as a more modest and realistic appreciation of our own professional role. (Harberger 1978, pp. S118–S119)

I hope by now it is clear why this argument is a bad argument for the Kaldor-Hicks compensation principle. Harberger wrongly assumes that to defend the use of welfare weights in applied economics is to defend the use of an *unabridged* welfarist SWF. But that is a mistake, as I have explained.

The same mistake is made by the economist John Creedy when he writes:

> [I]t is not uncommon to find authors using standard rhetorical devices to impose their own value judgements. Thus dogmatic statements along the lines that "positive pure time preference is morally indefensible" can often be found. However, it is worth remembering that zero pure time preference carries the implication that [a hypothetical policymaker] would be prepared to impose starvation on the current generation in order to produce a tiny benefit for a distant generation. (Creedy 2007, p. 9)

Now to make sense of this claim, we must suppose that Creedy assumes that the future generation will be sufficiently large that total well-being is increased by bestowing a tiny benefit on each of them even at the cost of starvation for present people. Suppose that is what he means. Where Creedy goes wrong is in assuming that "zero pure time preference carries the implication" that policymakers ought to implement whatever policy produces the most undiscounted well-being. I suspect this is something that many, if not the vast majority of economists believe. But I have explained why a zero pure time discount rate will *not* have that implication *if* it appears in a normatively abridged SWF. And I have argued that there are good reasons for economists to work with normatively abridged welfarist SWFs.

In light of the problems with the Kaldor-Hicks criterion that I discussed in section 3.15, and given the fallacy in the standard criticism of impartial SWFs rehearsed by Harberger and Creedy, I hope the discussion in the present chapter will lead some of the analysts that Goulder and Williams mention— the ones who prefer to use an evaluative criterion that focuses "only on one normative dimension"—to embrace a welfarist, temporally impartial, and normatively abridged SWF. Nothing in the social choice framework requires SWFs to rank outcomes and policies with respect to everything that matters. The use of an SWF to evaluate climate change policies does not thereby "arrogate to [economics] the solution to all of society's problems." Professional humility and temporally impartial welfarist SWFs are perfectly compatible.

6

Distribution

In chapter 5 I criticized Lawrence Goulder and Roberton Williams's claim, "In principle, a social welfare function will embrace all relevant normative dimensions (including both efficiency and distributional considerations)" (Goulder and Williams 2012, p. 1250024–16). I explained why it is coherent for an SWF to be normatively abridged, and I gave reasons for adopting an SWF of that sort. These reasons primarily related to normative factors that are agent-relative (such as Arrow's concern to give agents protection against unreasonably demanding obligations to others), and factors that are context-specific (such as Cline's and Dasgupta's view that one has stronger reason to refrain from harming others than one has to bestow a benefit upon them). When one opts for a utilitarian SWF whose job is to rank outcomes and prospects with respect to their capacity to promote overall well-being, one walls off that SWF from having to reflect agent-relative or context-specific factors. In that case, the utilitarian SWF may have to be combined with other non-utilitarian, non-welfarist considerations to perform an overall all-things-considered evaluation.

I also criticized Goulder and Williams on another point. When they say that an SWF will in principle embrace all normatively relevant factors, they single out "efficiency and distributional considerations" for special emphasis. By "efficiency" they mean Kaldor-Hicks efficiency (and possibly also Pareto efficiency), and by "distributional considerations" they mean how things like commodities and environmental amenities are distributed throughout a population. In contrast, I argued in section 3.15 that Kaldor-Hicks efficiency is normatively *ir*relevant, and in section 5.6 I suggested the better conception of efficiency is *efficiency in the production of impartially valuable well-being*. Meanwhile, though I sympathetically explained an axiomatic basis for utilitarianism in chapter 4, I certainly have not ruled out the possibility that a distribution of goods and services is more valuable if it leads to greater equality in well-being, other things equal.

I have, however, noted a problem for one SWF that is averse to inequalities in well-being. In section 4.3.1 I described what I called *Harsanyi-compliant prioritarianism*. I explained that this view, which sums concave transformations of individuals' well-being indicators, requires a quantitative notion of well-being that is not built up from expected utility theory. Yet since it is unclear where such a notion might come from, we have reason to treat the expected utility value functions that are summed in Harsanyian interpersonal aggregation as themselves well-being functions. And this yields an SWF that is utilitarian, not prioritarian.

In the theoretical literature on social welfare functions, prioritarianism is the leading framework for embedding social aversion to inequalities in well-being into an SWF. But owing to the attractions of using expected utility theory to construct indicators of individual well-being, philosophical prioritarians typically defend Harsanyi *non*-compliant prioritarianism. Since these prioritarians maintain that their quantitative notion of well-being can be built up from expected utility theory, they accept the premise of Harsanyi's aggregation theorem that requires individuals' betterness orderings of lotteries to obey the expected utility axioms. This means that these prioritarians must reject one (or both) of the aggregation theorem's other two main premises.

This chapter examines the case for various versions of Harsanyi noncompliant prioritarianism by considering the "Harsanyian woes" each is subject to.[1] I shall conclude that these woes are very high prices to pay, and that with the case for normative abridgement already strong, there is good reason to reject prioritarian SWFs while letting its underlying concerns with inequality influence wider, all-things-considered policy evaluation.

6.1 Axiomatic Prioritarianism

Axiomatic treatments of prioritarianism follow an approach that differs from the broad strategy underlying Harsanyi's aggregation theorem. I have said that prioritarians typically invoke expected utility theory to construct individuals' well-being indicators. But they do not initially require the general (or social) betterness ordering of prospects to obey the expected utility axioms. Rather, prioritarians first derive their SWF for

---

[1] The phrase is Hilary Greaves's (2015, p. 16). In this chapter I am indebted to Greaves's discussion, and to that in Fleurbaey (2010) and Adler (2019).

non-risky contexts, and then later supplement that SWF with an "uncertainty module" that extends the framework to contexts involving risk (Adler 2019, pp. 19–20).

The axiomatic approach for non-risky (or "deterministic") prioritarianism borrows from well-known axiomatizations of utilitarianism that differ from Harsanyi's. These alternatives begin with a set of outcomes expressible as interpersonal vectors of lifetime well-beings. I shall call these vectors *distributions*. The well-beings in these distributions are assumed to be determined by the cardinally measurable and interpersonally comparable well-being functions of the individuals who would live in the corresponding outcomes. For an unchanging population of individuals indexed by $i = 1, \ldots, N$, let us express these distributions as follows:

$$W = (w_1, w_2, \ldots, w_N)$$

d'Aspremont and Gevers (1977, p. 203) prove that if an ordering of such well-being distributions satisfies a certain set of axioms, then the only SWF that can represent that ordering is the utilitarian SWF:

$$V = \sum_{i=1}^{N} w_i$$

Their set of axioms is:

Anonymity: The general betterness ordering is sensitive only to the well-beings associated with each outcome, and not to the identities of the people whose well-beings they are. Thus, if an outcome x is changed to a new outcome y by keeping the well-beings the same but reassigning them to different people, y should have the very same ranking in the general betterness ordering as x.

Strong Pareto: If each individual's well-being is at least as great in outcome y as in outcome x, and if it is strictly greater in y for at least one person, then y comes higher in the general betterness ordering than x.

Independence of Irrelevant Alternatives (well-being version): Let distributions W_x and W_y list (respectively) individuals' lifetime well-beings in outcomes x and y. Then, when socially ranking W_x against W_y, it is never relevant what the individuals' well-beings would be in any outcome other than x and y.

Information invariance with respect to cardinal measurability and unit comparability: The general betterness ordering remains unchanged if instead of assessing well-beings using the functions $w_1, w_2, \ldots, w_N$, it is assessed using the functions $aw_1 + b_1, aw_2 + b_2, \ldots, aw_N + b_N$, for any positive constant a and any set of constants $b_1, b_2, \ldots, b_N$.

We encountered the Anonymity and strong Pareto axioms in chapter 4 (section 4.2). The Independence of Irrelevant Alternatives axiom says simply that when ranking two distributions of well-being against one another, one can focus on the well-beings in just those two distributions. This implies that how each compares to some third distribution is never relevant when comparing the first two.[2] Finally, the Information invariance axiom is related to the proposition from section 2.2 that a utilitarian SWF requires well-being indicators that are cardinal and unit comparable. d'Aspremont and Gevers show that when one begins with the requirement that the general betterness ordering must be invariant to positive affine transformations of each well-being indicator, with all such transformations using the same scaling factor a, then (if one adopts their other conditions) it follows that the only function able to represent that ordering is the utilitarian function.

Later, Eric Maskin (1978) proved that the utilitarian SWF is the only function that can represent an ordering of distributions when the ordering satisfies Anonymity, strong Pareto, Independence of Irrelevant Alternatives (well-being version), and these three further conditions:

Continuity: Take two distributions W and W'. Suppose that W is better than W'. Then there is some third distribution that is very close to W that is also better than W'.

Separability: When a number of distributions differ only in the well-being enjoyed by a subset of individuals G, then the distributions' relative ranking depends only on differences for the affected individuals in G.

Information invariance with respect to cardinal measurability and full comparability: The general betterness ordering remains unchanged if instead of assessing well-beings using $w_1, w_2, \ldots, w_N$, it is assessed using

---

[2] For more on this axiom, see Bossert and Weymark (2004, p. 1104). This is the "well-being version" because the most famous axiom with this name is Arrow's, which plays a key role in his so-called impossibility theorem (Arrow 2012). That theorem shows that only a dictatorial function can represent a social preference ordering when the function's arguments are restricted to individuals' preference orderings, and when certain other minimal axioms are imposed. A dictatorial social welfare function is one where a single individual's preference ordering determines the social ordering.

the functions $aw_1 + b, aw_2 + b, \ldots, aw_N + b$, for any single positive a and any single number b.

To define Continuity fully, we would need to specify what it means for one distribution to be "very close" to another. For example, the precise "sup norm" notion of distance defined the continuity axiom of Koopmans's that I discussed in section 4.1. Koopmans used the sup norm notion because it worked particularly well in the context of infinite distributions of well-being. That notion, however, conflicted with Anonymity. In contrast, Maskin is concerned with finite distributions of well-being, and because of this he is able to use a notion of continuity that is fully consistent with the Anonymity axiom that utilitarians also accept.

We can define Separability more formally as follows. Segment the population into two groups, G and H; now consider four distributions of well-bein $(W_G, W_H), (W'_G, W_H), (W_G, W'_H)$, and (W'_G, W'_H). The general betterness ordering is separable if, for all distributions, (W_G, W_H) is better than (W'_G, W_H) if and only if (W_G, W'_H) is better than (W'_G, W'_H). That is, whenever there is an unaffected group of individuals, the overall ranking of the two distributions is determined by the ranking of the distributions of well-being involving just the members of the affected group.[3]

Finally, Maskin's Information invariance axiom is similar to d'Aspremont and Gevers's, except that Maskin allows for interpersonal level comparisons as well as unit comparisons. This opens up the possibility that the general betterness ordering can be represented by an SWF that is sensitive to well-being levels in a way that the utilitarian SWF is not. But in fact Maskin proves that even when one admits interpersonal level comparisons into the analysis, only the utilitarian SWF represents orderings that obey Maskin's full set of axioms.

There have been other axiomatizations of utilitarianism in addition to these.[4] As noted above, a key feature of the ones presented here is that they do not proceed by assuming that the general betterness ordering obeys the axioms of expected utility theory. So they do not proceed by first assuming that the SWF must represent an ordering of prospects defined on a set of distributions of well-being. It therefore remains an open question how

---

[3] Here I borrow Broome's exposition of (strong) separability from Broome (2019b, p. 590).
[4] See Sen (1986) for a survey.

utilitarianism so axiomatized should handle contexts in which one cannot choose a given distribution for certain.

I have explained these alternative axiomatic approaches to utilitarianism because they display the general strategy taken by prioritarians in the SWF literature: first establish a deterministic prioritarian SWF for distributions, and then ask what approach to risk should be combined with that SWF. Of the axioms already mentioned, prioritarians embrace Anonymity, strong Pareto, Independence of Irrelevant Alternatives (well-being version), Continuity, and Separability. To these they add the following:

> *Pigou-Dalton (well-being version):*[5] Take two distributions, W_x and W_y, that differ only in the well-being of two individuals, q and r. Suppose that q is better off in terms of well-being than r in both distributions. And suppose that W_y is reached from W_x by a *pure, gap-diminishing transfer* from q to r. Then W_y comes higher than W_x in the general betterness ordering. (Adler 2019, p. 98)[6]

The Pigou-Dalton principle is a *distributive* axiom in the sense that it tilts in favor of more equal distributions of well-being. But it is not intrinsically concerned with "relativities"; that is, it is not intrinsically concerned with how one person fares relative to another. That is why Pigou-Dalton is consistent with the strong Pareto axiom: the Pigou-Dalton axiom does not automatically condemn making an already better-off person even better off while leaving an already worse-off person unaffected. If, for example, there is no way to diminish the gap in well-being between them, then the Pigou-Dalton principle is perfectly fine with an inequality-increasing benefit that goes to the better-off individual.

Together, the prioritarian's axioms entail that the general betterness ordering can be represented by a function having the following form (Adler 2012, ch. 5):

$$V_{Prior} = \sum_{i=1}^{N} g(w_i) \tag{6.1}$$

---

[5] I discussed this axiom in section 4.3.1.
[6] This is the "well-being version" of the Pigou-Dalton axiom because it is also possible to formulate a Pigou-Dalton principle for, say, generalized consumption. That principle would refer to distributions of generalized consumption and to pure gap-diminishing transfers of generalized consumption.

with g a strictly concave transformation of well-being. This is the generic prioritarian SWF. A more specific prioritarian function can be supported by the fact that no instance of (6.1) is invariant to rescalings of the well-being indicators that preserve only the interpersonal comparability of well-being units and levels (Adler and Treich 2015, p. 289). Ostensibly, that is a problem. For we know that prioritarians care about how well off people are and about how much they can be benefited; and it would seem to be problematic if a prioritarian betterness ordering changed when one switched from using one interpersonally comparable well-being scale to a different, equivalent scale. Thus to vindicate (6.1), it seems that prioritarians must identify an aspect of individuals' situation that is relevant to the general betterness ordering but that is not captured by fully comparable cardinal well-being indicators. They can do this by claiming that in addition to well-being units and levels, the general betterness ordering also cares about well-being *ratios* (Adler and Treich 2015, p. 290; Adler 2019, pp. 124–130).

To see the difference between scales that support talk of ratios and those that do not, consider Fahrenheit and Celsius versus pounds and kilograms. Temperatures in Fahrenheit and Celsius are positive affine transformations of one another: to convert to Fahrenheit from Celsius, multiply temperature in the latter by 1.8 and then add 32. These two scales therefore permit meaningful talk of ratios of temperature differences: the ratio of the difference between 0 and 10 degrees Celsius and 20 and 30 degrees Celsius is the same as the following ratio:

$$\frac{[1.8(10)+32]-[1.8(0)+32]}{[1.8(30)+32]-[1.8(20)+32]}$$

But some claims remain meaningless with the sort of unit and level comparability afforded by these two temperature scales. As Partha Dasgupta puts it:

> We are entitled to compare differences in temperatures. We can say, for example, that the difference in the temperatures at sites A and B is three times the difference in the temperatures at sites C and D; and so on. However, it makes no sense to say that one place is twice as hot as another place. (If it is true in Fahrenheit, it won't be true in Centigrade [i.e., Celsius], and if it is true in Centigrade, it won't be true in Fahrenheit!) (Dasgupta 2001, p. 22)

To make talk of percentage-based changes meaningful, the scale of measurement must feature a meaningful zero point, as in the case of weight. Pounds and kilograms are two different scales for measuring weight, but they share the same zero point—weightlessness. Whereas Fahrenheit and Celsius are two members of the same family of cardinal measures, pounds and kilograms are two members of the same family of ratio measures. With a ratio scale, it is meaningful to talk about percentage changes, in the way that it is meaningful to talk about the percentage change in weight that is added to an object if one straps a billiard ball to it. If this changes the object's weight by 10 percent when weight is measured in pounds, then it will also increase its weight by 10 percent when measured in kilograms instead.

Matthew Adler, a leading prioritarian, therefore adds the following axiom to the others I have so far associated with axiomatic prioritarianism (Adler and Treich 2015, p. 290; Adler 2019, pp. 124–130):

Information invariance with respect to common ratio rescalings of well-being functions: The general betterness ordering remains unchanged if instead of assessing well-beings using $w_1, w_2, \ldots, w_N$, it is assessed using the functions $aw_1, aw_2, \ldots, aw_N$, for any positive constant a.

It turns out that when one adopts this invariance axiom, there is only one instance of the general prioritarian SWF (6.1) that satisfies all of the other prioritarian axioms as well. This is the so-called Atkinsonian SWF (Adler and Treich 2015, p. 290; Adler 2019, pp. 154–156):

$$V_{Atkinson} = \sum_{i=1}^{N} \frac{w_i^{1-\gamma}}{1-\gamma} \qquad (6.2)$$

In the Atkinsonian SWF, the prioritarian transformation function g is an isoelastic function of individuals' well-beings, where those well-beings are measurable on a ratio scale and fully comparable. The parameter γ in (6.2) is an inequality aversion parameter. When $\gamma = 0$, (6.2) is equivalent to the utilitarian SWF: a transfer of one unit of well-being from a better-off person to a worse-off person makes the world neither better nor worse. Any γ larger than zero entails the Pigou-Dalton axiom, and as γ gets larger and larger, (6.2) becomes more and more "leak-tolerant."[7] An SWF is leak-tolerant when,

---

[7] I borrow the term from Adler (2019, p. 142).

instead of approving only of gap-diminishing transfers in which the beneficiary gains the same amount of well-being as the "donor" loses, the SWF sometimes also approves of transfers in which some of the "donated" well-being is lost in transit. As γ approaches infinity, the Atkinson SWF tolerates virtually *any* degree of leakage, so long as the beneficiary's well-being is increased by some amount and so long as the beneficiary is still worse off than the donor is after the transfer.

6.2 Prioritarianism under Risk

As I have mentioned, prioritarians standardly argue or assume that the strictly concave transformation g in equation (6.1) is logically distinct from the expected utility value functions that represent individuals' betterness orderings. This makes their prioritarianism Harsanyi non-compliant. It follows that standard prioritarianism must reject at least one of the other two axioms of Harsanyi's aggregation theorem, namely the ex ante strong Pareto principle and the principle that the general betterness ordering of lotteries also satisfies the requirements of expected utility theory. Unsurprisingly, then, the non-deterministic versions of prioritarianism that have received the most attention in the literature can be distinguished by which of those two axioms they violate.

I am now going to change the way I talk about uncertain prospects. In chapter 4, I used the language of the von Neumann–Morgenstern version of expected utility theory. There I described an uncertain prospect as a lottery that is articulated in terms of a set of possible outcomes, each of which is associated with a corresponding probability of coming about. Here, I will think of an uncertain prospect as an *act* that maps a set of possible and mutually exclusive *states of nature* to a set of outcomes. In this alternative articulation, one of these states is the actual state of nature, but we do not know which state that is. Each possible act then brings about an outcome m with a cumulative probability that is determined by the independent probabilities of all the states that would produce m given that act. In the vNM framework, an uncertain prospect is defined in terms of the cumulative objective probabilities associated with each possible outcome. In the alternative framework, probabilities may be subjective, and states of nature and their probabilities must be kept conceptually separate, even when the very same outcome would arise in multiple states of nature given a certain act.[8]

In what follows I shall rely on this alternative conceptual scheme because the choice between different uncertainty modules for prioritarianism sometimes turns on the acceptability of axioms that require the ability to compare two prospects' outcomes in a state-by-state fashion. Harsanyi's aggregation theorem has been proved for versions of expected utility theory articulated in terms of states, acts, and outcomes instead of lotteries and outcomes (e.g., in Mongin 1995). So it remains kosher to analyze different approaches to prioritarianism under risk by examining their respective Harsanyian woes.

Consider now the following social welfare function that combines deterministic prioritarianism with an uncertainty module that violates expected utility theory at the level of the general betterness ordering:

$$V_{EAP} = \sum_{i=1}^{N} g\left(\sum_{s \in S} p_s \cdot w_i(\mathbf{c}_i)\right) \qquad (6.3)$$

This is the *ex ante prioritarian* SWF. Here $\mathbf{c}_i$ can be interpreted as a vector of vectors—for example, a list of items that i consumes at a given time in i's life, and a list of all such lists, one for each time i is alive. For each possible act, the SWF (6.3) finds each individual's expected lifetime well-being given their well-being in each state s whose probability is p_s; the SWF then transforms these expectations with the strictly concave function g, and then sums the results across individuals. It is called ex ante prioritarianism because it applies the prioritarian transformation function to expected or "ex ante" well-being.

Ex ante prioritarianism obeys the ex ante strong Pareto axiom but violates expected utility theory at the level of the general betterness ordering. In fact, it does this in two different ways. First, it violates a very minimal principle of *Dominance*. To explain, consider this example:

> Consider a situation in which an impending climate change will alter the distribution of well-being on Earth. Suppose that only two scenarios are considered possible. In one scenario, the extreme latitudes gain and the low latitudes suffer, whereas the reverse occurs in the other scenario. Suppose

[8] For a canonical statement of this sort of decision theory framework, see Kreps (1988, ch. 9).

that in either scenario the distribution of well-being is ultimately much worse than in the absence of climate change. Therefore, one is sure that such climate change is harmful. However, if individual expected utilities are not diminished ex ante, because everyone may gain or lose depending on which scenario is realized, ex ante [prioritarianism] considers that climate change is harmless. This is strange since the same criterion considers that the change will ultimately be catastrophic. (Fleurbaey 2010, p. 650)

The example is constructed so that the prioritarian ranking of *non-risky* outcomes looks like this:

Best outcome:
   No climate change.
Tied for worst outcome:
   Climate change where extreme latitudes gain and low latitudes suffer.
   Climate change where low latitudes gain and extreme latitudes suffer.

Regardless of how climate change works out, therefore, it is definitely worse than an outcome without climate change. So if we faced a choice between (1) no climate change and (2) a 50 percent chance of one region suffering and a 50 percent chance of the other region suffering, we should choose (1). After all, for every possible state of nature, the distribution that results if we pick (1) is better than the distribution that will result if we pick (2). In this sense the prospect defined by (1) *dominates* the prospect defined by (2). And yet according to ex ante prioritarianism, (2) is just as good as (1). This is because each person's expected well-being is the same regardless of whether we choose (1) or (2). Dominance is a very basic axiom satisfied by all expected utility frameworks, and violating it seems deeply irrational. For this reason ex ante prioritarianism is deeply problematic (Fleurbaey 2010, p. 655).[9]

---

[9] Another way to put the same point is in terms of what Hilary Greaves calls the *principle of avoidance of foreseeable regret* (Greaves 2015, p. 38). The regret at issue is not the regret of tolerating seemingly catastrophic outcomes. "Ex ante" utilitarianism would also "consider climate change to be harmless" in the example above, but ex ante utilitarianism does not violate the principle of avoidance of foreseeable regret. This is because ex ante utilitarianism is studiously indifferent between an option that has as its certain outcome the avoidance of climate change and two other options whose certain outcomes involve one latitude's gaining in well-being while the other loses by an exactly offsetting amount. Ex ante prioritarianism, by contrast, ranks the certain prospect of climate change–avoidance higher than either of two alternative certain prospects in which one latitude gains while the other loses. Thus, while ex ante prioritarianism would be indifferent between the gamble and certain climate change–avoidance, once the dice have been thrown and

Ex ante prioritarianism also violates the expected utility axiom Independence. Independence is a principle of separability. Unlike Maskin's Separability axiom, which concerns separability in the dimension of people, Independence concerns separability of possible outcomes. It says, in effect, that if two prospects would have the very same outcomes in a specific set of states, then the general betterness ordering of these prospects can be determined by focusing on what would happen in the states where the outcomes differ. Independence has been the subject of much debate among economists and philosophers. But since ex ante prioritarians standardly accept that individuals' betterness orderings of prospects must satisfy Independence, it is at least curious they would abandon it in the context of the general betterness ordering. Nevertheless, their rejection of Dominance is much more troubling and is enough to induce most prioritarians to consider other ways of adding an uncertainty module to deterministic prioritarianism.

Thus consider now the *ex post prioritarian* SWF:

$$V_{EPP} = \sum_{s \in S} p_s \cdot \sum_{i=1}^{N} g(w_i(c_i)) \qquad (6.4)$$

Instead of summing concave transformations of expected well-being, V_{EPP} first uses (6.1) to find the deterministic prioritarian value associated with each possible outcome, and then computes the mathematical expectation of these "ex post" evaluations. Ex post prioritarianism derives its functional form by subjecting the general betterness ordering of prospects to the axioms of expected utility theory. It therefore fully complies with Dominance and Independence, unlike ex ante prioritarianism.[10]

---

one of the latitudes has gained and the other has lost, ex ante prioritarians would prefer to switch to the outcome in which climate change is avoided. Ex ante prioritarianism therefore courts foreseeable regret, *as judged by its own lights*.

[10] Strictly speaking, applying the axioms of expected utility theory to the general betterness ordering of prospects is consistent with the *transformed* ex post prioritarian social welfare function: $V_{TEPP} = \sum_{s \in S} p_s \cdot H(\sum_{i=1}^{N} g(w_i(c_i)))$. In this SWF, H reflects social risk aversion (Adler et al. 2014). Whereas a concave g expresses social aversion to inequalities in well-being across persons, a concave H expresses a final layer of risk-aversion with respect to sums of priority-transformed well-being. I shall ignore transformed ex post prioritarianism in order to focus on a problem for ex post prioritarianism that arises whatever the H function. Nevertheless, it is useful to see how a prioritarian SWF can incorporate distinct notions of social risk aversion, individual risk aversion, and social inequality aversion into one social welfare function. V_{TEPP} can in addition reflect a distinct notion of individual aversion to intertemporal fluctuations in consumption and well-being, depending on the functional form for lifetime well-being. This could go some way toward allaying

Table 6.1 Ex post prioritarianism violates ex ante strong Pareto

	Prospect I H	Prospect I T	expected well-being	Prospect J H	Prospect J T	expected well-being
w1	36	36	36	4	100	52
w2	49	49	49	4	100	52
STWB[a]	13	13		4	20	
ESTWB[b]		13			12	

[a] STWB = sum of transformed well-being.
[b] ESTWB = expected sum of transformed well-being.

Since ex post prioritarianism is also Harsanyi non-compliant, and since both its individual and general betterness orderings satisfy the axioms of expected utility theory, it must violate Harsanyi's ex ante strong Pareto axiom. As explained in 4.3.1, this axiom says that if a prospect A is at least as good for every individual as another prospect B, and if A is better than B for at least one individual, then A is generally better than B. To see the conflict between this principle and ex post prioritarianism, consider an example of Toby Ord's, shown in Table 6.1.[11]

In this example, Prospect I and Prospect J each involves the toss of a fair coin, which lands on Heads (H) 50 percent of the time and Tails (T) 50 percent of the time. For simplicity, I shall suppose throughout this chapter that the deterministic prioritarian SWF's concave transformation—its g function—is the square root function. This makes the sum of transformed well-being (STWB) in both outcomes of Prospect I 13. For Prospect J, the STWB is 4 in outcome H and 20 in outcome T. So the *expected* sum of transformed well-being (ESTWB) is 13 for I and 12 for J. Thus ex post prioritarianism ranks Prospect I over J in the general betterness ordering. And it does this even though *both* expected utilitarianism *and* ex post prioritarianism hold that Prospect J is better than Prospect I for every individual involved.

Ex post prioritarianism's evaluation of cases like Ord's would be very odd if that view were intrinsically concerned with relativities, since ex post

the concerns of some economists that standard models in climate economics conflate two or more of these distinct concepts. See Kelleher and Wagner (2018).

[11] Hilary Greaves credits Ord for this example in Greaves (2015, p. 37).

prioritarianism ranks Prospect *I* over Prospect *J* even though Prospect *J* is better for everyone *and* is the only prospect that guarantees ex post equality. As Hilary Greaves remarks, "It is thus abundantly clear that the manner in which Ex Post Prioritarianism violates the Ex Ante Pareto Principle cannot be rationalized by appeal to any intrinsic value of interpersonal equality" (Greaves 2015, p. 38).[12]

I have already noted that prioritarians are not intrinsically concerned with relativities. According to Adler, the best defense of deterministic prioritarianism invokes a specific conception of fairness, not equality. Adler calls this conception of fairness the *claims-across-outcomes* view. When Sam is worse off (in terms of well-being) than Sarah in the status quo, and when there is an alternative feasible outcome in which Sam's well-being is improved by the same amount that Sarah's is diminished (relative to the status quo), then so long as Sam will remain worse off, he has a stronger moral claim to the alternative than Sarah has to the status quo (Adler 2012, ch. 5, sect. I.B; Adler 2019, sect. 4.1.1.). Thus if fairness requires adjudicating between people's claims—as Adler believes it does—then we have moral reason to prefer the alternative outcome to the status quo. We have moral reason, in other words, to endorse the (well-being version of the) Pigou-Dalton principle.

Interestingly, Adler says that the claims-across-outcome view of fairness "*underwrites* the principle of Pareto-superiority," by which he means the strong Pareto principle (Adler 2012, p. 337, emphasis in original). As we have seen, this principle can approve of inequality-exacerbating policies that improve some people's well-being while leaving others unaffected. Adler writes:

> In short, a case of Pareto-superiority is a "no conflict" case in which some individuals have a claim in favor of one outcome, and all other individuals have no claim either way. If one uses the conceptual architecture of the claim-across-outcome view to think about problems of fairness, the principle of Pareto-superiority is compelling. Clearly a Pareto-superior outcome is fairer than the outcome it dominates. Where x is Pareto-superior to y, no one would have a complaint, in the across-outcome sense, if x were to obtain rather than y; while some would have a complaint, in the across-outcome sense, if y were to obtain rather than x. (Adler 2012, p. 335)

---

[12] As regards the violation of the ex ante Pareto principle itself, Greaves offers a second example in which ex post prioritarianism violates that principle even in cases involving just one person. See Greaves (2015, p. 37).

But this introduces a strong tension into Adler's overall prioritarian view. The problem is that his claims-based argument for the strong Pareto principle in the absence of risk is at odds with his ex post prioritarian rejection of the ex ante strong Pareto principle. After all, in Ord's case just above, *everyone* is better off with Prospect *J*, and yet ex post prioritarianism allows for the conclusion that *I* is generally better. If deterministic prioritarianism is justified because of its superior responsiveness to individuals' claims, and if this responsiveness in turn justifies the strong Pareto principle, then how can ex post prioritarianism be so *un*responsive to the fact that everyone in Ord's case has a stronger claim to Prospect *J*?[13]

Adler offers two responses to this line of argument. First, he observes that in a case like Ord's, although everyone's expected well-being is higher in Prospect *J*, it is still possible that *I* would in fact be better for everyone. This would be the case if we are in the state of nature where the coin will land on Heads. According to Adler, the ex ante strong Pareto principle is attractive only because decision-makers can find themselves in positions of imperfect information. If, instead, they could know which possible state of nature is the actual state, prioritarians could easily respect the only Pareto principles that matter in contexts of full knowledge, namely the strong Pareto principle and the Pareto Indifference principle (the latter of which says that if everyone is equally well-off in two distributions, then the distributions are level in the general betterness ordering). Adler appears to suggest that the presence of imperfect information, however pervasive it may be in life, is not a sufficiently strong reason to reject ex post prioritarianism in favor of the ex ante strong Pareto principle. He writes, "Indeed, the ex ante Pareto principles ... can require the choice of [one prospect] over [another] even though, in fact, no one will be better off with the [the first prospect] and some will be worse off" (Adler 2019, p. 137).

I do not see why it is a problem that ex ante Pareto's context of application is the context of imperfect information. Information's being imperfect is clearly a bad thing, yes; but it is not as if the badness of the informational context automatically infects a theory that is proposed for that context. In Ord's case, it is true that we do not know which state of nature we are in, the one where the coin lands Heads or the one where it lands Tails. But that is why we need a theory to navigate that context. The Harsanyi-Broome utilitarian framework is one such theory. Ex post prioritarianism is another. The

---

[13] Voorhoeve (2014) presses this argument against Adler.

fact that the Harsanyi-Broome framework's ex ante strong Pareto principle "reflect[s] imperfect information," as Adler puts it, does not seem to me to be the liability he suggests that it is.[14]

Adler has a second, better argument against the ex ante Pareto principle. He observes that if one wants to combine deterministic prioritarianism with Dominance, one is thereby logically required to reject the ex ante strong Pareto principle (as well as ex ante Pareto Indifference) (Adler 2019, p. 135). We have already seen that Dominance is a minimal and very compelling principle of choice under risk, and one that ex ante prioritarianism violates. For this reason, ex post prioritarianism is superior. But ex post prioritarianism cannot embrace both Dominance and ex ante strong Pareto, so Adler is prepared to reject the latter. He writes:

> The choice between [utilitarianism and prioritarianism] comes down, it seems, to a choice between the robust sensitivity to the distribution of well-being favored by the continuous-prioritarian approach (captured formally in the Pigou-Dalton principle) and the ex ante Pareto principles. The Pigou-Dalton axiom, coupled with the axioms of Continuity and Separability that are common ground for both sides in the debate, yields a ranking of well-being vectors—the continuous-prioritarian ranking—that necessarily conflicts with the ex ante Pareto principles, given Dominance. It is incoherent, in reflective equilibrium, to embrace Pigou-Dalton, Continuity, Separability, Dominance, *and* the ex ante Pareto principles all together. The utilitarian, facing this conflict, finds a coherent point of reflective equilibrium by embracing the ex ante Pareto principles and rejecting sensitivity to well-being distribution (Pigou-Dalton); the continuous prioritarian, by embracing Pigou-Dalton and rejecting the ex ante Pareto principles. (Adler 2019, p. 138, emphasis in original)

When he refers to "reflective equilibrium," Adler refers to the state of mind of a theorist who acknowledges that one must bite some bullets to accept her view, but who believes that her preferred view involves biting bullets that are more palatable than the ones her opponent must bite. Adler is in reflective equilibrium, he suggests, because he has examined the costs and benefits of embracing utilitarianism and ex post prioritarianism, and he finds the bullet of giving up ex ante strong Pareto more palatable than the bullet of

---

[14] For a related response, see Broome (2015, p. 262).

abandoning "robust sensitivity to the distribution of well-being." If Pigou-Dalton and Dominance should be retained, as Adler strongly believes they should, then ex ante strong Pareto has got to go.

This argument seems in part motivated by Adler's view, which we encountered in chapter 5, that all genuine moral values can and should be captured by a welfarist social welfare function. And indeed, if accepting a utilitarian SWF entailed that one cannot be sensitive to the distribution of well-being in *policymaking*, then this second argument of Adler's would be very powerful. Yet as I also noted in chapter 5, Adler himself allows for the possibility that the most defensible social welfare function will still not reflect all normatively relevant considerations: in his view, normatively important considerations of self-interest should be abridged from the SWF. But if it is acceptable for a prioritarian to exclude considerations of legitimate self-interest from her SWF, we should ask why it is not acceptable to abridge the Pigou-Dalton principle, as well. Now, we already know Adler's answer to this question: "The SWF construct... offers a framework for fully *ethical* choice," and self-interest is a non-ethical normative consideration (Adler and Treich 2015, p. 285, emphasis added). But surely the question "How much self-interest is legitimate or tolerable, whether in ourselves or in others, when we could improve the world by ignoring our own wishes?" is itself an ethical question. So why should one agree that considerations of self-interest are irrelevant to the content of "a framework for fully ethical choice"? If the answer is that by "fully ethical choice" Adler means "what maximizes welfarist value," then the proponent of the utilitarianism SWF can respond that her SWF concerns precisely that; but then she can remind us that it is very common in moral philosophy to distinguish the topic of what maximizes welfarist value from the topic of what, all things considered, ought to be done. That is, she can remind us that it is entirely coherent for a moral theorist to defend an SWF that is insensitive to the distribution of well-being, while at the same time embracing a wider moral theory that cares deeply about that normative aspect.

I have already made my own view clear: I believe it is tolerable and indeed desirable to adopt an SWF that is normatively abridged. If I am right about this, then as one who finds an aggregation-theorem-based utilitarian SWF attractive, I can achieve reflective equilibrium in another way. I can adopt a social welfare function that complies with the appealing ex ante strong Pareto axiom and is insensitive to the distribution of well-being; then I can insist that the non-utilitarian ethics of distribution bears on the all-things-considered evaluation of public policy.[15]

Consider now a final way to add an uncertainty module to deterministic prioritarianism. In response to the difficulties I have highlighted for ex ante and ex post prioritarianism, Marc Fleurbaey has formulated an SWF that "behave[s] like ex ante criteria when risk does not generate inequalities and like ex post criteria otherwise" (Fleurbaey 2010, p. 651). That is to say, like ex ante prioritarianism, Fleurbaey's SWF respects ex ante strong Pareto when inequality is absent in all possible outcomes (as it is in Ord's Prospect *J*); and like ex post prioritarianism, it respects Dominance when it can be known ex ante that one prospect will for sure result in a worse distribution than another, regardless of which outcome arises.

To explain further, consider contexts in which risk is absent—so that we can achieve any possible distribution we wish—and in which the relevant population is fixed. Now consider any deterministic prioritarian SWF of (6.1)'s form. This SWF ranks distributions of well-being in the same order as an SWF that ranks distributions by their *equally distributed equivalent*, or *EDE*. Relative to a given deterministic prioritarian SWF, V_{Prior}, a distribution's *EDE* is the constant well-being level $w_1^{EDE} = w_2^{EDE} = w_N^{EDE}$ that establishes the following equality:

$$V_{Prior}(w_1, w_2, \ldots, w_N) = V_{Prior}(w_1^{EDE}, w_2^{EDE}, \ldots, w_N^{EDE}) \qquad (6.5)$$

Thus, a distribution's equally distributed equivalent is the level of well-being such that if everyone in the population attained that level, the deterministic prioritarian SWF would assign the same value to it that it assigns to the distribution under consideration.[16]

---

[15] This is one of the stances that Greaves urges ex post prioritarians to consider in light of the problems for their view raised by contexts of risk. See Greaves (2015, pp. 34–35). It is also broadly a view that Adler himself once endorsed. See Adler and Posner (2006, pp. 154–158).

[16] Atkinson (1970) used the EDE concept to construct the inequality metric that now bears his name: $IN = \left[1 - \left(\frac{EDE}{B}\right)\right]$. Here B is the mean level of well-being in the well-being vector whose inequality the *IN* index is being used to evaluate. As Fleurbaey explains, *IN* is "a sensible inequality index, because $IN = 0$ whenever the distribution is egalitarian, and *IN* satisfies the Pigou-Dalton principle because any Pigou-Dalton transfer increases [the *EDE*] while leaving *B* unchanged, so that *IN* decreases" (Fleurbaey 2015, p. 208).

166   THE SOCIAL COST OF CARBON

Fleurbaey's innovation is to show that when one moves to contexts involving risk, one can avoid the problems I have raised for the first two versions of Harsanyi non-compliant prioritarianism by choosing instead to maximize the *expected EDE* (Fleurbaey 2010). For a given deterministic prioritarian SWF, $\sum_{i=1}^{N} g(w_i)$, that ranks distributions of well-being, the function that gives each distribution W's EDE is:

$$EDE(W) = g^{-1}\left[\left(\frac{1}{N}\right)\sum_{i=1}^{N} g(w_i)\right] \quad (6.6)$$

Thus the *expected equally distributed equivalent* (EEDE) SWF is:

$$V_{EEDE} = \sum_{s \in S} p_s \cdot g^{-1}\left[\left(\frac{1}{N}\right)\sum_{i=1}^{N} g(w_i)\right] \quad (6.7)$$

Consider now Table 6.2, which shows that maximizing the expected EEDE yields the same ranking of prospects as ex post prioritarianism in a case where ex ante prioritarianism violates Dominance.[17]

As indicated by their equal sums of transformed *expected* well-being (STEWs), this is a case where ex ante prioritarianism gives the same ranking

Table 6.2 EEDE respects Dominance

	Prospect K H	Prospect K T	expected well-being	Prospect L H	Prospect L T	expected well-being
w1	4	0	2	2	2	2
w2	0	4	2	2	2	2
STEW[a]			2.83			2.83
STWB[b]	2	2		2.83	2.83	
EDE[c]	1	1		2	2	
EEDE[d]		1			2	

[a] STEW = sum of transformed expected well-being.
[b] STWB = sum of transformed well-being.
[c] EDE = equally distributed equivalent.
[d] EEDE = expected equally distributed equivalent.

[17] I borrow this case from Fleurbaey (2010), p. 659.

score to Prospects *K* and *L*. It does this even though Prospect *L* dominates Prospect *K* in the following prioritarian sense: whether the coin toss turns out Heads or Tails, deterministic prioritarianism will rank the outcome under *L* higher than the corresponding outcome under *K*. This can be seen by comparing the sum of transformed well-being (STWB) values for each possible outcome; whether the coin lands Heads or Tails, Prospect *L* is better than Prospect *K*, from a prioritarian perspective. (Recall that I am assuming for the sake of argument that the deterministic prioritarian transformation function, g, is the square root function.) It therefore seems irrational for a prioritarian to be indifferent between the two prospects. And yet that is the stance adopted by the ex ante prioritarian. By contrast, EEDE prioritarianism ranks Prospect *L* higher than Prospect *K*, as indicated by the last row of the table. In fact, EEDE prioritarianism—like ex post prioritarianism—always respects Dominance.

Next, consider Table 6.3, a case that an ex post prioritarian SWF handles differently from both the EEDE SWF and the utilitarian SWF.[18]

In this case, Ada and Bianca are *identically situated*, in the sense that they face exactly the same prospects and thus will end up equal to one another in well-being regardless of which prospect is chosen and which outcome arises. The case is such that Prospect *M* maximizes both Ada's and Bianca's expected well-being. A utilitarian SWF will therefore rank *M* over *N*. By contrast, ex post prioritarianism ranks *N* over *M*. This is precisely the same conflict between ex post prioritarianism and ex ante strong Pareto that we observed in Ord's case above (Table 6.1). Finally, the EEDE prioritarian SWF yields the same ranking as the utilitarian SWF. This is the partial compatibility that Fleurbaey sought: unlike ex post prioritarianism, EEDE always complies with ex ante strong Pareto in cases in which every possible outcome exhibits perfect equality of well-being.

EEDE prioritarianism therefore avoids serious problems that afflict the other two ways of formulating Harsanyi non-compliant prioritarianism. But the EEDE has some serious problems of its own. I shall discuss two in particular. They both stem from the fact that the deterministic prioritarian g function is strictly concave, which makes EEDE's g^{-1} function strictly convex and therefore non-linear.

---

[18] This case is adapted from Adler (2019), p. 135.

Table 6.3 EEDE respects ex ante strong Pareto when ex post inequality is absent

	Prospect M ‖ H	Prospect M ‖ T	expected well-being	Prospect N ‖ H	Prospect N ‖ T	expected well-being
Ada	1	121	61	49	64	56.5
Bianca	1	121	61	49	64	56.5
STWB[a]	2	22		14	16	
ESTWB[b]		12			15	
EDE[c]	1	121		49	64	
EEDE[d]		61			56.5	

[a] STWB = sum of transformed well-being.
[b] ESTWB = expected sum of transformed well-being.
[c] EDE = equally distributed equivalent.
[d] EEDE = expected equally distributed equivalent.

First, consider Table 6.4, an expanded version of the case depicted in Table 6.3.[19]

This is what Adler calls a "Heartland case." Heartland cases compare two or more prospects and are defined by the following two features. First, the relevant population can be split into two exhaustive and mutually exclusive groups: those who are *sure to be unaffected* and those who are *identically situated*. In the case set out in Table 6.4, Carl and Don are sure to be unaffected. This is because the choice between Prospects O and P does not matter from the point of view of their well-being: regardless of whether the outcome is Heads or Tails, Carl's and Don's well-being would be exactly the same with O as it would be with P. Meanwhile, Ada and Bianca are identically situated. This means that while neither is sure to be unaffected—the difference between O and P *does* matter to their well-being—they will for sure end up equal in well-being: if Prospect O is chosen and Heads turns up, they will each enjoy 1 unit of well-being; if Prospect O is chosen and Tails turns up, they will each enjoy 121 units; and so on.

Now, it is clear how the utilitarian SWF will rank these two prospects. Since Carl and Don are unaffected and Ada and Bianca both do better with Prospect O, the utilitarian SWF complies with ex ante strong Pareto and ranks O over P. In contrast, we know that ex post prioritarianism

---

[19] Table 6.4 reproduces and expands a table from Adler (2019), p. 135.

Table 6.4 EEDE violates separability across people in a "Heartland Case"

	Prospect O H	Prospect O T	expected well-being	Prospect P H	Prospect P T	expected well-being
Ada	1	121	61	49	64	56.5
Bianca	1	121	61	49	64	56.5
Carl	100	16	58	100	16	58
Don	25	81	53	25	81	53
STWB[a]	17	35		29	29	
ESTWB[b]	26			29		
EDE[c]	18.06	76.56		52.56	52.56	
EEDE[d]	47.31			52.56		

[a]STWB = sum of transformed well-being.
[b]ESTWB = expected sum of transformed well-being.
[c]EDE = equally distributed equivalent.
[d]EEDE = expected equally distributed equivalent.

sometimes violates ex ante strong Pareto, and indeed that is what happens in this case: using the sum-of-square-root function as its deterministic prioritarian SWF, ex post prioritarianism gives a score of 29 to Prospect P and 26 to Prospect O. Finally, the last rows of Table 6.4 show that EEDE prioritarianism also violates ex ante strong Pareto in this Heartland case. Thus, while EEDE prioritarianism always respects the ex ante strong Pareto principle when there are no inequalities between people in any possible outcome, the EEDE version—like ex post prioritarianism—can violate that principle in Heartland cases that exhibit some outcome inequality.

But the cause of this violation is different for EEDE and ex post prioritarianism. Ex post prioritarianism violates ex ante strong Pareto in this Heartland case for the same reason that it violates ex ante strong Pareto when Ada and Bianca are the only relevant individuals (as they are in the case depicted by Table 6.3). Indeed, ex post prioritarianism never allows the evaluation to be swayed by the condition of individuals who are sure to be unaffected. It therefore treats that group as separable from the group of affected and identically situated individuals. In contrast, EEDE's evaluation of the Heartland case depends crucially on the presence of the sure-to-be-unaffected Carl and Don. As we saw in the previous case stated in Table 6.3, when Carl and Don were out of the picture, EEDE complied with ex ante strong Pareto and, therefore, let Ada's and Bianca's expected well-being carry the day. But in the Heartland case, the presence of Carl and Don induces the EEDE SWF to switch its ranking, even though they are sure to be unaffected and even though Prospect O still maximizes Ada's and Bianca's expected well-being. Thus the EEDE SWF violates ex ante strong Pareto in Heartland cases, and it does so because its convex g^{-1} function renders it nonseparable across people in risky contexts. In such contexts, therefore, EEDE prioritarianism *is* sensitive to relativities—to how people fare relative to one another. It differs in this respect from the utilitarian, the ex ante prioritarian, *and* the ex post prioritarian SWFs (Fleurbaey 2010, p. 664).

Fleurbaey has shown in addition that (to use Adler's term) any *minimally leak-tolerant* SWF that complies with Dominance will violate ex ante strong Pareto in at least some Heartland cases (Fleurbaey 2010, pp. 665–667). A minimally leak-tolerant SWF is an SWF that, in at least one conceivable case, approves of a leaky transfer of well-being from a better-off to a worse-off person. This result raises conflicts between the ex ante strong Pareto principle and *all* of the leading distribution-sensitive alternatives to the utilitarian SWF (Adler 2019, p. 142).[20]

The violation of ex ante strong Pareto in Heartland cases means that it is possible to construct examples in which the well-being levels of those who are dead become crucial to an EEDE-based evaluation of a policy that affects only the well-being of those who currently exist or will exist in the future (Fleurbaey 2010, p. 665; Greaves 2015, p. 39).[21] While Fleurbaey admits that this is a potentially troubling implication, he also offers reasons to think the violation of the "principle of the independence of the utilities of the dead" might not be so bad in practice (Fleurbaey 2010, pp. 665–669). But since the root cause of the violation is the concern for relativities induced by the convex g^{-1} function, which renders the EEDE evaluation nonseparable with respect to people, one should be especially interested in Fleurbaey's *egalitarian* defense of the violation. Here he is writing with Alex Voorhoeve:

> The unfairness which concerns egalitarians is essentially about how well some individuals' lives go in comparison to how well other, separate

---

[20] This includes all leximin, sufficientist, and rank-weighted views. For discussion of each of these, see Adler (2019, ch. 3).

[21] Fleurbaey adds: "An easy way out is to restrict attention to present and future generations in the evaluation, but it comes at the cost of intertemporal consistency. The evaluation then depends on the time at which it is made, and this seems a deep rationality failure" (Fleurbaey 2010, p. 665).

individuals' lives go. A situation in which, due to brute luck, Arnaldur's lifetime quality of life is okay and Bea's is very good is unfair. By contrast, a situation in which, due to brute luck, for one part of his life, Arnaldur has a merely okay quality of life and for another part of his life, he has a very good quality of life is not unfair in this way. Only in the former situation can Arnaldur legitimately complain of being unfairly disadvantaged vis-à-vis another. *He has this complaint even when his wellbeing cannot be improved and even when the better off Bea exists at a later point in time.* Suppose, for example, that Arnaldur develops a debilitating physical illness about which nothing can be done. Bea will also develop this illness, but because she belongs to a future generation, she will have access to a complete cure. Arnaldur can legitimately complain that this differential access to a cure is one way in which "life is unfair." (Voorhoeve and Fleurbaey 2016, pp. 943–944, emphasis added)

This conception of fairness is distinct from both Harsanyi's veil-of-ignorance conception (discussed in section 5.3) and Adler's claims-across-outcomes conception. Unsurprisingly, theories of fairness and equality are subjects of great debate among contemporary moral and political philosophers.[22] In fact, Broome has articulated a still different theory (Broome 1991, ch. 9). He argues in addition that fairness resists inclusion into a social welfare function whose aim is to represent an ordering of distributions of well-being: "the only way to give [fairness] proper recognition," he claims, "is to account for it separately" (Broome 2004, p. 39). This is an argument for a sort of normative abridgement.

Finally, here is the second problem induced by the EEDE SWF's convex g^{-1} function: it makes the EEDE SWF *catastrophe-seeking* in the sense captured by ranking option B above option A in the following example (Rheinberger and Treich 2016, p. 9):[23]

> Four passengers are aboard a sinking boat. There is only one lifeboat, with a design capacity of two people. The captain (whose code of honour requires him to go down with his boat) has the choice between the two following options:

---

[22] See, for example, Dworkin (2000, chs. 1 and 2); Cohen (1989); Parfit (1997); Anderson (1999); Temkin (2003); Hausman and Waldren (2011); Adler (2012, ch. 5, sect. I).

[23] Rheinberger and Treich (2016, p. 9) borrow this example from Gajdos et al. (2010).

[A] Put exactly half of the passengers onto the lifeboat. These passengers will survive for sure, whereas the passengers who remain on the sinking boat will die for sure. In order to choose who boards the lifeboat, the skipper designs a fair lottery, so each passenger has a probability of 0.5 of obtaining a place on the lifeboat.

[B] Let all the passengers board the lifeboat. The overcrowded lifeboat has a 50% chance of sinking, leading to the death of all of the passengers. If the lifeboat does not sink, all of the passengers will survive.

A social welfare function is catastrophe-seeking if it ranks B over A, catastrophe-averse if it ranks A over B, and catastrophe-neutral if A and B are level in its ordering. Note that in being catastrophe-seeking, an SWF does not necessarily prefer more expected deaths to fewer. Rather, it means the SWF treats it as a good thing when "individuals share a common fate" (Rheinberger and Treich 2016, p. 9).

It is not immediately clear how one should evaluate an SWF's penchant for catastrophe in this technical sense of the term; one might find oneself willing to "seek" catastrophes if, in reflective equilibrium, one wishes to be a prioritarian and thinks EEDE is the least implausible prioritarianism for contexts involving risk. But although a catastrophe-seeking tendency may not seem so problematic in the lifeboat example—where only the catastrophe-seeking welfare function prefers the option in which all four passengers might survive—it does seem to me a merit of the utilitarian social welfare function that it does not prefer that any and all deaths occur in the very same state of nature. To the extent that I am able to conjure a moral intuition about it, catastrophe-neutral SWFs seems to me more plausible than catastrophe-seeking ones. This adds to my doubts about the EEDE version of prioritarianism, and about its prospects for supplanting the utilitarian SWF.

* * *

In the end, the difficulties that face the three versions of prioritarianism that I have discussed in this chapter strike me as worth avoiding. This can be done by embracing normative abridgement and walling off the SWF from the considerations of fairness and inequality-aversion that underlie prioritarian alternatives to utilitarian SWFs. I have already argued that there are good reasons to exclude agent-relative and context-dependent considerations from one's SWF. Owing to the theoretical problems that afflict all three types of prioritarianism, as well as to the complex and protracted debates in moral philosophy concerning the correct theory of fairness, I believe it is all the more desirable to insulate SWF-based economic evaluations from these issues. Of course, if one takes that option, one has further reason to refrain from drawing quick policy conclusions from the results of SWF-based analyses.

On the other hand, if some form of prioritarianism *is* the proper social choice framework to use in calculating SCC figures, then there is still one further reason to doubt that the rankings given by a sound social choice social welfare function can be used to guide responsible climate policy. This further reason for doubt, which is equally a reason for utilitarianism and prioritarianism, concerns the ethics of valuing populations of different sizes. To this point, we have assumed that population size is invariant across every possible outcome. But at some point, a social choice framework must have something to say when population size varies endogenously across feasible well-being paths. It turns out that while no approach to so-called population ethics is obviously correct, the least implausible view provides very strong additional reasons to treat social welfare functions as normatively abridged.

7
Population

As I explained in chapter 4, the initial derivation of Harsanyi's aggregation theorem requires a "fixed-population" context. That is, it requires we assume that all and only the same people will exist in each possible outcome. Then, in section 4.3.3, I explained that by accepting an impartiality axiom, one can extend Harsanyi's theorem's reach to distributions that contain the same number of people, regardless of their identities. I have since gone on to consider other functional forms (in particular various kinds of prioritarianism), but I have continued to assume that the size of the relevant intertemporal population is fixed. However, the number of people who will ever exist is sure to differ depending on what is (or is not) done to address climate change. A sound SWF should be able to evaluate prospects whose defining outcomes exhibit radically different demographics.

When the size of a population cannot change, *total* utilitarianism and *average* utilitarianism yield the same ranking of outcomes, since average lifetime well-being will increase if and only if total well-being increases. When population can vary across possible outcomes, the difference between total and average utilitarianism becomes relevant. It may, for example, be possible to increase average lifetime well-being by reducing the global population's size while increasing the lifetime well-being of those who do live; alternatively, it may be possible to maximize total well-being by radically increasing the number of people who will live, even if a side effect is to decrease average lifetime well-being among those same people. In a passing remark, Harsanyi registered his view that his aggregation theorem's functional form—which is consonant with total utilitarianism—should not automatically be extended to variable-population contexts. He instead claimed that *average* utilitarianism "gives incomparably superior results" (Harsanyi 1977, p. 633n12).

Harsanyi did not explain why he found average utilitarianism superior as an approach to what is now known as "population ethics." But in the years since Harsanyi published that remark, the field of population ethics has turned up a surprising result: there is *no* approach to variable-population aggregation that is free of very counterintuitive implications. In this chapter

I will graze just the surface of this area of moral philosophy. My aim is to illustrate some of its challenges, and to reinforce the conclusion I have been defending in this part concerning the normative abridgement of social choice social welfare functions and the SCC concepts that emerge from them.

7.1 The Zero Level of Lifetime Well-being

Addressing questions in population ethics requires specifying a "zero level" of well-being.[1] To decide whether it is a good thing to add a new person to an existing population, one thing we should want to know is how good that life would be for the person who lives it. The zero level of lifetime well-being is, intuitively, the level such that it would be neither good nor bad for an individual to live a life with that amount of well-being. But how to make sense of this idea? Here it can be enticing to introduce the concept of a "life worth living." One might wish to say, for example, that the zero level of lifetime well-being is the level such that if one's life contains more well-being than that, then one has a life worth living, and if one's life contains less than that, then one does not have a life worth living. But what exactly does it mean to have a life worth living? It cannot mean that it would be better for the person to live that life than to not live at all, because we cannot compare how things go for a person when she lives with how they go for her when she does not exist: when she does not exist, there is not *any* way her life goes.

Here is John Broome's approach to the zero level of lifetime well-being (Broome 2004, pp. 233–235, 254). It does not invoke the concept of a life worth living. Take any person's life and construct a vector of the person's temporal well-beings from the time in which she is born to the time in which she dies. Now imagine she will live for just one additional time period. In that period, what level must her temporal well-being be in order for her lifetime well-being with the extra period to be exactly what it would have been had she not lived in that extra period, but had died instead? Call that level the "neutral level for continuing to live," and set this level as zero on the scale of *temporal* well-being. Now imagine a person who lives their full life at this neutral level for continuing to live. (For simplicity I will assume in this chapter that a "full life" involves living a specific number of time periods, and

---

[1] A zero level was also required by the ratio scale of measurable well-beings that feature in the Atkinson SWF that is stated as equation (6.2) in section 6.1.

that everyone in any population lives for that number of periods.) Now call a full life that exhibits zero temporal well-being at every time a "constantly neutral life." Finally, set the zero level of *lifetime* well-being to the level that is exhibited by a constantly neutral life.

I will take Broome's conception of the zero level of lifetime well-being for granted. I certainly have not defended it, and of course you do not have to accept it. You could choose your own approach to the zero level and then use it to flesh out the thought experiments I will introduce in the next section. Since the concept of a zero level of lifetime well-being will be important to that discussion, I wanted to introduce some definite notion for you to hold onto. Broome's conception gives us that, even if should turn out to be flawed.

7.2 Population Ethics

Let us now return to Harsanyi's preference for average utilitarianism. A classic result in population ethics is that average utilitarianism is subject to the so-called *Sadistic Conclusion* (Arrhenius 2000a, 2000b).

Figure 7.1 depicts three different scenarios, A, B, and C. In each, the width of a bar indicates the size of a population, and the height represents the level of lifetime well-being enjoyed by each person in that population. Suppose scenario A is the baseline situation, and that it depicts a large population each member of which enjoys a rather high level of lifetime well-being. Assume also that the horizontal line at the bottom of A's bar represents the zero level of lifetime

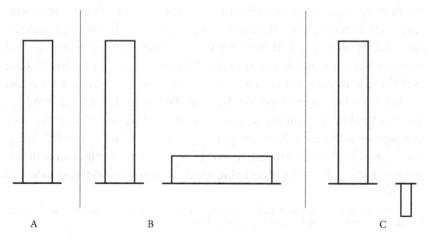

Figure 7.1 The Sadistic Conclusion.

well-being. Now suppose it were feasible to move from the baseline scenario A either to scenario B or to scenario C. B would include all the people who exist in A, and would also include a great many additional people, all of whom have lifetime well-being levels much below the level enjoyed by those who live in both A and B. However, all of these new people will have lives with positive well-being, as indicated by the fact that the second bar in B rises above the zero level. Like B, the scenario depicted by C also includes all the people who exist in A. And again like B, C would be brought about by adding a new group of people. C's new group is much smaller than B's new group, and everyone in C's new group has *negative* lifetime well-being.

Here, now, is the Sadistic Conclusion: *Moving from A to C can be better than moving from A to B*. This is "sadistic" because it is hard to see how it could possibly be better to add lives with negative lifetime well-being than it is to add lives with positive well-being. But average utilitarianism allows for this. For it is easy to imagine an example in which we would bring down A's average level of lifetime well-being more by adding the new lives in B than we would by adding the new lives in C. Since it seems extremely implausible that C could be better than B, the Sadistic Conclusion has been invoked as an argument against average utilitarianism (Arrhenius et al. 2021, p. 117).

The Sadistic Conclusion is not the most famous result in population ethics, however. That honor belongs to the so-called *Repugnant Conclusion*, which presents a challenge to average utilitarianism's main rival, total utilitarianism. Consider Figure 7.2.

Here again, scenario A depicts a large population of people, each of whom enjoys rather high lifetime well-being. Scenario Z differs from A in three key respects. First, Z includes an *entirely different* population of people, all of whom have the same positive level of lifetime well-being. Second, Z's population is *very* large—much larger than A's; this is depicted by Z's dashed horizontal line. Finally, the uniform, positive level of lifetime well-being that is enjoyed by Z's members is *much* lower than the level enjoyed by A's members.

Here is the canonical formulation of the Repugnant Conclusion:

> For any possible population of at least ten billion people, all with a very high quality of life, there must be some much larger imaginable population whose existence, if other things are equal, would be better, even though its members have lives that are barely worth living. (Parfit 1984, p. 388)

Suppose that scenario A in Figure 7.2 depicts Parfit's first population; it therefore has "ten billion people, all with very high quality of life." Scenario

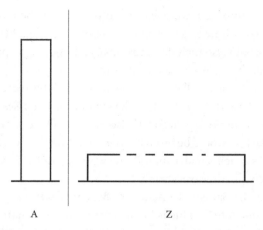

Figure 7.2 The Repugnant Conclusion.

Z is then intended to depict Parfit's second, much larger population, all of whose members "have lives that are barely worth living." Total utilitarianism allows that scenario Z is better than scenario A, if the population in Z is large enough to make Z contain more *total* well-being than is contained in A. Even most devotees of total utilitarianism believe this implication is a serious theoretical liability for the view.

So far, I have simply drawn our attention to some untoward implications of just two prominent approaches to valuing population in an SWF-based framework. I have not offered an argument for either of these approaches; certainly I have not offered anything like the axiomatic defenses that we explored in chapters 4 and 6. Yet it turns out that if one builds up variable-population total utilitarianism from more fundamental assumptions—all of which are consistent with Harsanyi's aggregation theorem—one encounters along the way a form of utilitarianism that can evade the Repugnant Conclusion. The derivation, which comes from Broome (2004, pp. 199–201) and which I rehearse in this chapter's Appendix, gives what has come to be known as *critical-level utilitarianism*:[2]

$$V = \sum_{i=1}^{} (w_i - v) \tag{7.1}$$

---

[2] See also Blackorby et al. (2005, ch. 5).

This formulation says that the value of a distribution is the sum of the "standardized" lifetime well-beings of all the individuals who exist in the outcome. Individuals' lifetime well-beings are standardized by subtracting from each the *critical level* of well-being, v. Importantly, the critical level is not necessarily the same as the zero level of lifetime well-being. Whereas the zero level of well-being implicates judgments about how *personally* good or bad a life is for the person who lives it, the critical level is the level that a person's lifetime well-being must surpass in order for it to be *generally* good that she existed—good, that is, according to the general betterness ranking. If person i's lifetime well-being in outcome x is exactly at the critical level, then critical-level utilitarianism holds that x has the same rank in the general betterness ordering as any outcome whose distribution is identical to x's, except for the absence of i's well-being indicator (because i does not live in those other outcomes). Likewise, if i's lifetime well-being in outcome y is *below* the critical level, then the general betterness ordering will rank y below any outcome whose distribution is identical to y's, except for the absence of i's well-being indicator. This remains so even if the critical level is set at a rather high level of lifetime well-being. If the critical level is set high enough, a person might have a life that is, for *her*, very enjoyable, even though the general betterness ordering deems her well-being too low to mend the wound she imposes on the universe just by virtue of existing in the first place. The critical level is an indicator of how serious a wound this is.

Total utilitarianism is a version of critical-level utilitarianism. It is the version in which the critical level is set at the zero point of lifetime well-being. According to total utilitarianism, there is no wound the universe sustains merely by virtue of someone's existing; if that person's life contains a positive level of well-being, then total utilitarianism treats that as a good thing, and that person's existence is better, in general terms, than her not existing (other things equal).

Critical-level utilitarianism can evade the Repugnant Conclusion if the critical level is set strategically. Suppose, for example, that it is set between the level of lifetime well-being enjoyed in Figure 7.2's scenario A and the level enjoyed in Z. In that case, the general betterness ordering will view each life in A as a net good, and each life in Z as a net bad. This will be so even though every life in Z is good on balance for the person who lives it. Such is the evaluative power embodied in the choice of the critical level.

If the critical level is set fairly low, then a version of the Repugnant Conclusion reemerges. Although a positive critical level can rule out the specific version Parfit formulated, with its reference to lives that are *barely* worth living, the force of the Repugnant Conclusion will remain if scenario A in Figure 7.2 is worse than a scenario in which myriad people have lives that are still quite low in lifetime well-being.

On the other hand, if we set the critical level high enough to rule out any such repugnant conclusion, we reinvite a sadistic conclusion (Arrhenius 2000b). This is because critical-level utilitarianism allows for the total negative value embodied in many lives of misery to be less bad than the total negative value created by many, many more lives whose standardized well-being is just barely negative. Recall that a life's standardized well-being is negative just in case its lifetime well-being is below the critical level. So if the critical level is set high enough to avoid all intuitively troubling repugnant conclusions, it will also assign negative standardized well-being to lives whose lifetime well-being is just below the critical level. But these can still be quite good lives for the people who live them. Indeed, they will *have to* be good lives if the critical level is selected to evade repugnant conclusions. Yet when there are many, many such lives, their combined negative value accumulates, and this can make an outcome that features only good lives worse than one featuring only lives of misery.

7.3 Population Ethics and Normative Abridgement

There are many more approaches to valuing population than the few I have discussed so far. But it is well-known within the field of population ethics that none of them is free of unpalatable implications (Arrhenius 2000b, 2000a; Greaves 2017b). Indeed, Budolfson and Spears (2018) formulate an "extended version" of the Repugnant Conclusion and show that this version is implied by every conception of betterness that appears in the population ethics literature, including "rank-dependent" conceptions that do not simply sum well-being (or standardized well-being) across persons. Budolfson and Spears therefore conclude that "the repugnant conclusion does not tell against any [conception of betterness]. In light of these results, the idea that the repugnant conclusion must be avoided cannot remain the leading methodological principle in" population ethics (Budolfson and Spears 2018, p. 31).[3]

I am inclined to agree with this conclusion, and for two additional reasons. First, for all of its problems, the Repugnant Conclusion is much less repugnant than the Sadistic Conclusion. No plausible general betterness ordering of outcomes will say it is better to create new people with miserable lives than to create new people with lives that are personally good for them. One should therefore make peace with the Repugnant Conclusion if one's best alternatives are "sadistic" views like average utilitarianism and critical-level utilitarianisms that adopt relatively high critical levels.

Second—and more important for my purposes—if normative abridgement is a genuine theoretical option, as I have argued it is, then it is quite unclear what the repugnance of the Repugnant Conclusion amounts to in practice. Compare the Repugnant Conclusion with what Tim Mulgan calls the Repugnant Obligation Conclusion:

> If any agent faces a choice between two actions whose outcomes correspond to [Figure 7.2's] A-world and Z-world, then she is obliged to opt for Z over A. This remains true even if the result is a Z-life rather than an A-life both for herself and for all her nearest and dearest. For instance, if an agent can transform an A-world into a Z-world by a process that creates a new species of Z-creature while greatly reducing the well-being of everyone who already exists, then she ought to do so. (Mulgan 2006, p. 61)

If there is indeed a gap between the set of normative considerations that a cogent conception of general betterness reflects, on the one hand, and the full set of sound normative considerations, on the other, then it is not necessarily incoherent to accept the Repugnant Conclusion while rejecting the Repugnant Obligation Conclusion. Of course, it would be nice to know exactly how conclusions from the subdomain of ethics concerned with general betterness—the area that philosophers call *axiology*—fit into responsible deliberation about what ought to be done, all things considered. Most moral philosophers, including myself, believe that axiological considerations are always *relevant* to normative conclusions about right and wrong action. But there is still much work to be done before we understand the precise way in

---

[3] This is also the message of Zuber et al. (2021).

which all relevant normative considerations combine to support final practical conclusions. That is the view, at any rate, of most philosophers who, like me, deny that axiological considerations exhaust the realm of policy-relevant normative considerations.

As more support for normative abridgement, consider next what Broome calls the *intuition of neutrality*, an intuition that Broome thinks most of us have:

> [W]e think the lifetime wellbeing of a person who is added to the world is in itself ethically neutral ... It is neither a good thing nor a bad thing ... Our moral instinct is to care about people, and to care about making people's lives go well. This is caring for the people there are; we want their lives to go better. We have no natural interest in having more people about. A famous remark of Jan Narveson puts it succinctly: "We are in favour of making people happy, but neutral about making happy people." (Broome 2005, pp. 399–400)

Broome, for his part, endorses a version of critical-level utilitarianism whose critical level is just somewhat above the zero level of well-being. Broome therefore accepts that a population of ten billion people, all of whose lives are very high in well-being, can be worse than a much larger population of individuals, all of whose lives are just above Broome's low critical level. Moreover, since his critical level is positive, Broome must also accept the Sadistic Conclusion (Broome 2004, pp. 212–213, 259). Finally, since critical-level utilitarianism is inconsistent with the intuition of neutrality, Broome ultimately rejects that intuition, despite admitting that it "grips me strongly" (Broome 2004, p. v). But now what is the practical upshot? At one point, Broome wrote:

> Think about a couple who might have a child. Our intuition is that their having a child is neither better nor worse than their not having one. But we now know this intuition is mistaken except in the special case where the child happens to live at exactly the single neutral level [i.e., at exactly the critical level]. So if the couple have a child, that will generally be either better or worse than their not having one. Suppose it is better. Then the couple are in a position to make the world better by having a child. But even so, we might think they have no moral responsibility to do so. We might think they are doing nothing wrong if they choose not to. This normative

conclusion about rightness and wrongness may be part of what the neutrality intuition is pointing to.

Possibly the intuition might be given a coherent interpretation in these normative terms. And possibly it may apply to grand issues such as global warming as well as to a couple's decision about a child. Global warming will be very good or very bad because of its effect on population. But possibly we may have no moral responsibility towards population, and we may be entitled to ignore the goodness or badness of this effect. (Broome 2005, pp. 412–413)

Since writing those words, Broome has offered the sketch of a view concerning how a (roughly) total utilitarian conception of betterness links up with practical obligation. He believes that while *individuals* may not have overwhelmingly strong obligations to make the world better—as judged by a utilitarian SWF—*governments* do have "a categorical duty" to improve the world, for example by ensuring clean water everywhere, controlling malaria and tuberculosis, providing for basic needs, and radically reducing greenhouse gas emissions (Broome 2012, pp. 65, 67). So while prospective parents may be permitted to make choices that do not jibe with an SWF's ordering (like the choice not to conceive happy children), governments should take even greater heed of what maximally improves the world—as judged, again, by the correct SWF.

Mulgan's Repugnant Obligation Conclusion is, however, still a problem for Broome's thesis concerning political obligation. It is impossible to believe there could be an all-things-considered, final normative duty for a government (or a coalition of governments) to trade an A-world for a Z-world. To make this point in a different way, consider the following hypothetical caricature of our actual world and its relationship between unchecked climate change and population dynamics. (Please do not think I believe that this is likely to happen if we leave climate change unchecked. This is purely to construct an example.) Suppose that if we brought greenhouse gas emissions to a halt by 2050, we would secure something like an A-world for all those who live until the year 4000, when our solar system will suffer an exogenous extinction event, ending sentient life within it. Now assume that if we let climate change go unchecked, living standards until the year 4000 will plummet to well-being levels just barely above the zero level of lifetime well-being, but there will also be many more people who ever live, since (let us assume) fertility increases rapidly as poverty increases. If we could somehow know that this latter scenario would be like the Z-world in containing more total well-being than the climate-controlled A-world, that would certainly not give us decisive reason to refrain from controlling climate change. But Z could very well be ranked above A by whatever conception of betterness survives critical philosophical scrutiny of the sort displayed in this part of the book.[4]

The argument I have just given has led at least one leading philosopher of economics to conclude that *there is no such thing as general betterness*. For, if there were such a thing, then the best conception of it would be Broome's critical-level utilitarianism, and that conception tells us that Z-worlds can be better than A-worlds, and that is too absurd a conclusion to be true. But Broome's argument (which draws heavily on Harsanyi's aggregation theorem) is so logically tight that its flaw must lie with its initial assumption that general betterness orderings have any relevance at all to responsible policy choice. This is Daniel Hausman's line of reasoning (Hausman 2005). Though I take it seriously, I am personally not yet ready to accept Hausman's axiological nihilism. But I *do* think Hausman's broad line of reasoning strongly supports the conclusion that general betterness orderings, if they carry any normative weight, are radically normatively abridged.

If a sound conception of general betterness is (at best) radically normatively abridged, it poses a problem for certain attempts to reconcile disagreements in population ethics. Arrhenius, Budolfson, and Spears, for example, argue that in the case of climate change policy, it does not much matter which of

---

[4] As Zuber et al. note, it is an empirical question whether a sufficiently large Z-population is compatible with the earth's environmental and resource constraints. If it is not, then even without invoking normative abridgement one may be able to conclude that a population ethics "approach that entails the Repugnant Conclusion need not entail any repugnant recommendations in practice" (Zuber et al. 2021, p. 381). Dasgupta (2019) defends a conception of population ethics that he calls "generational-relative utilitarianism." This is a form of discounted utilitarianism that is supplemented with additional weights to reflect a generation's agent-centered prerogative of self-concern. As Dasgupta formalizes this conception in an SWF, it is fully consistent with the Repugnant Conclusion (Dasgupta 2019, p. 91). But when applying his specific economic model to "test" his conception against total utilitarianism, Dasgupta finds that total utilitarianism prefers large populations with low average well-being, whereas his generation-relative utilitarianism prefers smaller populations with higher average well-being. The cause of this divergence is his model's *empirical* assumption that resources will be distributed equally between members of the current generation and members of the next generation they will bring into existence. Since members of the current generation wish to keep their own well-being fairly high, generation-relative utilitarian allows them to create a smaller subsequent generation with which to share available resources. Dasgupta advances his theory as a normatively *un*abridged answer to population questions. And it is certainly a virtue of the approach that it does not entail Mulgan's Repugnant Obligation Conclusion. But since his framework's underlying *philosophical* conception of population ethics is consistent with the Repugnant Conclusion, it should be viewed either as normatively abridged and in need of supplementation, or else as a mistaken unabridged theory of population policy.

average utilitarianism and total utilitarianism is true. Drawing on more respectable empirical assumptions than the ones I mused on two paragraphs back, these authors explain that both average utilitarianism and total utilitarianism support completely decarbonizing the world economy as soon as possible (Arrhenius et al. 2021, pp. 120–122). They then conclude that when theoretically inconsistent approaches to population ethics converge on a policy, this shows "that we can know whether to implement the policy without knowing the correct population axiology" (Arrhenius et al. 2021, p. 122).

But in fact, if all axiologies are normatively abridged, then this type of convergence does not deliver knowledge about "whether to implement the policy." It can deliver knowledge only about whether implementing the policy would be best *from the abridged perspective of general betterness*. Indeed, Arrhenius et al. admit that if policymakers do not aim singlemindedly to maximize an SWF, then it can be crucial which of the rival population axiologies is true. If general betterness is genuinely normatively relevant, then whenever other normative considerations support a policy different from the one deemed best by an SWF, it becomes even more important to know just how bad the SWF judges that alternative policy to be. And average utilitarianism and total utilitarianism can give very different answers to *that* question, as Arrhenius et al. themselves note (Arrhenius et al. 2021, pp. 122–123). Yet in their discussion of this point, the only considerations they allow to cut against the dictates of general betterness are considerations of "bounded political capital" (Arrhenius et al. 2021, p. 123). If my analysis in this part of the book is correct, the phenomenon of normative abridgement attenuates the practical upshot of axiological convergence even before realpolitik enters the picture.

* * *

If one has not pored over the difficult philosophical issues I have explored in this part of the book—if one has not engaged in what Nicholas Stern labels "agonizing reflections" (Stern 2015, p. 204)—then one is not justified in drawing quick inferences from the results of an SWF-based evaluation to practical recommendations or policy conclusions. And despite my own agonizing reflections, I have not come close to providing an airtight defense of the conception of general betterness I personally favor. That conception is grounded in (1) Harsanyi's aggregation theorem, (2) a principle of impartiality that extends the theorem from same-people to same-number contexts,

(3) the extension to variable-population contexts provided by critical-level utilitarianism, and (4) a critical level set equal to the zero level of lifetime well-being to evade all sadistic conclusions. The result is a (finite) non-discounted total utilitarian approach to interpersonal aggregation (i.e., the "people part" of aggregation), extended to handle variable-population contexts.[5]

One lesson from Part I is that the general equilibrium social cost of carbon figures should exclude normative considerations *in their construction*, whereas their *use* in policymaking always raises important normative questions. By contrast, we have seen in this part that social choice SCC figures deeply implicate ethics in both contexts—construction and use. Still, if it turns out that the most defensible SWF is indeed normatively abridged, then even unimpeachable social choice SCC figures are very incomplete guides to morally responsible climate policy.

Appendix: Deriving Critical-Level Utilitarianism

The following derivation of critical-level utilitarianism is taken from Broome (2004, pp. 200–201).

Harsanyi's theorem tells us that if two distributions involve the lifetime well-beings of the same set of people, the following value function places these vectors of lifetime well-being into a ranked ordering:

$$V = \sum_{i \in \Pi} a_i \cdot w_i \qquad (7.2)$$

where Π is the relevant set of members of this population.

In order to extend this theorem to contexts in which the number of people in each outcome is the same while the sets of people in each outcome might

---

[5] I explained in section 4.3.4 how one can use Harsanyi's aggregation theorem a second time to round out the "people route" to (a finite version of) the standard SWF in social choice climate economics. This second application is used to aggregate temporal well-beings within each life. I also explained there that this approach to same-lifetime aggregation cannot account for the desirability of certain patterns of temporal well-being in a life. It is interesting that at the end of *Weighing Goods*, Broome explores the possibility that pattern goods are "not axiologically significant" (Broome 1991, p. 234). Although he does not discuss what it might mean for pattern goods to be normatively relevant even if they are not axiologically significant—that is, even if they are not relevant to individuals' betterness orderings—I think Broome's discussion can be read as raising that possibility. This would enable one to accept the aggregation-theorem-based route to same-lifetime aggregation as yet one more normatively abridged aspect of a betterness ordering.

POPULATION 187

be different, let us set all a_i values equal to 1. (See section 4.3.3 for the reasoning behind this move.) I will therefore omit explicit reference to these weights.

Now consider two distributions of lifetime well-beings, A and A'. Let the populations of these distributions be Π and Π', respectively; and let the number of people in each population be n and n', respectively, with $n' > n$. Finally, let the vector of Π's members' lifetime well-beings be w_1, w_2, w_3, and so on, with the counterpart vector for Π' being w'_1, w'_2, w'_3, and so on.

Now take A and enlarge it by adding an additional person whose lifetime well-being is exactly at the critical level, v. This new distribution is equally as good as A; that is entailed by the meaning of the critical level.

Enlarge the distribution further, adding individuals with lifetime well-beings at the critical level, until $(n' - n)$ people have been added. The resulting distribution now has n' people. This distribution is also equally as good as A. Its total lifetime well-being is

$$\left[\sum_{i \in \Pi} w_i\right] + (n' - n)v \tag{7.3}$$

This new distribution now has the same number of people in it as does A'. By Harsanyi's theorem, we know that it will be better than A' just in case it has more total well-being. We write this condition as:

$$\left[\sum_{i \in \Pi} w_i\right] + (n' - n)v > \sum_{i \in \Pi'} w'_i \tag{7.4}$$

Rearranging this a bit gives:

$$\left[\sum_{i \in \Pi} w_i\right] - nv > \left[\sum_{i \in \Pi'} w'_i\right] - n'v \tag{7.5}$$

Because the sizes of Π and Π' are n and n', respectively, we can rewrite this again as:

$$\sum_{i \in \Pi} (w_i - v) > \sum_{i \in \Pi'} (w'_i - v) \tag{7.6}$$

This condition tells us when the new distribution that we created by enlarging A is better than A'. But since that new distribution is equally as good as A, it also tells us when A is better than A'. The same reasoning can be used for any two distributions, no matter how many people they contain. That is, distributions of lifetime well-being can be placed into a ranked ordering using the following *critical-level utilitarian* social welfare function:

$$V = \sum_{i \in \Pi} (w_i - v) \qquad (7.7)$$

where v is the critical level of well-being. And this is equation (7.1).

PART III
POLICY ANALYSIS

8
The Social Cost of Carbon in Applied Climate Change Policy Analysis

In this book I have distinguished four different social cost of carbon (SCC) concepts and explained their respective welfare economic foundations. I have also examined in some detail the moral philosophy that bears on the brand of climate change economics I have called social choice climate economics. From all of this I have drawn the general conclusion that while the four SCC concepts are importantly distinct from one another, they share the following important feature: no SCC concept reflects the full set of ethical considerations to which sound climate policy must respond. Each SCC concept is, in that sense, normatively abridged.

Despite this, each of the four SCC concepts is related to its own distinct task in climate change policy analysis. For this reason, it is a mistake to refer to "the" social cost of carbon or "the" discount rate: each SCC concept gives rise to its own time series of discount rates and its own time series of SCC values.

Nor should one infer from widespread disagreement about discounting that SCC estimates are unreliable tools for climate policy. The conclusion here may be correct, but the line of reasoning is flawed. For it is possible that once analysts come to appreciate the differences between the various SCC concepts, disagreements over the relevant parameters will be narrowed and perhaps eliminated. Put differently, it is not surprising to find disagreement over discounting parameters when some commentators are focused on one type of social cost of carbon, others are focused on another type, but each camp believes it is studying "the" social cost of carbon. Once analysts have a better grasp on the conceptual distinctions between various concepts, they can revisit their disagreements over discounting parameters and perhaps find that the basis for disagreement has evaporated.

Even if that should turn out to be so, there are many other reasons to be skeptical that SCC estimates should play a prominent role in climate change policy analysis. I mentioned one such reason in the Preface: every existing

SCC estimate is predicated upon a model that omits major categories of climate-related harms from its damage function. For example, in November 2023 the U.S. Environmental Protection Agency (EPA) announced new SCC figures that it will use in its analyses of proposed greenhouse gas regulations (EPA 2023). Still, EPA was very clear that its estimates are weakened by the fact that "[t]here are still many important categories of climate impacts and associated damages that are not yet reflected in these estimates due to data and modeling limitations" (EPA 2023, p. 81). As examples of such omitted categories, EPA lists damages from extreme weather events, increased precipitation, ocean acidification, infectious diseases, climate-related displacement and migration, lack of access to safe drinking water, increasingly intense and frequent coastal storms, negative impacts on biodiversity and on animal and livestock health, and threats posed to tourism and recreation industries as well as to national security. In light of these omissions, EPA warns that it is "likely that the SC-GHG [social cost of greenhouse gases] estimates presented in this report underestimate the marginal damages from GHG emissions" (EPA 2023, p. 86). Moreover, as I noted in the Preface, SCC estimates uniformly ignore the intrinsic value of nature and non-human animals. Thus even if it is reasonable to hope that improved conceptual clarity can narrow disagreements on (for example) discounting parameters, that welcome result would not mean that various SCC estimates can be used reliably to perform the analytical tasks they are addressed to in climate economics. My own view is that since every SCC estimate omits myriad climate impacts, those estimates are distinctly unsuited for these analytical tasks. I therefore doubt that climate change policymaking should rely heavily on SCC-based analysis.

But not everyone will agree with me on this, and I hope that those who continue to lean on SCC estimates in their policy analyses will take seriously the conceptual distinctions and philosophical argument I have provided in this book. Let me recapitulate these very briefly.

8.1 Summary

I have distinguished between four SCC concepts, grouped into two families. Two of these concepts belong to what I have called the social choice family. These concepts stem from a social welfare function that represents a normative ordering defined on a set of well-being paths, where these paths are in turn constructed out of interpersonally comparable indicators of well-being. The remaining two SCC concepts belong to what I have called the general equilibrium family. I have explained how these concepts relate to what I termed character functions, which provide analytically useful ways to refer to Pareto efficient allocations, but which have no connection whatsoever to the task of representing an ordering of paths of consumption or well-being. Furthermore, character functions can be articulated using interpersonally *non*comparable utility functions.

Each of these families—the social choice family and the general equilibrium family—consists of two SCC concepts: one baseline SCC, and one optimal SCC. A social choice baseline SCC (SC-BASE SCC) can in principle be used in a social choice cost-benefit analysis of a greenhouse gas abatement project. If the SC-BASE SCC were soundly constructed and reflected all relevant climate-related impacts, the cost-benefit test in which it features could reveal whether undertaking the relevant project would move the world from its status quo intertemporal path of well-being to a path that is ranked higher by the social welfare function (SWF) that underlies the SC-BASE SCC estimate. In contrast, the social choice optimal SCC (SC-OPT SCC) is the SWF-based SCC—or more accurately, the time series of SWF-based SCCs—that would prevail along the feasible intertemporal path of well-being that is ranked highest by the chosen SWF. This time series of SCCs is "optimal" solely because of its connection to the SWF's ranking. Yet as I explained in chapter 5, if this ranking is normatively abridged—if, that is, it does not rank paths with respect to everything that matters to ethically responsible climate policy—then optimal social choice SCCs will not necessarily be indicators of ethically compelling climate policies.

The general equilibrium family also contains one baseline SCC concept and one optimal SCC concept. The baseline general equilibrium SCC (GE-BASE SCC) turns out to be the SCC concept that is employed in the brand of cost-benefit analysis that is predicated not on a social welfare function, but on the Kaldor-Hicks compensation principle. If it is constructed using faithful representations of people's actual preferences, then the GE-BASE SCC is an indicator of aggregate willingness to pay for the marginal abatement of carbon dioxide.[1] Those who accept the Kaldor-Hicks version of cost

---

[1] I noted in section 3.15 that those who construct SCC figures for use in Kaldor-Hicks-based cost-benefit analysis typically do not think of these estimates as rooted in general equilibrium theory. But as I explained there, the GE-BASE SCC concept is precisely the SCC concept that is standardly employed by Kaldor-Hicks-based cost-benefit analysis.

benefit analysis commonly interpret a project's passing that test to mean that those who would benefit from marginal abatement could fully compensate those who would be harmed and still be better off than they were prior to the abatement project. This use of GE-BASE SCC figures is theoretically problematic, for two reasons. First, passing a cost-benefit test that uses a GE-BASE SCC does not in fact tell us that the abatement project can be undertaken in a Pareto-improving manner. This is the key implication of the so-called Boadway paradox that I discussed in section 3.15. Second, those who predicate cost-benefit analysis upon the Kaldor-Hicks compensation principle typically adopt a different interpretation of the results of their cost-benefit tests. Instead of using such tests simply to determine whether abatement could be Pareto-improving, proponents of Kaldor-Hicks-based cost-benefit analysis hold that when a project passes such a test, that is sufficient to deem the project a good thing to do.[2] I explained in section 3.15 why that use of GE-BASE SCCs is normatively untenable. To address that evaluative task, one instead needs a social choice baseline SCC.

The second general equilibrium SCC concept is that of an optimal general equilibrium SCC (GE-OPT SCC). As explained in section 3.12, there are as many GE-OPT SCCs as there are Pareto efficient allocations. (Actually, there are even more than that, for each Pareto efficient allocation is associated with a *time series* of GE-OPT SCC figures.) Each of these gives the Pigouvian tax (or series of taxes, one for each year) that must be imposed upon emitters in order to decentralize a given Pareto efficient allocation. In the social choice framework, one hopes to identify the single social welfare function that ranks all feasible paths from best to worst. But in the general equilibrium framework, every Pareto efficient allocation is associated with a character function. These character functions say absolutely nothing about

---

[2] For example, Al McGartland, the director of the EPA's National Center for Environmental Economics, writes: "The Kaldor–Hicks criterion . . . allows for some to be made worse off by [an] economic change. *For there to be an increase in social welfare*, Kaldor–Hicks requires a 'potential' Pareto improvement, which occurs when those who gain from the economic change would be willing to compensate the losers and still be better off" (McGartland 2021, pp. 345–346n8, my emphasis). I have emphasized the phrase "For there to be an increase in social welfare"; McGartland's use of this phrase reflects a shift from using the compensation principle solely to identify potential Pareto improvements to using it as an indicator of a real increase in the well-being of society. That shift is theoretically unwarranted, but in my experience it is very common. Often when I mention the Kaldor-Hicks principle in conversation with an economist who has produced an environmental cost-benefit analysis that measures benefits and costs solely in terms of people's willingness to pay, I am met with a chuckle or an incredulous stare (or both). It appears more common for such applied welfare economists to conceive of their methods as a rough-and-ready approach to measuring real changes in social welfare—that is, as a rough-and-ready approach to a social choice cost-benefit analysis.

which efficient allocation is the best allocation, or which is the allocation that ought to be targeted by climate change policy. Thus just as GE-BASE SCCs cannot legitimately be used to evaluate the desirability of marginal abatement projects, GE-OPT SCCs cannot be used to indicate the desirability of any Pareto efficient intertemporal allocation. At best, GE-OPT SCCs tell us what the carbon tax level should be if we wish to guide the economy onto a given Pareto efficient trajectory using only tax and transfer policies.

We therefore have four SCC concepts, each of which addresses a specific task in climate change policy analysis. No one of these is "the" task for climate change economics or for climate change policy analysis, and so no one of the SCC concepts is "the" proper social cost of carbon concept. Still, I have argued that at least one of the four SCC concepts—the GE-BASE SCC—is theoretically unsuited for the task to which it is addressed. Because of the Boadway paradox, the GE-BASE SCC cannot be used to identify policies that could be Pareto-improving when accompanied by compensation. Moreover, since the Kaldor-Hicks compensation principle is normatively spurious, that leaves the GE-BASE SCC concept with no further role to play in climate change economics or climate change policy analysis. It follows that if one wishes to use an SCC to evaluate a marginal CO_2 abatement project or policy, the only SCC concept available for that purpose is that of a baseline social choice SCC. If one wishes to know whether an abatement project could be Pareto-improving, one will have use other tools of economic analysis to answer that question. No SCC can serve that function.[3]

---

[3] For example, one will have to model policies that combine abatement with adjustments to consumption, and then ask whether the result is one that leaves some people better off than they were before the policy and no one worse off. Louis Kaplow describes such a method, and relates it conceptually to Lindahl pricing (Kaplow 1996, p. 521). By this he means that a combination of taxes and transfers can be used to address a public good or externality in a Pareto-improving way. At times Kaplow says that the test for whether Pareto-improving policies are available is "the simple cost-benefit test" (e.g., Kaplow 1996, pp. 514, 517). But he does not seem to have the Kaldor-Hicks cost-benefit test in mind. Instead, he appears to mean that if what the potential gainers are willing to pay is greater than what the potential losers are willing to accept, then a Pareto improvement is possible. This is a straightforward consequence of the Samuelson condition for the efficient provision of public goods, which I discussed in section 3.8. It does not follow from this that a policy that has a net positive willingness to pay can be combined with transfers to yield a Pareto-improving outcome. An inference of that sort is blocked by the Boadway paradox. Yet it does follow that *some* abatement policy can be combined with *some* fiscal policy to yield a Pareto improvement. But the way to test whether a set of changes can be Pareto-improving is to model the abatement policy and fiscal measures directly, and to determine whether they would leave everyone indifferent between the pre- and post-policy outcome. Then, if the fiscal measures involve tax increases on the "winners" from the policy, and if the policy-cum-fiscal measures have left the government with net positive revenue, then this surplus can be rebated back to the population in a uniform way to yield a Pareto improvement over the pre-policy situation. Kaplow admits that this result depends on a technical assumption about the structure of consumers' preferences that may be violated in the real world (Kaplow 1996, p. 518.).

When it comes to optimal social cost of carbon concepts, both the SC-OPT SCC and the GE-OPT SCC concepts are theoretically well-founded and normatively relevant. Yet because of normative abridgement (and also because of the problem of omitted damages), sound optimal social choice SCCs are not necessarily indicators of sound—that is, ethically responsible—climate policy. Nor should we adopt without argument the standard assumption among economists that whatever else is true of the intertemporal path of consumption that climate policy should target, that path should be Pareto efficient. Perhaps, for example, social policy should be more averse to risk than actual individuals are themselves.[4]

Upon this background, I want in the rest of this chapter to consider further the question of which SCC concepts, if any, should play a role in real-world climate policy analysis. My answer to this question will be driven by facts about real-world institutions. To preview the conclusions I shall draw, my view is that while the SC-BASE and GE-OPT SCC concepts are highly relevant for climate policy analysis, the SC-OPT concept is much less so, and the GE-BASE concept should (as I have argued) play no role at all. Moreover, by invoking the conceptual distinctions and arguments that are core to this book, I believe we can reasonably hope to settle some of the long-standing disputes about welfare weighting, discount rates, and "optimal" carbon taxes that many believe to be irresolvable and matters solely for personal subjective judgment.

Although each baseline SCC concept and each optimal SCC concept is in principle addressed to a distinct analytical task, I shall organize this chapter around two themes, *climate change cost-benefit analysis* (in which the baseline SCC concepts figure) and *climate policy targets and taxes* (which are commonly analyzed in light of optimal SCC estimates).

8.2 Climate Change Cost-Benefit Analysis

One of the most important contexts in which baseline SCC estimates figure is that of cost-benefit analyses conducted by the U.S. federal government. The U.S. federal government uses baseline SCC estimates in analyses of proposed environmental regulations as well as in analyses of various forms

---

[4] This would be so if the ex post prioritarian SWF were a defensible unabridged choice function. For in violating the ex ante strong Pareto axiom, ex post prioritarianism is more risk-averse than are individuals' own well-being orderings.

of federal spending. My discussion of applied climate change cost-benefit analysis will focus exclusively on this context.[5]

8.2.1 The Interagency Working Group and the EPA

As I noted in the Preface, the U.S. federal government created an Interagency Working Group on Social Cost of Carbon (IWG) in the early years of the Obama administration. The goal was to compute official estimates of the SCC that all federal agencies could use, rather than leaving each agency to devise its own estimate. The IWG was disbanded under President Trump and then reestablished by President Biden under a new name—the Interagency Working Group on Social Cost of Greenhouse Gases. The broader title reflected IWG's new mandate to estimate not just the social cost of carbon dioxide (SCC), but also the social costs of methane and nitrous oxide. I shall refer to all iterations of the Interagency Working Group with the abbreviation *IWG*.

From the beginning, the IWG sought to produce GE-BASE SCC estimates. It did this because its conception of cost-benefit analysis was explicitly predicated on the Kaldor-Hicks compensation principle (IWG 2010, p. 18). This is a long-standing norm within the U.S. federal government (see OMB 1992, 2003).[6] Indeed, when in 2017 the National Academies of Sciences, Engineering, and Medicine issued an IWG-requested report on how to improve IWG's current SCC methodology, the report included the following qualification:

> In benefit-cost analysis, the benefit of a commodity is measured by what people are willing to pay for it. It is important to note that willingness to pay is constrained by ability to pay... Distributional effects [of an environmental regulation] can also be reflected in benefit-cost analysis using welfare weights, although this is rarely done in practice and is not permitted in [federal] regulatory impact analysis. (NAS 2017, p. 23n4)

---

[5] I am indebted to R. Daniel Bressler and Noah Kaufman for very helpful comments on this section.
[6] The U.S. federal government's staunch commitment to the Kaldor-Hicks brand of cost-benefit analysis has one significant exception. I will discuss this below in section 8.2.3.

IWG's SCC estimates therefore did not reflect welfare weighting and were constructed using market interest rates as discount rates (IWG 2010, pp. 18–19).

On President Biden's first day in office, he issued Executive Order 13990, which was titled "Protecting Public Health and the Environment and Restoring Science to Tackle the Climate Crisis" (Executive Office of the President 2021). This order not only reinstated the IWG, but it also tasked the IWG with publishing "interim" updated SCC values within thirty days, and with publishing "final" SCC figures within a year. It also charged the IWG with publishing, by June 1, 2022, recommendations for how to "revise methodologies for calculating the SCC . . . to the extent that current methodologies do not adequately take account of climate risk, environmental justice, and intergenerational equity" (Executive Office of the President 2021, p. 7040). Many commentators interpreted this last part of the order as calling for a shift from Kaldor-Hicks-based cost-benefit analysis to the social welfare function-based brand that I described in chapter 2. This would have required a shift from the use of GE-BASE SCC estimates to the use of SC-BASE SCC estimates.

But that is not what has happened—yet. Although the IWG did issue its interim SCC updates in February 2021, these merely updated the Obama-era SCC figures for inflation (IWG 2021). Since that update, nothing further has been heard from the IWG. Instead, it was the EPA that in November 2023 released its own updated SCC estimates that it intended to use in evaluating new environmental regulations of the U.S. oil and natural gas sector.

In its report on the SCC updates, EPA was explicit about the theoretical basis of its new estimates:[7]

> The developers of the damage functions used in this report applied valuation methods that are consistent with the theoretical underpinnings of EPA's benefit-cost analysis (BCA)—the Kaldor-Hicks criterion. (EPA 2023, p. 164)

> While EPA will continue to assess the broader literature on BCA, social welfare, and equity as it seeks to apply the best available science in its analyses, this report develops [SCC] estimates that are considered to be

---

[7] Throughout this chapter I have replaced EPA's use of "SC-GHG" (i.e., social cost of greenhouse gases) with "SCC." I want to avoid confusing EPA's use of "SC-" with mine throughout this book, where it has been shorthand for "social choice" rather than "social cost."

generally consistent with the Kaldor-Hicks criterion that guides all the other elements of the EPA's BCAs. (EPA 2023, p. 168)

I have already criticized these theoretical commitments. Here I want to highlight three further methodological choices EPA made because of them.

8.2.1.1 Discounting

The first concerns discount rates. As I explained in section 3.15, GE-BASE SCCs are constructed by discounting future marginal consumption damages using baseline real interest rates as discount rates. Although this was indeed EPA's broad methodology, its specific approach to discounting was novel and worth examining a bit further.

When the Obama-era IWG constructed baseline SCCs with the aim of implementing the Kaldor-Hicks compensation principle, it too discounted future monetized damages at rates that it conceptualized as market interest rates. But instead of allowing interest rates to vary from year to year, or even decade to decade, the IWG used three constant discount rates—2.5, 3, and 5 percent (IWG 2010, p. 1). Here is how it worked.

IWG used three models that had been created by independent scholars in climate economics. These were the DICE model, the FUND model, and the PAGE model. Each of these models incorporates assumptions about the ways in which cumulative emissions translate into atmospheric CO_2 concentrations, the way concentrations translate into temperature changes, and the ways that temperature changes translate into monetized climate damages in a given future year. IWG modified these models in one key way: it adopted a single set of assumptions concerning equilibrium climate sensitivity (ECS), which is the amount of warming that follows a doubling of atmospheric CO_2 concentrations. Each model came preprogramed with its own assumptions about this, but IWG replaced these with a single representation that attached different probabilities to different ECS values. This stochastic treatment of ECS was then used in the following way to construct 150,000 paths of marginal climate damages.

Taking one model at a time, IWG calibrated the model to focus on a specific baseline scenario. This is a scenario that incorporates assumptions concerning growth trends in population, GDP, and CO_2 emissions. The model was then asked to return an intertemporal path of global consumption that reflected these baseline assumptions as well as the model's projection of the climate damages that would follow from those assumptions. This is where the stochastic treatment of ECS is important: to compute a climate-affected baseline consumption path, IWG selected an ECS value at random from the pre-selected probability distribution. The resulting climate-affected baseline consumption path therefore reflects one model's view of how the world might turn out, given the baseline assumptions, the model's own assumptions about climate dynamics and climate economics, and the stochastic treatment of the ECS parameter.

Next, all of these assumptions (including the specific pre-selected ECS value) were held fixed, and the model was told to compute the consumption path that would result if a single extra ton of CO_2 were added into the atmosphere in the initial period. Then, by comparing the climate-affected baseline path with the path that reflects one extra ton of CO_2, the model yields a time path of marginal climate damages that can be attributed to the influence of that extra ton. The model was then used to repeat this procedure 9,999 more times, to yield a total of 10,000 baseline- and model-specific marginal damage paths, each of which was associated with a specific ECS value chosen at random from the ECS probability distribution. Finally, and still using the first model, IWG performed exactly the same procedure four more times, each time using a different set of baseline assumptions (i.e., different assumptions concerning the population, GDP, and CO_2 emissions over time). The result was 50,000 model-specific paths of marginal climate damages.

The other two models were then used to perform the same procedure, to yield a final total of 150,000 intertemporal marginal damage paths. Next, IWG took the first of its discount rates—2.5 percent—and used it to compute a present value damage estimate for each of the 150,000 damage paths. Then it averaged these estimates and reported the average as the SCC-for-the-2.5-percent-discount-rate. After doing the same thing for the other two discount rates, IWG had three SCC estimates for the initial time period. These were its headline SCC values, which it supplemented by reporting the 95th percentile value when using the 3 percent discount rate. This is the value that is at least as large as 95 percent of the 150,000 individual SCCs-for-the-3-percent-discount-rate. IWG interpreted this final SCC figure as "represent[ing] higher-than-expected impacts from temperature change further out in the tails of the SCC distribution" (IWG 2010, p. 1).

When recently constructing its own updated SCC estimates, EPA changed several aspects of the Obama-era IWG's procedure. EPA did this in response to the 2017 report from the National Academies, which made recommendations for updating IWG's approach to (1) modeling the baseline scenarios, (2) modeling climate dynamics, (3) estimating the climate damages caused by greenhouse gas–related temperature increases, and (4) discounting. In response to the National Academies's recommendations concerning categories (1)–(3), EPA stopped relying on DICE, FUND, and PAGE and instead pieced together its own integrated assessment model from what it determined to be state-of-the-art work in the modeling community. I will not discuss these modeling updates here. I want instead to explain the changes EPA made to IWG's discounting methodology.

Although EPA made fundamental updates to the model components connected with the first three topics listed above, it preserved a good deal of IWG's abstract SCC methodology. Because many of its model's parameters were stochastic, EPA continued to produce thousands of model runs which were then used to compute a distribution of SCC estimates. Yet instead of running three different models thousands of times, as IWG did, EPA chose to calibrate its single model in three different ways; it then ran the model 10,000 times under each of those calibrations. Specifically, EPA adopted three different damage modules, whose job is to translate temperature increases into monetized climate damages in different years. For each damage module, EPA ran its model in a "baseline" mode 10,000 times. This yielded 10,000 baseline projections of climate-impacted global consumption from 2020 to 2300. Each of these projections reflected a specific set of parameter values that were selected randomly from their respective probability distributions. Then, for each of these 10,000 projections, the parameter values that led to it were held fixed and the model was run once more with the added assumption that a single extra ton of CO_2 was "pulsed" into the atmosphere in the analysis's first time period. This in turn yielded 10,000 new consumption paths. EPA then computed the year-by-year differences in consumption between each baseline run and its corresponding "pulsed" run. The result was 10,000 damage-module-specific time paths of marginal climate damages. This process was then repeated with the other two damage modules, resulting in three sets of 10,000 marginal damage paths. Crucially, each of these 30,000 marginal damage paths is computed by comparing a specific baseline run of the model with its respective "pulsed" variant (EPA 2023, pp. 77–81).

Coming now to its discounting methodology, EPA preserved IWG's commitment to a "descriptive" approach to discounting on which market interest rates are used as discount rates. Like the IWG, EPA adopted this approach explicitly because it fits best with the Kaldor-Hicks brand of cost-benefit framework that EPA also endorsed (EPA 2023, pp. 62–64). But unlike IWG,

202 THE SOCIAL COST OF CARBON

EPA did not discount time paths of marginal climate damages using constant discount rates. Instead, EPA followed the National Academies report's recommendation that federal SCC estimates be computed using what it called a "Ramsey-like approach" to descriptive discounting (NAS 2017, pp. 18, 179–182). The Ramsey-like approach allows interest rates to fluctuate over time along each possible baseline consumption path. The reasoning goes like this. Suppose that individual consumers have intertemporal preferences that can be represented by the following utility function:

$$U_t = \sum_{i=0}^{L} u(c_{t,t+i}) \cdot \frac{1}{(1+\varepsilon)^i} \tag{8.1}$$

where U_t is the lifetime utility of individuals born in period t; each individual lives for $L+1$ periods; $c_{t,t+i}$ is the temporal consumption in period $t+i$ of an individual born at t; and ε is the individual's rate of pure time preference. Now let each consumer's temporal utility function u take the standard isoelastic form:

$$u = \frac{(c_{t,t+i})^{1-\sigma}}{1-\sigma} \tag{8.2}$$

Then under these assumptions, the formula for deriving consumers' personal, preference-based marginal rates of substitution between consumption in adjacent time periods—that is, their personal consumption discount rates—takes the familiar Ramsey form:[8]

$$\mu_t = \varepsilon + \sigma \cdot g_t \tag{8.3}$$

where g_t is the growth rate of the individual's consumption from period t to $t+1$. Moreover, we know from section 3.15 that agents with these preferences will adjust their savings behavior until the following version of the Ramsey rule holds at every time τ in which they live:

$$r_\tau = \varepsilon + \sigma \cdot g_\tau \tag{8.4}$$

Here r_τ is the prevailing market interest rate at τ.

---

[8] See section 2.4.

By assuming consumers have preferences that entail personal versions of the Ramsey rule, EPA used this rule to project a time path of real interest rates corresponding to each of the 30,000 baseline run of its model. First, it picked what it (and many other economists) consider to be three plausible candidates for being the near-term interest rate—1.5, 2.0, and 2.5 percent. Then it drew on recent work by Newell et al. (2022) and Rennert, Prest, et al. (2022) that combined these three near-term interest rates with other economic phenomena to infer the values of the ε and σ parameters from each consumer's intertemporal utility function. This process culminated in three pairs of "Ramsey parameters," one pair for each of the posited near-term interest rates (EPA 2023, pp. 67–73).

With these three pairs of Ramsey parameters in hand, EPA returned to the 30,000 baseline consumption paths it had already computed using its core model and the three damage modules. For each of these baseline paths, EPA used equation (8.3), along with the three pairs of Ramsey parameters, to compute three different time paths of consumption discount rates along each baseline path. It then invoked equation (8.4) to derive a time path of real interest rates for each path of consumption discount rates. Finally, it used these interest rates to discount the path of marginal damages that it had previously associated with each baseline path. This yielded three SCC figures for that path of marginal damages. Thus since each of three damage modules was used to compute 10,000 paths of marginal climate damages, and since each path of marginal damages was discounted using three different time paths of interest rates, EPA ended up with nine groups containing 10,000 SCC figures each. It then averaged the SCC values within each group, and reported its results for 2020. These results are given in Table 8.1.

Table 8.1 EPA SCC figures by near-term interest rate and damage module. Adapted from EPA (2023, p. 78).

Emissions Year	2.5% DM 1[a]	2.5% DM 2[b]	2.5% DM 3[c]	2.0% DM 1	2.0% DM 2	2.0% DM 3	1.5% DM 1	1.5% DM 2	1.5% DM 3
SCC in 2020	$110	$120	$120	$190	$190	$200	$330	$310	$370

[a] "DM 1" = Damage Module 1.
[b] "DM 2" = Damage Module 2.
[c] "DM 3" = Damage Module 3.

I have set out these details because I want to make it very clear that EPA's "Ramsey-like" discounting methodology is very different from Ramsey's own general approach to discounting. For one thing, Ramsey worked within social choice welfare economics, whereas EPA strictly avoids making the assumptions concerning interpersonal comparisons of well-being that the social choice framework requires (EPA 2023, pp. 95–96, 95n140, 168). For another, I explained at the end of section 2.7 that it is perfectly coherent in the social choice framework for consumption discount rates to depart markedly from the interest rates that prevail in any real-world market. This is because discount rates in the social choice framework are normative hurdle rates: they are the rates of return a consumption investment must meet in order for the investment to move the world from its baseline consumption path to one that is ranked higher than it by the social welfare function from which the discount rates are derived. But this is not the role that discount rates play in EPA's Kaldor-Hicks-based brand of cost-benefit analysis. Instead, EPA wants to know whether the aggregate willingness to pay for marginal CO_2 abatement exceeds the amount that present abaters would have to be compensated in order to be indifferent between abating and not abating. To arrive at the necessary willingness to pay indicator, EPA must discount future willingness to pay using real interest rates. (I explained the rationale for this in section 3.15.) So while it is true that EPA employs certain mathematical techniques that stem from Ramsey's work, these two uses are decidedly distinct.[9]

8.2.1.2 Welfare Weighting

Because of its commitment to Kaldor-Hicks-based cost-benefit analysis, EPA stated very clearly in its 2023 report that its SCC figures did not reflect the use of welfare weights:

> The [SCC] by design, and consistent with the economic theory and methods for benefit-cost analysis, is an aggregation across individuals of their willingness to pay to avoid the marginal damages of climate change. (EPA 2023, p. 95)

---

[9] Thus if a "prescriptive" approach to discounting necessarily invokes a normative social welfare function (and therefore an interpersonally comparable notion of well-being), then EPA's approach to discounting is not prescriptive, despite making use of Ramsey's formulae. This conflicts with Newell et al. (2022)'s reference to the National Academies' "hybrid descriptive/prescriptive recommendation" on discounting (p. 1018). I interpret these authors as claiming that a discounting framework is prescriptive whenever it makes use of Ramsey's mathematical tools and analysis. But that is a misapprehension.

The result was a set of SCC figures that did not attempt "to reflect a decreasing marginal utility of income" (EPA 2023, p. 168). Since "willingness to pay is constrained by ability to pay," as the National Academies' report stressed (NAS 2017, p. 23n4), EPA's SCC estimates systematically treated a given harm suffered by poorer people in poorer countries as less bad than an equivalent harm experienced by richer people in richer countries.

To its credit, EPA did not express complete indifference to the measurement bias that attends Kaldor-Hicks-based cost-benefit analysis. It announced that it "will continue to assess the broader literature on BCA [benefit-cost analysis], social welfare, and equity," and it noted:

> In addition to conducting a Kaldor-Hicks based BCA, EPA has and will continue to conduct detailed analyses of environmental justice concerns of climate change in its rulemakings as required and appropriate and the distributional outcomes of climate change in detailed quantitative analyses, so as to ensure that decision-makers and the public have robust information as to the damages of climate change and their distributional effects. (EPA 2023, p. 168)

To put this in my terms: EPA acknowledges that Kaldor-Hicks-based cost-benefit analyses are normatively abridged, and it is committed to providing decision-makers not only with aggregate SCC values, but also with disaggregated information concerning the impacts of climate change on different populations. This is precisely the sort of supplementary information that one should want decision-makers to receive and respond to if one accepts the following three conclusions of this book: (1) Kaldor-Hicks cost-benefit analysis is unjustified, (2) SCC figures should reflect welfare weights, and (3) even properly welfare-weighted SCCs are normatively abridged and cannot be used as reliable guides to ethically sound climate change policy.

8.2.1.3 VSLs

One of the most controversial aspects of Kaldor-Hicks-based cost-benefit analysis is its approach to valuing the badness of deaths and the benefits of preventing them. It does this with a concept known as the *value of a statistical life* (VSL). The idea is to value prevented deaths using the same willingness-to-pay methodology that is used for valuing non-mortality benefits. But whereas non-mortality benefits are valued in terms of what people are willing to pay to achieve *them*, mortality-related benefits are valued in terms of what people are willing to pay for a *chance* to receive them.

To explain further, suppose that next year you will face a 5-in-100,000 chance of being killed by air pollution that is emitted by a local factory. And suppose there is a filter the factory could put on its smokestacks that would reduce this chance by 1-in-100,000. How much would you be willing to pay for this degree of risk-reduction? Imagine that each member of your community of 100,000 people is willing to pay $100 to secure this level of risk-reduction. Then, according to the standard implementation of the Kaldor-Hicks framework, your community's VSL is $100 · 100,000 = $10,000,000.

The logic behind the VSL concept and its mathematics is easy to comprehend when viewed alongside the Kaldor-Hicks basis for cost-benefit analysis. If it will cost the factory's owners some amount of money to purchase, install, and run the filter, then a policy that requires them to do so will pass a Kaldor-Hicks compensation test only if the "winners" from the policy—that is, those who benefit from the risk-reduction—are willing to pay more for it than the policy's "losers" would have to pay to implement it. So if the winners each benefit by having their risks of dying reduced by 1-in-100,000, and if each is willing to pay $100 to achieve that benefit, then the community's total willingness to pay for that level of risk-reduction is $10,000,000. Now one can compare that total willingness to pay with the cost of implementing the abatement measure, and this would (so the Kaldor-Hicks reasoning goes) tell us whether requiring factory owners to install the filters constitutes a potential Pareto improvement.

Because VSLs aim to value only the reductions in risk that certain policies secure, rather than the actual deaths that are prevented, EPA says that the term "value of statistical *life*" is "inapt" (EPA 2023, p. 165). Many other economists agree. Yet it is important to stress that we *are* talking about lives here: any environmental regulation that is evaluated by EPA using VSL measures is a regulation that will, if implemented, prevent deaths that will occur without the regulation. And those who will die without the regulation will, of course, lose their lives. Renaming the VSL concept will not change that fact.[10]

---

[10] Nor will it change the fact that the EPA employs the VSL concept in an effort to evaluate what it calls "the net harm to society from emitting a metric ton of [greenhouse gases] to the atmosphere in a given year"; this is a harm whose conceptual flip-side is "the societal net benefit of reducing emissions . . . by a metric ton" (EPA 2023, p. 1). Thus, no matter how many times EPA cites the concept of a potential Pareto improvement in footnotes or deep into its reports, EPA's most prominent statements

The main controversy concerning the use of VSLs is connected to the problems with valuing non-mortality benefits in terms of willingness to pay. Since poorer people have less ability to pay for prospective benefits, their willingness to pay for them will often be lower than rich people's willingness to pay. This is as true for a piece of clothing as it is for a filter that reduces one's chances of dying from poisonous ambient air pollution, or for a government regulation that reduces one's chances of being killed by climate change's impacts. Accordingly, when EPA computed its updated SCC figures, its model valued deaths across the world differently depending on the per capita income of the country in which the death was projected to occur. For example, while EPA valued a death in the United States in 2020 at $10.05 million (in 2020 U.S. dollars), it valued deaths in other countries by assuming that everyone worldwide is willing to pay the same absolute percentage of per capita income for reductions in mortality risks (EPA 2023, p. 49n84). This made EPA's approach to valuing lives income-sensitive, which in turn profoundly influenced its SCC calculations. This is because the outcomes associated with temperature-related mortality risks make up the largest share of damages in the damage modules used by EPA (EPA 2023, p. 165), and because the vast majority of climate-induced temperature-related deaths will occur in low- and medium-income countries (Bressler et al. 2021).[11]

It is worth noting here that the utilitarian social choice framework (which I sympathetically presented in Part II) also values risk reductions in an income-sensitive way. The utilitarian framework values mortality risk reductions by valuing the expected changes in well-being that such reductions secure. This is what Bressler (2021, p. 9) calls the "opportunity cost of life methodology to valuing the lost life from climate change": this method values deaths according to the (expected) well-being that is lost

about the analytical relevance of cost-benefit analyses generally, and of the SCC specifically, concern the question of whether a given environmental regulation is "a welfare-enhancing improvement to society" (EPA 2010, p. A-7). This framing of the aims of cost-benefit analysis firmly harks back to the social choice conception of cost-benefit analysis.

[11] There is an important technical issue to note here. EPA chose to use purchasing power parity (PPP)–adjusted income data when it monetized climate damages and calculated VSLs for different countries around the world. But as Heal and Bressler (2023, p. 4) explain, "because PPP-adjusted dollars are hypothetical and not an actual unit of exchange, this conversion undermines the appeal to the Kaldor-Hicks potential compensation criterion. And this is not a minor issue, as the differences between PPP-adjusted money and market-money are very large, especially in developing countries." See Bressler and Heal (2022, sect. 3.4) for details. While I will have nothing further to say about this inconsistency with EPA's otherwise broad loyalty to the Kaldor-Hicks compensation principle, I will return to a different and equally significant inconsistency in section 8.2.3.

when mortality risks are not reduced. This approach is income-sensitive because a higher income translates into higher consumption opportunities and thus higher well-being.[12] More well-being is therefore lost when a higher-income person dies prematurely than when a lower-income person dies, other things equal. So although a utilitarian SCC captures the intuition that more well-being is created when a lower-income person is given an extra dollar than when a higher-income person acquires it, utilitarianism can violate moral intuitions about which deaths are more important to prevent.[13] But if my arguments in Part II are correct, we should expect a utilitarian social choice framework to issue some counter-intuitive normative conclusions. There is nothing problematic about this, so long as we appreciate that the utilitarian social choice framework should not be treated as the final normative arbiter in policy evaluation. No normatively abridged evaluative framework can play that role. Still, it *would* be a strike against utilitarianism if, like a Kaldor-Hicks-based framework, it could not even account for the diminishing marginal well-being of income (or consumption). For if one's concern is to evaluate the degree to which different policies promote social welfare, one's framework must be articulated in terms of well-being, and not merely in terms of the monetary metric of willingness to pay.

8.2.2 Biden's Executive Order and OMB's New Circular A-4

While EPA was working on its updated SCC estimates, the U.S. Office of Management and Budget (OMB) released a draft update of its Circular A-4, the primary cost-benefit analysis guidance document for federal regulatory agencies (OMB 2023a). IWG had been ordered by President Biden on his first day in office to make recommendations concerning just this update, but for some reason that did not happen (at least not publicly).

In any case, the April 2023 Public Review draft of OMB's update to Circular A-4 was a landmark event. If approved, it would have reversed the

---

[12] I should note, however, that the model Bressler employs in that paper, which is a variant on the DICE model, does not include a representation of interpersonal or regional inequality. At any given time in the model, all consumers enjoy the same level of per capita global consumption. This precludes one source of income-sensitivity of the sort described in the text, namely sensitivity to income (or consumption) differences across countries. The model could still display income-sensitivity with respect to deaths that occur at different times, however.

[13] Adler et al. (2014, p. 83) explain that by calibrating their parameters in just the right way, members of the prioritarian family of social welfare functions can avoid utilitarianism's "wealth sensitivity."

federal prohibition against welfare weighting that the National Academies cited when it called for updated SCC methodologies that remained grounded in the Kaldor-Hicks brand of cost-benefit analysis (OMB 2023a, pp. 65–66). The draft guidelines would not have *required* agencies to use welfare weighting, however: if an agency did not feel comfortable moving to a social choice brand of cost-benefit analysis, the draft guidelines would permit them to stick with the Kaldor-Hicks version. At the same time, the draft guidelines continued to "recommend . . . a descriptive approach to discounting" that identifies discount rates with interest rates reflecting consumers' intertemporal preferences concerning consumption, saving, and borrowing (OMB 2023b, p. 18). This would encourage regulatory agencies to avoid the normative approach to pure time discounting that I defended in section 5.5.

8.2.3 The Peer Reviewers Strike Back

After releasing its April 2023 draft updates to Circular A-4, OMB requested comments from the public and also engaged the independent consulting firm ICF International to oversee a process of external peer review. In August 2023 OMB released the peer reviews of nine external experts, all of them economists (ICF International 2023).

To the peer reviewers, the most controversial change in the new draft Circular was its openness to welfare weighting. Some reviewers were entirely opposed to allowing agencies to use welfare weighting. Others characterized the change as "premature" or "problematic" (ICF International 2023, pp. 51, 91). No reviewer endorsed the draft's stance that a regulatory agency should be allowed to treat a welfare-weighted cost-benefit analysis as its primary economic analysis. Several reviewers did, however, support allowing agencies to use welfare-weighted cost-benefit analyses "to supplement traditional ways of estimating benefits and costs" (ICF International 2023, p. 37).

I want to set out and briefly discuss five arguments that were made by peer reviewers in connection with welfare weighting. Doing this will enable me to recapitulate some key observations, conclusions, and lines of reasoning that I set out in Parts I and II. It will also reveal an internal inconsistency between the draft Circular's treatment of welfare weighting and its treatment of discounting. No peer reviewer criticized the draft's broad endorsement of descriptivism about discount rates (although several quibbled with the rates

OMB presented as "default" values). But as we shall see, OMB's main argument in favor of descriptivism about discount rates is inconsistent with its own emphatic—and correct—response to certain peer reviewers' skepticism about welfare weighting.

8.2.3.1 "Equity-weighted estimates... appear to be a solution in search of a problem."

One peer reviewer, Joseph Aldy, characterized welfare weighting as unnecessary, calling it "a solution in search of a problem." Aldy first observed that "by far the single largest monetized outcome in executive branch RIA [regulatory impact analysis] is reduction in mortality risk, which is monetized with the value of statistical life (VSL)." But in using VSLs, federal agencies invariably use "a common VSL across all populations." That is to say, federal guidelines actually do not allow a higher VSL to be applied to richer populations or a lower VSL to poorer populations, as would be required to faithfully implement the Kaldor-Hicks compensation principle. Thus: "Not a single RIA out of the nearly 50 RIAs produced by EPA for final Clean Air Act rules over this time period [1997–2020] monetizes an outcome measure as a function of income (or other sociodemographic characteristic)." The result is a "status quo practice that reflects an implicit, equity-weighted [i.e., welfare-weighted] approach to valuing benefits" (ICF International 2023, p. 6).

The use of a population-average VSL is a major departure from a strictly Kaldor-Hicks brand of cost-benefit analysis. This is one reason why Heal and Bressler (2023) assert that "the current BCA [benefit-cost analysis] practice used by the Federal Government and EPA... in fact differs substantially from a Kaldor-Hicks consistent BCA" (p. 2). Why has the federal government departed in this way from the pure Kaldor-Hicks methodology? I believe there are two main reasons. The first concerns convenience: a population-average VSL does not require data on how willingness to pay for mortality risk reductions varies across individuals.

The second reason concerns fear of backlash from the public and from lawmakers. In 2002, EPA published an analysis of President George W. Bush's Clear Skies Initiative, which sought to reduce emissions from sources of electric power. As part of the analysis, EPA monetized the value of mortality risk-reductions using a cousin of the VSL known as the value of a statistical life year (VSLY). In a sensitivity analysis, EPA heeded its Scientific Advisory Board's advice that "the appropriate way to account for age differences [in willingness to pay for mortality risk reductions] is to obtain the values for risk reductions from the age groups affected by the risk reduction" (EPA 2002, p. 35). Drawing on a study of citizens in the United Kingdom, EPA ended up with VSLY numbers for seventy-year-olds that were 37 percent lower than the VSLYs for forty-year-olds (EPA 2002, p. 35). This in turn "led to a political firestorm. Protesters adopted slogans such as 'seniors on sale—37% off,'" and a U.S. senator "proposed legislation banning all demographic adjustments to VSL" figures (Viscusi 2011, pp. 130–131).

Because agencies employ a uniform VSL to value all deaths in the United States, the VSL used to value deaths among low-income people is higher than it would be if it were computed solely on the basis of their actual willingness to pay for mortality risk reductions. In this respect, a uniform VSL has some of the hallmarks of welfare weighting, which would increase a low-income person's willingness to pay by applying a weight that accounts for the greater value that money has for her, compared to the value it has for a high-income person. This is why Aldy calls the use of a uniform VSL a form of "implicit" welfare weighting.[14]

There are two main problems with Aldy's argument that a uniform VSL renders explicit welfare weighting unnecessary. The first is that this method does not account for the differential impact of the *costs* of reducing mortality risks. Consider, for example, a project whose costs and benefits are fully concentrated on the lowest-income population. Even if it would reduce the well-being of every member of this population, such a project could still pass an unweighted cost-benefit analysis that uses a population-average VSL. If unweighted costs are compared with a VSL that is larger than what the VSL *would be* if it reflected the lowest-income population's actual willingness to pay, then the project may pass the cost-benefit test even though it might cost the affected population more than it offers them in benefits.[15] A cost-benefit analysis that instead welfare-weighted both benefits and costs would never yield this perverse conclusion. So instead of being a "solution in search of a problem," welfare weighting actually solves a problem that afflicts the current methodology that Aldy defends.

The second problem with Aldy's argument is that it completely ignores the methodology that EPA had used to compute its new SCC estimates that it released for public and peer review in November 2022. Those estimates

---

[14] The U.S. federal government's departure from a faithful Kaldor-Hicks approach to valuing mortality risk-reductions is further discussed by Adler (2020) and Bressler and Heal (2022).
[15] This problem is a central theme in Sunstein (2004), and is also discussed in Adler (2020, p. 32).

did reflect the use of a uniform, population-average VSL to value climate-related deaths *in the United States*; but EPA's estimates also reflected income-sensitive VSLs for the populations in the 183 other countries in EPA's model (EPA 2022, pp. 44, 129). Specifically, EPA began with the single VSL for the United States—$10.05 million in 2020—and then computed VSLs for each other country by multiplying the U.S. VSL by the ratio of per capita income in the target country to the per capita income in the U.S. (EPA 2022, p. 129).[16] (EPA made no changes to this methodology before finalizing its new SCC figures in November 2023 (EPA 2023, p. 166).) Thus, if a country's per capita income was less than the U.S.'s, its VSL was lower too. For example, EPA's analysis treated one death in the United States as worth 57.6 deaths in the Democratic Republic of the Congo.[17] This conflicts with Aldy's claim that "Agencies apply a common VSL to affected populations—at least within a given point in time" (ICF International 2023, p. 6).

When discussing this new income-sensitive VSL methodology in its November 2023 SCC report, EPA quoted the following guidance issued by its Scientific Advisory Board (SAB) in 2011:

> While it is clear from economic theory that individual [willingness to pay] may vary with individual and risk characteristics, the SAB acknowledges that the objectives, methods, and principles underlying benefit cost analysis and particularly the values of mortality risk reductions and other non-market goods are often misunderstood or rejected as inappropriate by many participants and commentators on the policymaking process. In the past, for example, the Agency was criticized for considering VSLs that differ by individuals' age . . . The proposed change of terminology [from VSL to Value of Risk Reduction (VRR)] and application of VRRs that differ with individual and risk characteristics provide an opportunity for constructive engagement with the public and other interested parties concerning these topics. (EPA 2011, p. 7; quoted in EPA 2023, pp. 166–167)

Evidently, EPA thought its SCC estimates offered just such "an opportunity for constructive engagement with the public" on the putative virtues of income-sensitive VSLs. Conspicuously, it did not see it as an opportunity to adopt income-sensitive VSLs for subpopulations within the United States.

---

[16] This same approach was also employed by Rennert, Errickson, et al. (2022, Methods, eq. (5)).
[17] I thank R. Daniel Bressler for supplying this figure.

Aldy is mistaken to cite the implicit welfare weighting of uniform VSLs as evidence that explicit welfare weighting is "a solution in search of a problem." In EPA's SCC methodology, only lower-income Americans enjoy the benefit of this implicit sort of welfare weighting. Those in sub-Saharan Africa do not.[18] In the end, welfare weighting is the only solution that can simultaneously address the two problems I have raised in connection with Aldy's claim.

8.2.3.2 "It is not clear how to interpret these numbers."
In his peer review of the Public Review draft of Circular A-4, William Pizer raises three other putative problems with welfare weighting. I will address these in this and the following sections.[19]

Let me begin by restating a useful example Pizer constructs to motivate his criticisms of welfare weighting. I have made some changes to the way in which the example is presented, but none of these affects the points Pizer uses it to make. The example involves a large group of individuals that can in turn be separated into five subgroups of equal size. While the individuals in each subgroup enjoy the same income level, income differs across groups. These figures are reported in the row of Table 8.2 labeled "Income." In Pizer's version, the respective levels in this row correspond to the household income levels associated with different income quintiles within the United States, as reported by a nonpartisan think tank. To keep things simple, I shall interpret the figures as income levels for individuals, not households. Indeed, I shall assume that each subgroup contains just one individual; the total weighted benefits reported in the rightmost column reflect this assumption.

Table 8.2 lists five stylized policies that we can imagine a federal agency wanting to evaluate using the sort of welfare-weighted cost-benefit analysis that OMB endorsed in the draft of Circular A-4. The draft states that in computing welfare weights, agencies should assume that all individuals share the same isoelastic well-being function of the form $\frac{I_q^{1-\eta}}{1-\eta}$. Here I_q denotes

---

[18] Strictly speaking, relatively low-income people in sub-Saharan African countries will have their willingness to pay for mortality risk reductions implicitly welfare weighted to equal the population-average willingness to pay in their country. I doubt this would mollify them, since someone with their exact same income in the United States would have their VSL implicitly welfare weighted to equal the population-average VSL in the U.S.

[19] In his discussion, Pizer enumerates four problems, not three. The fourth is related to the fact "that the calculation of weighted net benefits will necessarily depend on the granularity of the calculations ... Thus average values increase as quintiles become deciles, etc." (ICF International 2023, p. 86). This is not an ethical issue, but one concerning possible data limitations and the need to ensure that data sets are compatible with one another. Since the problem does not seem to play a major role in Pizer's critique of welfare weighting, I shall not examine it further. For more on this issue, see Morgenstern et al. (2023, pp. 9–10).

Table 8.2 An example from William Pizer. Adapted from ICF International (2023, p. 85). Income and policy benefits are unweighted and in U.S. dollars. Welfare weights are constructed with the third quintile serving as the reference quintile.

	Lowest quintile	Second	Third	Fourth	Highest quintile	Total weighted benefits	Policy rank by total weighted benefits
Income	14,859.00	41,025.00	70,879.00	115,462.00	269,356.00		
Welfare weight	8.91	2.15	1	0.51	0.15		
Policy I benefits	10	10	10	10	10	127.21	3
Policy II benefits	50	0	0	0	0	445.56	1
Policy III benefits	0	0	0	0	50	7.71	4
Policy IV benefits	25	25	0	0	0	276.53	2
Policy V benefits	31.03	0	0	0	0	276.53	2

the income of individuals in subgroup q, and η denotes the function's (absolute value) of the elasticity of the marginal well-being of income. The draft Circular recommends using 1.4 as the value of η.

(From a theoretical perspective, it is a mistake to focus on income rather than consumption. Individuals derive well-being from their actual consumptions, not from their income, some of which can be saved. Saving converts current consumption opportunities into future consumption opportunities; it therefore does not contribute to current well-being. The report references income because that is the metric for which agencies have the best data. Here I will follow OMB and refer to income rather than consumption. Everything I say will apply also to the theoretically preferred context in which consumption is the focus.)

Suppose now that the five policies listed in Table 8.2 would each be paid for by reducing the income of the individual in the middle of the income distribution (i.e., the individual in the third quintile). Given this assumption, the quintile-specific welfare weights to be applied to policy benefits are listed in the row labeled "Welfare weight." Because the draft guidelines use the same functional form that I used when explaining welfare weights in chapter 2, the guidelines instruct agencies to compute welfare weights using the same method I described in section 2.5, where the context involved consumption inequalities across regions rather than income inequalities across quintiles.[20]

The five policies and their unweighted monetized benefits for the individuals in each quintile are given in the last five rows of Table 8.2. Note that the first four policies all generate $50 in unweighted benefits (and thus all generate an average benefit of $10 per person). The outlier, Policy V, will become relevant when I come to Pizer's third concern with welfare weighting.

Pizer motivates his first concern by observing that Policy II's total weighted benefits exceed Policy IV's total weighted benefits by an average of roughly 34 dollars. By this he means that if one takes the difference between the two policies' total weighted benefits and then divides that difference by 5, one gets roughly 34. Likewise, Policy I exceeds Policy III by roughly 24 weighted dollars per person. Pizer then expresses his concern: "It is not clear how to interpret these numbers or compare them" (ICF International 2023, p. 86).

I agree that it is hard to interpret or compare differences in the metric Pizer asks the reader to focus on—a project's *per-person benefit as denominated in welfare-weighted dollars*. But I do not see why that metric

---

[20] See in particular the welfare weights that feature in equation (2.15). Cf. OMB (2023a, p. 65n114).

should be considered meaningful over and above its relation to a project's *total* welfare-weighted dollar benefit. That total enables one to compare the project's benefits with its costs to determine whether the project offers a net increase in total well-being. By using the third quintile as the reference quintile, the weights in Table 8.2 can facilitate a cost-benefit test in which any unweighted costs for the third-quintile individual are subtracted from the total weighted benefits. Suppose, for example, that each project would cost this individual (and only this individual) $130. In that case, Table 8.2 tells us that while Policies II and IV would both increase overall well-being, Policies I and Policy III would each *reduce* overall well-being.

Thus one useful way to interpret the total weighted benefits listed in Table 8.2 is as *break-even levels*: if a given project had costs for the individual in the third quintile that were equal to that project's total weighted benefits, then the project would neither increase nor decrease the amount of well-being in the world. So to rank different policies with respect to their net welfare-weighted dollar benefits is to rank them in terms of their relative capacities for increasing well-being in the world. Beyond that, I do not see what additional meaning or significance Pizer might want these numbers to possess.

Consider now an altered version of Pizer's example, which is given in Table 8.3. The welfare weights in this second version have been constructed using the *highest income quintile* as the reference quintile.

Note first that the values listed in the "Total weighted benefits" column of Table 8.3 differ from the counterpart values in Table 8.2. This is because the weights also differ, to account for the change in the reference quintile. For precisely this reason, a recent effort to calculate the social cost of methane found that the figure was $8,290 when the reference region was the United States, whereas it was just $134 when it was sub-Saharan Africa (Errickson et al. 2021, p. 569).[21] The implication is that the average American would lose as much well-being if she had to pay $8,290 in abatement costs as the average individual in sub-Saharan Africa would lose if she had to pay $134.

Second, observe that while the two tables differ in the *values* reported under "Total weighted benefits," the tables' respective *rankings* of the policies by their total weighted benefits are the same. Here is a sense in which an "average weighted benefits" metric is relevant: holding population size

---

[21] Errickson et al. (2021)'s calculation assumed that $\eta = 1$.

Table 8.3 The same example as in Table 8.2, but with welfare weights now constructed using the highest quintile as the reference quintile.

	Lowest quintile	Second	Third	Fourth	Highest quintile	Total weighted benefits	Policy rank by total weighted benefits
Income	14,859.00	41,025.00	70,879.00	115,462.00	269,356.00		
Welfare weight	57.77	13.94	6.48	3.27	1		
Policy I benefits	10	10	10	10	10	824.60	3
Policy II benefits	50	0	0	0	0	2,888.30	1
Policy III benefits	0	0	0	0	50	50.00	4
Policy IV benefits	25	25	0	0	0	1,792.59	2
Policy V benefits	31.03	0	0	0	0	1,792.59	2

fixed across policies, this metric will rank policies in the same way as the total weighted benefits metric does. And that ranking conveys the policies' relative capacities to create gross gains in well-being. A policy's capacity to create *net* gains in well-being is of course also a function of the project's costs. But Pizer's concern was how to understand the idea of a project's weighted benefits, not with the concept of a project's costs.

This is a good time to correct a possible misapprehension: although my examples have not involved this possibility, the welfare-weighted brand of cost-benefit analysis does allow for project costs to be spread across individuals in different income or consumption groups. I have been talking as if any project costs will be borne by just one individual (or else equally by all individuals in a given income quintile). Only on this condition can the cost-benefit test subtract total *unweighted* dollar costs from total weighted benefits and be a reliable indicator of a policy's capacity to increase well-being in the world. But if costs will instead be dispersed throughout the population, then *both* group-specific benefits *and* group-specific costs must be welfare-weighted. When this occurs, it does not matter which group is chosen to be the reference group whose income or consumption level features in the formulae underlying the weights. That group's identity matters only when it is the group whose monetary costs and benefits will go unweighted in the calculation. But even that is somewhat misleading, since that group's costs and benefits will actually be weighted by a factor of 1.0.

On November 9, 2023, OMB released its finalized update to Circular A-4. In a companion document subtitled "Explanation and Response to Public Input," OMB wrote:

> One commenter opposing the use of weights that account for diminishing marginal utility argued that income-weighted net benefit estimates are difficult to interpret. OMB disagrees. Income-weighted estimates of net benefits are interpretable as the regulation's effect on total welfare, where welfare is denominated in units of dollars for the median American. By contrast, traditional net benefit estimates—though now familiar—are in fact more difficult to interpret. Kaldor-Hicks efficiency estimates of net benefits roughly (i.e., ignoring the Scitovsky paradox, etc.) represent the amount of dollars that could be hypothetically transferred from the winners of a regulatory change to the losers of the regulatory change, up to the point where the winners become indifferent to the change . . . The interpretation of traditionally-weighted estimates of net benefits is at least, in OMB's view,

less straightforward than consistently income-weighted estimates of net benefits. (OMB 2023d, p. 45)

This is a landmark passage. To my knowledge, it represents the very first time the U.S. federal government has published remarks critical of the Kaldor-Hicks methodology. And while it directly concerns only Pizer's claim that welfare-weighted estimates are difficult to interpret—with OMB disagreeing with Pizer—the passage also cites one of the serious problems for Kaldor-Hicks-based cost-benefit analysis that I discussed in section 3.15, namely the Scitovsky paradox. This willingness to criticize Kaldor-Hicks and to endorse alternative bases for federal cost-benefit analysis constitutes immense progress by the U.S. government.

8.2.3.3 Welfare weighting "presumes a particular distribution of costs and benefits is best."

The second problem Pizer raises concerns "whether equity weighting would rank policies in the way that society would desire." He believes it would not, because welfare-weighted cost-benefit analysis "tends to become dominated by distributional concerns that favor giving all the benefits to the poorest while implying very specific trade-offs." In contrast, Pizer observes, even President Biden's historic Justice40 initiative seeks to steer only a significant *portion*—namely 40 percent—of climate policies' benefits to low-income marginalized communities. "Notably [Justice40] does not suggest that increasing the direction of all net benefits to the very poor is desired," Pizer writes (ICF International 2023, p. 86). Pizer seems to be claiming that welfare weighting is problematic because it ignores non-utilitarian values and principles that many believe are relevant to climate policy and to public policy more generally.

This line of criticism is misplaced, as I explained in Part II. The results of welfare-weighted cost-benefit analysis need not mirror actual societal preferences, nor the policy preferences of moral philosophers. To be useful, the results need only tell us something normatively important about the policy issue at hand. And welfare-weighted cost-benefit analysis does that: it tells us about a policy's impact on overall well-being. That normative dimension is relevant and important to study, even if it is not the whole story and thus even if it must be combined with other relevant considerations in a more holistic form of policy analysis. To use the language of Part II, Pizer ignores the possibility that welfare weighting can facilitate a useful evaluative analysis that is nevertheless self-consciously normatively abridged.[22]

Pizer admits that "[a]n emphasis on distributional outcomes is important," and that Kaldor-Hicks-based cost-benefit analysis is insensitive to distributional considerations (ICF International 2023, pp. 86, 85). But he does not recommend against using the Kaldor-Hicks version. Moreover, he correctly emphasizes "that recognizing declining marginal utility of income is not the same as deciding that maximizing (arithmetic) average utility is the societal goal" (ICF International 2023, p. 86). So by rejecting welfare-weighted cost-benefit analysis but not its Kaldor-Hicks counterpart, Pizer is actually rejecting one normatively abridged version of cost-benefit analysis for another. But if he is not entirely hostile to normatively abridged evaluation, why does Pizer caution against welfare-weighted cost-benefit analysis? Is it again because he finds welfare-weighted cost and benefit numbers too hard to interpret?

I do not think so. I think Pizer has another reason, to which I now turn.

8.2.3.4 Welfare weighting can "easily dominate the analysis."

Pizer's final concern is actually the concern he raises first in his peer review. It is that welfare weighting allows policies' distributional effects to "easily dominate what might be other (total benefit) differences among policies" (ICF International 2023, p. 86). To see what he means, compare Policy V with Policies I, III, and IV in Tables 8.2 and 8.3. Take first Policy IV and Policy V. Although these two policies offer the same amount of total *weighted* benefits, Pizer observes that Policy IV offers nearly $19 more in "total benefits," by which he means $19 more in unweighted willingness to pay. Likewise, although Policy III ranks higher than Policy V in terms of what Pizer calls "total benefits," Policy V ranks well above Policy III in terms of *weighted* benefits. The same is true of the comparison between Policy I and Policy V. Indeed, if the welfare weights are constructed using the richest quintile as the reference quintile, then a project that gives $1,000 only to that quintile will be equivalent in welfare-weighted terms to a project that gives $17.31 only to the poorest quintile. Pizer's worry is that welfare-weighted cost-benefit analysis conceals this vast difference in total unweighted benefits.

---

[22] In this respect Pizer's argument is similar to the argument of Harberger's that I criticized in section 5.6.

This was a common complaint among other peer reviewers as well. Glenn Blomquist, for example, writes:

> The second reason [not to use welfare weights in the primary analysis] is to preserve the core of benefit-cost analysis that has provided crucial information about allocative efficiency effects of regulations. It may be the sole source of information about overall efficiency in the policy process. The primary net benefit estimate should be based on this core analysis. This core benefit-cost analysis is the regulatory analysis that has survived more than forty years under seven different presidents. Mixing analysis that weights net benefits based on analyst-specified values risks the integrity of the BCA that has made it useful. (ICF International 2023, p. 19)

And Joseph Cordes writes:

> The acknowledged purpose of benefit cost analysis is to assess whether a particular policy change, such as a government regulation, enhances economic efficiency. While, from a welfare-analytic perspective, government regulations should be both economically efficient, and have desirable (or at least acceptable) distributional outcomes, the two objectives are distinct. The public interest is best served by presenting separate impacts of regulation on efficiency and equity rather than by attempting to combine the effects in a single weighted benefit-cost measure. (ICF International 2023, p. 51)

Rather than ignore the importance of normative abridgement, Pizer, Blomquist, and Cordes are asserting it. They are claiming that the dimension of "total unweighted benefits" is so important that it must be evaluated and reported on separately. Note that this view is entirely consistent with the view that total welfare-weighted benefits constitute a second, normatively relevant evaluative dimension. So the issue ultimately comes down to the question of whether these peer reviewers are correct that a policy's total unweighted benefit really is an important policy consideration. Of course we know that it cannot be important as an indicator of a policy's total well-being, since it studiously ignores the diminishing marginal well-being of consumption. So in the end, it can be important only as an indicator of what Blomquist and Cordes refer to as a policy's "efficiency," by which they mean "potential Pareto efficiency." But I have already rehearsed the severe problems raised by this evaluative concept, and none of these reviewers seeks to rebut them.[23] Contra Cordes, it is simply not true that "the purpose" of cost-benefit analysis is to assess a policy's potential Pareto efficiency. That is the purpose of only one brand of cost-benefit analysis, and it is a brand that rests on intolerably unstable ground.

8.2.3.5 "There is no empirical evidence for interpersonal comparisons of well-being."

The final objection to welfare weighting that I will examine is related to the well-being function's elasticity parameter. OMB claims that this parameter can be calibrated empirically "from a survey of empirical evidence regarding risk aversion, self-reported happiness measures, the elasticity of intertemporal substitution [i.e., individuals' preferences for smoothing consumption over time], and the income elasticity of the value of statistical life (VSL)" (OMB 2023d, p. 50). All of these bases, except perhaps for the self-reported happiness measures, bottom out in people's preferences.

OMB acknowledges that welfare-weighted cost-benefit analysis requires that well-being be measurable on a cardinal scale (OMB 2023d, pp. 47–48). In defending this assumption, OMB principally cites theorems from expected utility theory that state the conditions under which individuals' preference orderings of lotteries can be represented by a cardinal utility function (OMB 2023d, p. 48). Now, when an individual's preferences can be represented by such a function, that fact licenses the following sort of inference: if the individual prefers outcome x to outcome y, and also y to z, then if the difference between the utilities of x and y is equal to the difference between the utilities of y and z, the individual is indifferent between getting y for sure and facing a lottery in which she gets x if a fair coin lands on heads and z if it lands on tails. Suppose all individuals' preferences can be represented with cardinal utility functions. Is that enough for welfare-weighting?

It is not. As I explained in section 2.2, social choice climate economics, which includes welfare-weighted cost-benefit analysis, requires both that well-being be cardinally measurable *and* that individuals' well-being functions be interpersonally comparable. And several peer reviewers correctly raised concerns about OMB's entitlement to make that second assumption (ICF International 2023, pp. 18, 52, 57, 106). As I explained in section 3.4, the utility functions constructed and used in most empirical

---

[23] See in particular section 3.15.

economic modeling are intended only to represent individuals' preference orderings, not the ordering of outcomes and lotteries in terms of a person's *well-being*. Well-being is a substantive philosophical notion that is simply not relevant to many exercises in contemporary welfare economics. But even if one makes the philosophical assumption (as I think OMB does) that well-being is nothing over and above preference satisfaction, the assumption of interpersonal comparability requires a further philosophical rationale. It is not simply entailed by the fact (if it is a fact) that individuals' preferences over lotteries obey the expected utility axioms. At best that gives us cardinality, and interpersonal comparability is something else entirely.

OMB gets close to giving such a rationale when it writes:

> OMB agrees that the appropriate default assumption is that individuals are similar to one another, and therefore observed evidence on the income elasticity of marginal utility is best explained by commonalities in the diminishing marginal utility of income (absent a persuasive and evidence-backed alternative explanation). (OMB 2023d, p. 47)

I too invoked premises about human similarity in section 4.3.2 to support the claim that interpersonal comparisons of well-being are possible. But the kind of premise I referred to was, again, a substantive philosophical judgment about what makes a life go well. OMB wants to avoid such commitments and to instead infer conclusions about well-being from people's revealed preferences over lotteries. I agree with the peer reviewers that OMB's discussion and treatment of this issue is inadequate.

One way to proceed—and to proceed "descriptively"—would be to convene demographically representative focus groups whose task would be to rank various consumption lotteries in terms of which lotteries are best from the standpoint of promoting an individual's well-being. Philosophers of economics could be enlisted to explain the point of the exercise, why the expected utility framework is relevant to it, and why the assumption of interpersonal comparability is so important. Economists could then structure the elicitation exercise so that the expected utility axioms are obeyed, with violations (e.g., intransitive rankings) flagged for reconsideration and reevaluation by the group. An approach like this would not only address the peer reviewers' concern about interpersonal comparisons, but it would also address one peer reviewer's worry that the use of welfare weights forces policy analysts to sacrifice "scientific objectivity" (ICF International 2023,

p. 19). It would do this by acknowledging that welfare weighting invokes inherently philosophical assumptions, while at the same time putting the philosophical onus on a representative group of community members, rather than on the analysts themselves.

Designing and deploying such focus groups would certainly be more time intensive than consulting the econometric literature on revealed risk-aversion. But I believe it is work OMB should undertake nonetheless.[24]

8.2.4 Discounting, Revisited

In its Preamble to the April 2023 draft update to Circular A-4, OMB wrote:

> The primary argument for the use of a descriptive approach [to discounting] in the context of benefit-cost analysis is that it enables policymakers "to base resource allocation on the tradeoffs that society actually makes." (OMB 2023b, p. 18)

Although I think it is reasonable to calibrate the necessary well-being function descriptively using focus groups, there is a serious problem with OMB's call for a thoroughgoing descriptivism in the context of discounting. In defending its stance on welfare weighting, OMB said the job of welfare-weighted cost-benefit analysis is to assess a "regulation's effect on total welfare" (OMB 2023d, p. 45). And it emphasized this interpretation when rebutting Pizer's charge that to endorse welfare weighting is to endorse utilitarian public policy: OMB replied, correctly, that an agency can be interested in understanding a policy's impact on overall well-being without committing itself to the view that maximizing well-being is the only proper

---

[24] Nesje et al. (2023) present results from a survey of philosophers asking for their own considered judgments about how to calibrate the parameters of the Ramsey formula (i.e., equation (2.10)), as well as the growth rate of per capita consumption. The authors then compare philosophers' answers to the answers given by economists in a previous survey (Drupp et al. 2018). I was one of the philosophers who was invited to participate, but I respectfully declined. I did so because I did not think that many philosophers or economists heed the important distinctions I have sought to clarify in this book. That includes the distinction between social choice and general equilibrium climate economics, as well as the distinction between normatively abridged and unabridged orderings of intertemporal paths of well-being. I therefore did not think that the submitted answers could be interpreted reliably or compared meaningfully. Of course, I do not think that members of a citizen focus group should be taught all of the material from this book before they are asked to participate in the ranking exercise I describe in the text. But I do think that some degree of expert facilitation could ensure that the focus group results really do address the philosophical questions at issue.

aim of public policy. But then what would happen if OMB asserted this same stance in the context of discounting future well-being?

I answered this question in section 5.5: if an evaluation is concerned to rank policies solely with respect to their ability to improve the world by adding well-being to it, then there is no good reason for pure time discounting. A policy that would reduce well-being by one unit today and increase it by $1 + \varepsilon$ units next year is a policy that would increase the amount of well-being in the world, so long as ε is positive. This fact remains true even if people or governments display temporal impatience about well-being in their own decision-making. The "tradeoffs that society actually makes" are one thing; the impact that policies actually make on well-being is another. If—as OMB insists—welfare-weighted cost-benefit analysis need not rank policies in accordance with society's policy preferences concerning the distribution of well-being, then why must welfare-weighed cost-benefit analysis reflect the intertemporal trade-offs that society actually makes?

The one answer I find in OMB's discussion is this: OMB wishes to "establish an objective evidentiary basis for the specific parameters the government uses when developing the analytical basis for policymaking" (OMB 2023b, p. 19). This impulse is understandable; government officials do not want agency analyses to reflect the personal values and preferences of those who will perform the analysis. It is reasonable to want more objectivity than that. Still, the first question that analysts should ask is, "Which parameters do we need to select values for?" I have agreed that cost-benefit analysts need to set parameter values for the well-being function that is used to perform welfare weighting. And I have suggested that these values should be chosen democratically, on the basis of dialogue with citizen focus groups. But when it comes to the other normative parameter that features in the Ramsey formula for consumption discount rates, namely the pure time discount rate, it is a mistake to think that it should be anything other than zero. This is *not* because public policy should adopt a strong future-oriented stance—perhaps it should, perhaps it should not. Rather, it is because welfare-weighted cost-benefit analysis concerns the degree to which different policies improve the world by contributing well-being to it. And if *that* is its task, then to use a positive pure time discount rate is to produce a warped picture of a policy's capacity to perform along the relevant evaluative dimension. For this reason, OMB should have required agencies to use a pure time discount rate of zero.

As I noted in section 4.2, a pure time discount rate of zero is problematic when an analysis's time horizon is infinite. To my knowledge, no federal cost-benefit analysis has ever adopted an infinite time horizon. The EPA's updated SCC estimates used a time horizon of 2020–2300 (EPA 2023, p. 77n130). And in its 2017 report on updating the federal government's SCC methodology, the National Academies said only that the time horizon should "extend far enough in the future to provide inputs for estimation of the vast majority of discounted climate damages" (NAS 2017, p. 10). So it is very possible this issue with an infinite time horizon will not arise in practice.

But even if it does arise, it would remain ethically unacceptable to treat a unit of well-being next year (or in a hundred years) as contributing less to total welfare than is contributed by a unit of well-being today. If the aim of the analysis is to assess policies' impacts on total welfare, then welfare should be totaled; it should not be discounted and then totaled. If it cannot be totaled for technical reasons, then of course that is a problem, but it is a problem that must not be solved on the backs of future people whose well-being contributes just as much to the overall goodness of an outcome as the well-being of present people.

8.2.5 The Future of Federal SCCs in the United States

As of this writing, there has been no word from the Interagency Working Group on Social Costs of Greenhouse Gases since February 2021, when it updated the Obama-era SCC figures to account for inflation. At that time, IWG's headline SCC estimate for a ton of CO_2 emitted in 2020 was $51 (IWG 2021, p. 5). Since then, EPA released its own comprehensive SCC update, which underwent external peer review in the summer of 2023 (Versar Inc. 2023) and was finalized without changes in November 2023 (EPA 2023). EPA's "central" SCC estimate for 2020 is now $190, which is more than 3.7 times higher than IWG's figure. In light of the radio silence from IWG, it appears possible that EPA's estimates will serve as the de facto figures for the entire federal government.

As we have seen, EPA did not use welfare-weighted cost-benefit analysis in its comprehensive SCC update. Instead, it restated its long-standing commitment to the Kaldor-Hicks brand of cost-benefit analysis, which was independently endorsed in 2021 in a scholarly venue by the director of EPA's National Center for Environmental Economics (McGartland 2021). Meanwhile, only one peer reviewer of EPA's updated methodology recommended that EPA consider the use of welfare weights in future SCC computations (Versar Inc. 2023, pp. 143, 151–153).[25] Indeed no other peer reviewer even mentioned the topic of welfare weighting. Thus despite OMB's recent embrace of welfare weighting, it is possible that federal agencies in the United States will, for the foreseeable future, have access only to non-weighted SCC figures. That is too bad.

8.3 Carbon Taxes and Climate Targets

When it comes to the selection of climate targets and the setting of carbon prices, I have somewhat less to say. I have sought to distinguish between two optimal SCC concepts, one stemming from social choice climate economics and one from general equilibrium climate economics. A central conclusion of Part II was this: although optimal social choice SCCs might give us information concerning marginal abatement costs along the consumption path that best promotes overall well-being, that path may be very different from the path public policy ought to aim at. I also said that it seems to me difficult to know exactly how to combine the objective of promoting overall well-being with other reasonable policy objectives. Since I personally find philosophical utilitarianism overly demanding and too insensitive to individual rights, I do not believe public policy should strive simply to maximally promote the aggregate of intertemporal well-being. But this is not a book on political philosophy and I have not sought to defend these views against reasonable criticism. So here I merely register my hesitation about shaping public policy in response to optimal social choice SCC figures. I hope I have explained the sense in which these are "optimal" SCCs, and why policymakers should not be beguiled into thinking they are touchstones for ethically responsible climate policy.[26]

Anyway, the world has largely shunned that way of setting climate policy targets. The historic Paris Agreement adopted the alternative goal of

> Holding the increase in the global average temperature to well below 2 °C above pre-industrial levels and to pursue efforts to limit the temperature increase to 1.5 °C above pre-industrial levels, recognizing that

---

[25] That peer reviewer was the climate economist Gernot Wagner.
[26] They should also avoid being beguiled for a second reason I have already mentioned: contemporary SCC figures entirely fail to capture many important categories of climate damage.

this would significantly reduce the risks and impacts of climate change. (COP 2015, p. 2)

Each of these temperature targets implies its own *carbon budget*—the amount of greenhouse gases that can be emitted into the atmosphere without overshooting the target (IPCC 2018, p. 12). Climate scientists cannot know for certain what these budgets are, but they can specify what remains of carbon budgets that would give the world a decent chance of staying under the chosen threshold (Lamboll et al. 2023).

Another non-optimizing concept that is implied by a temperature target is a *net-zero date*. Scientists have known for a while that stabilizing global temperatures requires net zero CO_2 emissions (Matthews and Caldeira 2008). And at least since the IPCC's special report *Global Warming of 1.5°C* (IPCC 2018), which detailed the severe risks to humans and ecosystems associated with warming greater than 1.5 degrees above the pre-industrial average, the international community has increasingly rallied around the goal of reaching net-zero CO_2 emissions round about the middle of this century. With this exogenous, internationally salient target in mind, Kaufman et al. (2020) modeled the carbon prices that would be required in the near term to place the United States on straight-line pathways to net-zero CO_2 emissions by three different target dates. They found that near-term carbon prices "in 2025 of US$32, US$52, and US$93 per metric ton (in 2018 dollars) [are required] for consistency with net-zero targets in 2060, 2050, and 2040, respectively" (p. 1012). Moreover, "more stringent and successful complementary policies (that is, air quality regulations that lead to higher coal retirements, more aggressive energy efficiency measures, and more aggressive early-stage deployment support for certain low-carbon technologies) lowered the CO_2 prices by US$10–US$20 per ton" (p. 1012).

Kaufman et al. (2020) begin from the view that climate policy need not—indeed should not—strive to "perfectly balanc[e] costs and benefits" (p. 1013). I have defended that view myself, at least in the context of social choice climate economics. But my reasons have been different. Like many other climate economists, Kaufman et al. are impressed by the wide range of uncertainty in published SCC studies—a range running from negative values to over $2,000 (p. 1010). This range reflects empirical uncertainties about baseline trajectories, climatic dynamics, and annual monetized impacts, as well as theoretical uncertainties concerning discount rates and the treatment of risk. Another prominent economist has cited these same uncertainties to conclude that integrated assessment models are "close to useless as tools for policy analysis" (Pindyck 2013, p. 860). Yet even if we can resolve all of these uncertainties, I have argued that social choice optimal SCCs are radically normatively abridged and, therefore, that it may be ethically irresponsible to focus singlemindedly on balancing abatement costs against these SCCs. Such a focus risks ignoring ethically relevant considerations that are (or ought to be) excluded from welfarist social choice frameworks—considerations like rights, justice, fairness, and the intrinsic value of nature.

For its part, the world community has been principally motivated not by achieving an optimal balance of costs and benefits, but by precautionary concerns about catastrophic risks. And these concerns are growing stronger by the year. I think there is no chance the international community is going to replace this target-based approach to climate policy with one grounded in the aim of maximizing intertemporal well-being by balancing social choice SCCs and marginal abatement costs. For all these reasons, I do not think the concept of an optimal social choice social cost of carbon is an important concept for climate policy.

What about the goal of exactly balancing unweighted costs and unweighted benefits of abatement in a general equilibrium context? Here I am more open-minded. We know from chapter 3 that a balance of this sort is required for Pareto efficiency in the presence of pollution externalities. We also know (from the same chapter) that optimal general equilibrium SCCs equal the carbon taxes that are needed, along with suitable transfers, to support Pareto efficient allocations in a decentralized fashion: each intertemporally Pareto efficient allocation is associated with its own time-series of GE-OPT SCCs, which in turn gives the time-series of pollution taxes needed to support that allocation. With this result in hand, one could then use Negishi's method (from section 3.11) to calculate the carbon taxes and transfers associated with Pareto efficient allocations that are Pareto superior to our current inefficient baseline. This establishes an important connection between the concept of an optimal general equilibrium SCC and Pareto-improving climate policy.[27]

---

[27] One does not have to use Negishi's method to compute Pareto-improving prices and transfers. His method computes an economy's competitive equilibrium by varying Pareto weights in a schematic character function until the implied prices associated with an efficient allocation leave all individuals with final consumptions that are equal in market value (at those prices) to the market value of their endowments. An alternative *excess demand* approach varies prices until aggregate excess demand is zero in all markets. In this second approach, one assumes that consumer budgets balance, and then varies prices until supply equals demand. In Negishi's approach, one assumes market

The economist Duncan Foley and the moral philosopher John Broome have long stressed the fact that much greenhouse gas mitigation can be Pareto-improving, if compensating intertemporal transfers are actually carried out (Foley 2009; Broome 2010, 2012, ch. 3; Broome and Foley 2016). While this is an intriguing prospect—Broome calls it "the very most important thing about climate change" (Broome 2010, p. 102)—Broome is very clear that it is not without ethical blemish. He explains:

> [Pareto-improving climate policy] has the further, serious demerit that it is unjust. Under business as usual emitters benefit from emitting greenhouse gas, at the expense of receivers. Under [Pareto-improving climate policy] emitters are paid to reduce their emissions by the receivers. Receivers in effect bribe emitters not to harm them. This benefits both emitters and receivers, but only relative to the initial unjust state of business as usual. [Pareto-improving climate policy] perpetuates the injustice. (Broome 2012, p. 46)

Pareto-improving climate policy requires those who suffer the harms of climate change—the future "receivers"—to pay those of us today—the present emitters—who are causing the harm in the first place. Even if this is feasible, and even if everyone's situation would be improved if future generations shouldered the costs of present mitigation, the ethically superior policy might be for us to just stop causing harm. Broome agrees. But he worries that meaningful climate action will not occur unless it is made to be in the self-interest of fossil fuel companies and their investors.

If Broome is right about this, and if policymakers agree, then for the purposes of crafting Pareto-improving legislation and treaties, it will be optimal general equilibrium SCC figures that are relevant. This is significant in part because GE-OPT SCCs raise none of the philosophical issues I grappled with in Part II.[28] If one hopes to get the whole world on board with a climate target that has been computed using a policy optimization IAM, it is better for the IAM's objective function to be an empirically

---

clearance, and varies the weights (and thus the prices) until consumer budgets balance. See Mas-Colell et al. (1995, p. 631). For a quantitative analysis of Pareto-improving climate policy that uses the excess demand method, see Kotlikoff et al. (2021).

[28] Broome also makes this point; see Broome (2018, p. 240).

tractable general equilibrium character function than a philosophically knotty social choice social welfare function.[29]

Broome and Foley admit that to engineer the unprecedented intergenerational transfers required for Pareto-improving climate policy, "there needs to be a major development in the international financial system. We need a new financial institution, a World Climate Bank" (Broome and Foley 2016, p. 157). I do not know whether pushing for a World Climate Bank would be a responsible use of political capital in the world as it exists today. Evaluating that proposition would require a foray into political science and political philosophy that I cannot undertake here. But if it *is* true that substantial mitigation can be had without anyone's making a sacrifice, and if a social cost of carbon concept is part of the story of how this is possible, then perhaps there are good reasons after all to introduce at least one SCC as "the most important number you have never heard of."

---

[29] There is, however, a serious philosophical issue that must be addressed before one can conclude that general equilibrium SCCs capture future people's willingness to pay for abatement in the present. The problem has to do with the fact that our decisions in the present affect the identifies of those who will be born in the future. This means that any person in the far future who will experience climate impacts would not have existed if we had substantially curbed our emissions in, say, 1995. This is because the policies that would have reduced emissions that much also would have changed the world enough to change who procreated with whom, and when. In light of this, it is not clear that future individuals would be willing to pay much at all to induce us to abate our emissions, since significant abatement now would guarantee *those* individuals' non-existence in the future. Kelleher (2015) and Broome (2018) state the problem more fully, and Broome (2018) presents what I think is the right solution to adopt within general equilibrium climate economics.

References

Acemoglu, D. 2009. *Introduction to Modern Economic Growth*, Princeton, NJ: Princeton University Press.

Ackerman, F., and Stanton, E. A. 2010. *The Social Cost of Carbon: A Report for the Economics for Equity and the Environment Network*, Cambridge, MA: Economics for Equity and the Environment Network.

Adler, M. D. 2008. "Future Generations: A Prioritarian View," *The George Washington Law Review* (77), p. 1478.

Adler, M. D. 2012. *Well-Being and Fair Distribution: Beyond Cost-Benefit Analysis*, New York: Oxford University Press.

Adler, M. D. 2016. "Extended Preferences," in *The Oxford Handbook of Well-Being and Public Policy*, M. D. Adler and M. Fleurbaey (eds.), Oxford: Oxford University Press, pp. 476–517.

Adler, M. D. 2019. *Measuring Social Welfare*, Oxford: Oxford University Press, p. 336.

Adler, M. D. 2020. "What Should We Spend to Save Lives in a Pandemic? A Critique of the Value of Statistical Life," *Covid Economics* (33), pp. 1–45.

Adler, M. D., Hammitt, J. K., and Treich, N. 2014. "The Social Value of Mortality Risk Reduction: VSL versus the Social Welfare Function Approach," *Journal of Health Economics* (35), pp. 82–93.

Adler, M. D., and Posner, E. A. 2006. *New Foundations of Cost-Benefit Analysis*, Cambridge, MA: Harvard University Press.

Adler, M. D., and Treich, N. 2015. "Prioritarianism and Climate Change," *Environmental & Resource Economics* (62:2), pp. 279–308.

Anderson, E. S. 1999. "What Is the Point of Equality," *Ethics* (109:2), pp. 287–337.

Anthoff, D., Tol, R. S., and Yohe, G. 2009. "Discounting for Climate Change," *Economics: The Open-Access, Open-Assessment E-Journal* (Vol. 3). https://www.degruyter.com/document/doi/10.5018/economics-ejournal.ja.2009-24/pdf.

Armstrong, A. 2017. "Trump Administration Drops Social Cost of Carbon from $51 to $1," *S&P Global Marketplace Intelligence*. https://platform.mi.spglobal.com/web/client?auth=inherit#news/article?id=42286458&cdid=A-42286458-11818.

Arrhenius, G. 2000a. "Future Generations: A Challenge for Moral Theory," Ph.D. thesis, Acta Universitatis Upsaliensis.

Arrhenius, G. 2000b. "An Impossibility Theorem for Welfarist Axiologies," *Economics & Philosophy* (16:2), pp. 247–266.

Arrhenius, G., Budolfson, M., and Spears, Dean. 2021. "Does Climate Change Policy Depend Importantly on Population Ethics? Deflationary Responses to the Challenges of Population Ethics for Public Policy," in *Philosophy and Climate Change*, M. Budolfson, T. McPherson, and D. Plunkett (eds.), Oxford: Oxford University Press, pp. 111–136.

Arrow, K. J. 1950. "A Difficulty in the Concept of Social Welfare," *Journal of Political Economy* (58:4), pp. 328–346.

Arrow, K. J. 1951. *Social Change and Individual Values*, New York: John Wiley & Sons.

Arrow, K. J. 1995. *Intergenerational Equity and the Rate of Discount in Long-Term Social Investment*, Unpublished paper presented to IEA World Congress.

Arrow, K. J. 1999. "Discounting, Morality, and Gaming," in *Discounting and Intergenerational Equity*, P. R. Portney and J. P. Weyant (eds.), New York: Resources for the Future, pp. 13–21.

Arrow, K. J. 2012. *Social Choice and Individual Values: Third Edition*, New Haven, CT: Yale University Press.

Arrow, K. J., and Hahn, F. H. 1983. *General Competitive Analysis*, Amsterdam: Elsevier Science.
Arrow, K., Cline, W., Maler, K., Munasinghe, M., Squitieri, R., and Stiglitz, J. 1996. "Intertemporal Equity, Discounting, and Economic Efficiency," in *Climate Change 1995: Economic and Social Dimensions of Climate Change: Contribution of Working Group III to the Second Assessment Report of the Intergovernmental Panel on Climate Change*, J. P. Bruce, H. Lee, and E. F. Haites (eds.), Cambridge: Cambridge University Press, pp. 127–144.
Asheim, G. B. 2010. *Justifying, Characterizing and Indicating Sustainability* (Vol. 3), Dordrecht: Springer Science+Business Media.
Asheim, G. B. 2012. "Discounting While Treating Generations Equally," *Climate Change and Common Sense: Essays in Honour of Tom Schelling*, Robert W. Hahn and Alistair Ulph (eds.), Oxford: Oxford University Press, pp. 131–146.
Atkinson, A. B. 1970. "On the Measurement of Inequality," *Journal of Economic Theory* (2:3), pp. 244–263.
Auffhammer, M. 2017. *Social Cost of Carbon* (video). https://www.youtube.com/watch?v=BNdS1o2GoPQ.
Baumstark, L., Bauer, N., Benke, F., Bertram, C., Bi, S., Gong, C. C., Dietrich, J. P., Dirnaichner, A., Giannousakis, A., and Hilaire, J. 2021. "REMIND2. 1: Transformation and Innovation Dynamics of the Energy-Economic System within Climate and Sustainability Limits," *Geoscientific Model Development* (14:10), pp. 6571–6603.
Beckerman, W., and Hepburn, C. 2007. "Ethics of the Discount Rate in the Stern Review on the Economics of Climate Change," *World Economics* (8:1), pp. 187–210.
Bewley, T. F. 2009. *General Equilibrium, Overlapping Generations Models, and Optimal Growth Theory*, Cambridge, MA: Harvard University Press.
Blackorby, C., Bossert, W., and Donaldson, D. J. 2005. *Population Issues in Social Choice Theory, Welfare Economics, and Ethics* (Vol. 39), Cambridge: Cambridge University Press.
Blackorby, C., and Donaldson, D. 1990. "A Review Article: The Case against the Use of the Sum of Compensating Variations in Cost-Benefit Analysis," *The Canadian Journal of Economics/Revue Canadienne d'Economique* (23:3), pp. 471–494.
Boadway, R. W. 1974. "The Welfare Foundations of Cost-Benefit Analysis," *The Economic Journal* (84:336), pp. 926–939.
Boadway, R. W., and Bruce, N. 1984. *Welfare Economics*, Oxford: Basil Blackwell.
Bossert, W., and Weymark, J. A. 2004. "Utility in Social Choice," in *Handbook of Utility Theory: Volume 2 Extensions*, Salvador Barberà, Peter J. Hammond, and Christian Seidl (eds.), New York: Springer Science+Business Media, pp. 1099–1177.
Brennan, G. 2008. "Lessons for Ethics from Economics?" *Philosophical Issues* (18), pp. 249–271.
Bressler, R. D. 2021. "The Mortality Cost of Carbon," *Nature Communications* (12:1), p. 4467.
Bressler, R. D., and Heal, G. 2022. *Valuing Excess Deaths Caused by Climate Change*, NBER Working Paper 30648, November. https://www.nber.org/papers/w30648.
Bressler, R. D., Moore, F. C., Rennert, K., and Anthoff, D. 2021. "Estimates of Country Level Temperature-Related Mortality Damage Functions," *Scientific Reports* (11:1), p. 20282.
Broome, J. 1990. "Bolker-Jeffrey Expected Utility Theory and Axiomatic Utilitarianism," *The Review of Economic Studies* (57:3), pp. 477–502.
Broome, J. 1991. *Weighing Goods: Equality, Uncertainty and Time*, Oxford: Basil Blackwell.
Broome, J. 1992. *Counting the Costs of Global Warming*, Cambridge, UK: White Horse Press.
Broome, J. 1994. "Discounting the Future," *Philosophy & Public Affairs* (23:2), pp. 128–156.
Broome, J. 1999a. "Utility," in J. Broome, *Ethics Out of Economics*, Cambridge: Cambridge University Press, pp. 19–28.
Broome, J. 1999b. *Ethics Out of Economics*, Cambridge: Cambridge University Press.
Broome, J. 1999c. "Extended Preferences," in J. Broome, *Ethics Out of Economics*, Cambridge: Cambridge University Press, pp. 29–43.
Broome, J. 2004. *Weighing Lives*, Oxford: Oxford University Press.
Broome, J. 2005. "Should We Value Population," *Journal of Political Philosophy* (12:4), pp. 399–413.

Broome, J. 2008. "The Ethics of Climate Change," *Scientific American* (June), pp. 97–102.
Broome, J. 2010. "The Most Important Thing about Climate Change," in *Public Policy: Why Ethics Matters*, J. Boston, A. Bradstock, and D. Eng (eds.), Canberra: ANU E Press, pp. 101–116.
Broome, J. 2012. *Climate Matters: Ethics in a Warming World*, New York: W. W. Norton & Company.
Broome, J. 2015. "General and Personal Good: Harsanyi's Contribution to the Theory of Value," in *The Oxford Handbook of Value Theory*, I. Hirose and J. Olson (eds.), Oxford: Oxford University Press, pp. 249–266.
Broome, J. 2018. "Efficiency and Future Generations," *Economics & Philosophy* (34), pp. 1–21.
Broome, J. 2019a. "The Well-Being of Future Generations," in *The Oxford Handbook of Ethics and Economics*, M. D. White (ed.), Oxford: Oxford University Press, pp. 901–927.
Broome, J. 2019b. "Lessons from Economics," in *The Oxford Handbook of Ethics and Economics*, M. D. White (ed.), Oxford: Oxford University Press, pp. 583–606.
Broome, J., and Foley, D. 2016. "A World Climate Bank," in *Institutions for Future Generations*, A. Gosseries and I. González-Ricoy (eds.), Oxford: Oxford University Press, pp. 156–169.
Budolfson, M., and Spears, D. 2018. "Why the Repugnant Conclusion Is Inescapable," Unpublished manuscript, December.
Calvin, K., Patel, P., Clarke, L., Asrar, G., Bond-Lamberty, B., Cui, R. Y., Di Vittorio, A., Dorheim, K., Edmonds, J., and Hartin, C. 2019. "GCAM V5. 1: Representing the Linkages between Energy, Water, Land, Climate, and Economic Systems," *Geoscientific Model Development* (12:2), pp. 677–698.
Cass, D. 1965. "Optimum Growth in an Aggregative Model of Capital Accumulation," *The Review of Economic Studies* (32:3), pp. 233–240.
Cline, W. R. 1992. *The Economics of Global Warming*, Washington, D.C.: Institute for International Economics.
Cline, W. R. 1998. "Equity and Discounting in Climate-Change Decisions," in *Economics and Policy Issues in Climate Change*, W. D. Nordhaus (ed.), New York: Resources for the Future, pp. 97–104.
Cline, W. R. 2012. "Intergenerational Discounting and Global Economic Policies," remarks given at the Peterson Institute for International Economics conference Ethics and Globalization: Trade-offs Behind Policy Choices, January 7, Washington, D.C.
Cohen, G. A. 1989. "On the Currency of Egalitarian Justice," *Ethics* (99:4), pp. 906–944.
Conference of the Parties of the UNFCCC (COP). 2015. "Paris Agreement," UN Climate Change. https://unfccc.int/files/meetings/paris_nov_2015/application/pdf/paris_agr eement_english_.pdf.
Creedy, J. 2007. "Policy Evaluation, Welfare Weights and Value Judgements: A Reminder," *Australian Journal of Labour Economics* (10:1), p. 1.
d'Aspremont, C., and Gevers, L. 1977. "Equity and the Informational Basis of Collective Choice," *The Review of Economic Studies* (44:2), pp. 199–209.
Dasgupta, P. 1982. *The Control of Resources*, Cambridge, MA: Harvard University Press.
Dasgupta, P. 2001. *Human Well-Being and the Natural Environment*, Oxford: Oxford University Press.
Dasgupta, P. 2005. "Three Conceptions of Intergenerational Justice," in *Ramsey's Legacy*, H. Lillehammer and D. H. Mellor (eds.), Oxford: Oxford University Press, pp. 149–169.
Dasgupta, P. 2008. "Discounting Climate Change," *Journal of Risk and Uncertainty* (37), pp. 141–169.
Dasgupta, P. 2011. "The Ethics of Intergenerational Distribution: Reply and Response to John E. Roemer," *Environmental and Resource Economics* (50:4), pp. 475–493.
Dasgupta, P. 2012. "Time and the Generations," in *Climate Change and Common Sense*, R. Hahn and A. Ulph (eds.), Oxford: Oxford University Press, pp. 101–130.
Dasgupta, P. 2019. *Time and the Generations: Population Ethics for a Diminishing Planet*, New York: Columbia University Press.

Dasgupta, P., and Heal, G. M. 1979. *Economic Theory and Exhaustible Resources*, Cambridge: Cambridge University Press.

Dasgupta, P., Sen, A., and Marglin, S. 1972. *Guidelines for Project Evaluation*, New York: United Nations.

Deaton, A. 1992. *Understanding Consumption*, Oxford: Oxford University Press.

Debreu, G. 1954. "Representation of a Preference Ordering by a Numerical Function," in *Decision Processes* (Vol. 3), R. M. Thrall, C. H. Coombs, and R. L. Davis (eds.), New York: Wiley, pp. 159–165.

Dennig, F., and Emmerling, J. 2017. "A Note on Optima with Negishi Weights," Unpublished manuscript.

Dietz, S., and Hepburn, C. 2013. "Benefit-Cost Analysis of Non-marginal Climate and Energy Projects," *Energy Economics* (40), pp. 61–71.

Digas, B., Rozenberg, V., and Kuklin, A. 2014. "A New Version of Integrated Assessment Model MERGE," *International Journal of Environmental Research* (8:4), pp. 1231–1240.

Drupp, M. A., Freeman, M. C., Groom, B., and Nesje, F. 2018. "Discounting Disentangled," *American Economic Journal: Economic Policy* (10:4), pp. 109–134.

Dworkin, R. 2000. *Sovereign Virtue: The Theory and Practice of Equality*, Cambridge, MA: Harvard University Press.

Environmental Protection Agency (EPA). 2002. *Technical Addendum: Methodologies for the Benefit Analysis of the Clear Skies Initiative*. https://archive.epa.gov/clearskies/web/pdf/tech_adden.pdf.

Environmental Protection Agency (EPA). 2010. *Guidelines for Preparing Economic Analyses (Appendix A)*. https://www.epa.gov/sites/default/files/2017-08/documents/ee-0568-50.pdf.

Environmental Protection Agency (EPA). 2011. *EPA Science Advisory Board (SAB) Letter to Administrator Jackson on SAB's Review of Valuing Mortality Risk Reductions for Environmental Policy: A White Paper*. https://www.epa.gov/system/files/documents/2022-03/86189901_0.pdf.

Environmental Protection Agency (EPA). 2022. "Report on the Social Cost of Greenhouse Gases: Estimates Incorporating Recent Scientific Advances (External Review Draft)," U.S. Environmental Protection Agency. https://www.epa.gov/system/files/documents/2022-11/epa_scghg_report_draft_0.pdf.

Environmental Protection Agency (EPA). 2023. "EPA Report on the Social Cost of Greenhouse Gases: Estimates Incorporating Recent Scientific Advances," U.S. Environmental Protection Agency. https://www.epa.gov/system/files/documents/2023-12/epa_scghg_2023_report_final.pdf.

Errickson, F. C., Keller, K., Collins, W. D., Srikrishnan, V., and Anthoff, D. 2021. "Equity Is More Important for the Social Cost of Methane Than Climate Uncertainty," *Nature* (592:7855), pp. 564–570.

Executive Office of the President. 2021. "Protecting Public Health and the Environment and Restoring Science to Tackle the Climate Crisis (Executive Order 13990)," *Federal Register* (86 FR 7037), pp. 7037–7043. https://www.govinfo.gov/content/pkg/FR-2021-01-25/pdf/2021-01765.pdf.

Fankhauser, S., Tol, R. S., and Pearce, D. W. 1997. "The Aggregation of Climate Change Damages: A Welfare Theoretic Approach," *Environmental and Resource Economics* (10), pp. 249–266.

Feldman, A. M., and Serrano, R. 2006. *Welfare Economics and Social Choice Theory*, New York: Springer Science+Business Media.

Fleurbaey, M. 2010. "Assessing Risky Social Situations," *Journal of Political Economy* (118:4), pp. 649–680.

Fleurbaey, M. 2015. "Equality versus Priority: How Relevant Is the Distinction," *Economics & Philosophy* (31:2), pp. 203–217.

Foley, D. 2009. "The Economic Fundamentals of Global Warming," in *Twenty-First Century Macroeconomics: Responding to the Climate Challenge*, J. M. Harris and N. R. Goodwin (eds.), Cheltenham: Edward Elgar Publishing, pp. 115–126.

Foley, D. K. 1970. "Lindahl's Solution and the Core of an Economy with Public Goods," *Econometrica: Journal of the Econometric Society* (38:1), pp. 66–72.
Gajdos, T., Weymark, J. A., and Zoli, C. 2010. "Shared Destinies and the Measurement of Social Risk Equity," *Annals of Operations Research* (176:1), pp. 409–424.
Gilboa, I. 2012. *Rational Choice*, Cambridge, MA: MIT Press.
Ginsburgh, V., and Keyzer, M. 2002. *The Structure of Applied General Equilibrium Models*, Cambridge, MA: MIT Press.
Gorman, W. M. 1955. "The Intransitivity of Certain Criteria Used in Welfare Economics," *Oxford Economic Papers* (7:1), pp. 25–34.
Goulder, L. H., and Williams, R. C., III. 2012. "The Choice of Discount Rate for Climate Change Policy Evaluation," *Climate Change Economics* (3:04), p. 1250024-1–1250024-18.
Greaves, H. 2015. "Antiprioritarianism," *Utilitas* (27:1), pp. 1–42.
Greaves, H. 2017a. "Discounting for Public Policy: A Survey," *Economics & Philosophy* (33:3), pp. 391–439.
Greaves, H. 2017b. "Population Axiology," *Philosophy Compass* (12:11), p. e12442.
Hammond, P. 1998. "The Efficiency Theorems and Market Failure," *Elements of General Equilibrium Analysis*, pp. 211–260.
Harberger, A. C. 1978. "On the Use of Distributional Weights in Social Cost-Benefit Analysis," *Journal of Political Economy* (86:2, Part 2), pp. S87–S120.
Harsanyi, J. C. 1953. "Cardinal Utility in Welfare Economics and in the Theory of Risk-Taking," *Journal of Political Economy* (61:5), pp. 434–435.
Harsanyi, J. C. 1955. "Cardinal Welfare, Individualistic Ethics, and Interpersonal Comparisons of Utility," *Journal of Political Economy* (63:4), pp. 309–321.
Harsanyi, J. C. 1977. "Morality and the Theory of Rational Behavior," *Social Research*, pp. 623–656.
Hausman, D. M. 2005. "Review of John Broome's Weighing Lives," *Ethics* (114:445), pp. 718–722.
Hausman, D. M., and Waldren, M. S. 2011. "Egalitarianism Reconsidered," *Journal of Moral Philosophy* (8:4), pp. 567–586.
Heal, G. 1998. *Valuing the Future*, New York: Columbia University Press.
Heal, G. 2005. "Intertemporal Welfare Economics and the Environment," in *Handbook of Environmental Economics* Volume 3, K.-G. Mäler and J. Vincent (eds.), Amsterdam: Elsevier, pp. 1105–1145.
Heal, G. 2009. "The Economics of Climate Change: A Post-Stern Perspective," *Climatic Change* (96:3), pp. 275–297.
Heal, G. M., and Bressler, R. D. 2023. "Public Comment on the EPA External Review Draft of Report on the Social Cost of Greenhouse Gases: Estimates Incorporating Recent Scientific Advances." https://www.regulations.gov/comment/EPA-HQ-OAR-2021-0317-2464.
Hicks, J. R. 1939. "The Foundations of Welfare Economics," *The Economic Journal* (49:196), pp. 696–712.
Hope, C. 2005. "Integrated Assessment Models," in *Climate Change Policy*, D. Helm (ed.), Oxford: Oxford University Press, pp. 77–98.
Howarth, R. B. 1996. "Climate Change and Overlapping Generations," *Contemporary Economic Policy* (14:4), pp. 100–111.
Howarth, R. B. 1998. "An Overlapping Generations Model of Climate-Economy Interactions," *Scandinavian Journal of Economics* (100:3), pp. 575–591.
ICF International. 2023. *External Peer Review for OMB, Proposed OMB Circular No. A-4, "Regulatory Analysis."* https://www.whitehouse.gov/wp-content/uploads/2023/08/A4-Peer-Reviewer-Comments_508c-Final.pdf.
Interagency Working Group on Social Cost of Carbon (IWG). 2010. "Social Cost of Carbon for Regulatory Impact Analysis under Executive Order 12866," Interagency Working Group on Social Cost of Carbon. https://www.epa.gov/sites/default/files/2016-12/documents/scc_tsd_2010.pdf.

Interagency Working Group on Social Cost of Greenhouse Gases (IWG). 2021. *Technical Support Document: Social Cost of Carbon, Methane, and Nitrous Oxide Interim Estimates under Executive Order 13990*. https://www.whitehouse.gov/wp-content/uploads/2021/02/TechnicalSupportDocument_SocialCostofCarbonMethaneNitrousOxide.pdf.

Intergovernmental Panel on Climate Change (IPCC). 2014. "Summary for Policymakers," in *Climate Change 2014: Mitigation of Climate Change. Contribution of Working Group III to the Fifth Assessment Report of the Intergovernmental Panel on Climate Change*, O., R. Pichs-Madruga, Y. Sokona, E. Farahani, S. Kadner, K. Seyboth, A. Adler, I. Baum, S. Brunner, P. Eickemeier, B. Kriemann, J. Savolainen, S. Schlömer, C. von Stechow, T. Zwickel and J.C. Minx (eds.), Cambridge: Cambridge University Press, pp. 1–30.

Intergovernmental Panel on Climate Change (IPCC). 2018. "Summary for Policymakers," in *Global Warming of 1.5°C. An IPCC Special Report on the Impacts of Global Warming of 1.5°C Above Pre-industrial Levels and Related Global Greenhouse Gas Emission Pathways, in the Context of Strengthening the Global Response to the Threat of Climate Change, Sustainable Development, and Efforts to Eradicate Poverty*, V. Masson-Delmotte, P. Zhai, H.-O. P.rtner, D. Roberts, J. Skea, P.R. Shukla, A. Pirani, W. Moufouma-Okia, C. P.an, R. Pidcock, S. Connors, J.B.R. Matthews, Y. Chen, X. Zhou, M.I. Gomis, E. Lonnoy, T. Maycock, M. Tignor, and T. Waterfield (eds.), Cambridge: Cambridge University Press, pp. 3–24.

Johansson, P.-O. 1991. *An Introduction to Modern Welfare Economics*, Cambridge: Cambridge University Press.

Jones, C. 2005. *Applied Welfare Economics*, Oxford: Oxford University Press.

Kaldor, N. 1939. "Welfare Propositions of Economics and Interpersonal Comparisons of Utility," *The Economic Journal* (49:195), pp. 549–552.

Kamm, F. M. 2008. "Should You Save This Child? Gibbard on Intuitions, Contractualism, and Strains of Commitment," in *Reconciling Our Aims: In Search of Bases for Ethics*, Barry Stroud (ed.), Oxford: Oxford University Press, pp. 120–144.

Kaplow, L. 1996. "The Optimal Supply of Public Goods and the Distortionary Cost of Taxation," *National Tax Journal* (49:4), pp. 513–533.

Kaplow, L., and Weisbach, D. 2011. "Discount Rates, Social Judgments, Individuals' Risk Preferences, and Uncertainty," *Journal of Risk and Uncertainty* (42:2), pp. 125–143.

Kaufman, N., Barron, A. R., Krawczyk, W., Marsters, P., and McJeon, H. 2020. "A Near-Term to Net Zero Alternative to the Social Cost of Carbon for Setting Carbon Prices," *Nature Climate Change* (10:11), pp. 1010–1014.

Kehoe, T. J., Levine, D. K., and Romer, P. M. 1992. "On Characterizing Equilibria of Economies with Externalities and Taxes as Solutions to Optimization Problems," *Economic Theory* (2:1), pp. 43–68.

Kelleher, J. P. 2015. "Is There a Sacrifice-Free Solution to Climate Change," *Ethics, Policy & Environment* (18:1), pp. 68–78.

Kelleher, J. P. 2017a. "Descriptive versus Prescriptive Discounting in Climate Change Policy Analysis," *Georgetown Journal of Law and Public Policy* (15), pp. 957–977.

Kelleher, J. P. 2017b. "Pure Time Preference in Intertemporal Welfare Economics," *Economics & Philosophy* (33:3), pp. 441–473.

Kelleher, J. P., and Wagner, G. 2018. "Prescriptivism, Risk Aversion, and Intertemporal Substitution in Climate Economics," *Annals of Economics and Statistics* (132), pp. 129–149.

Kolstad, C., Urama, K., Broome, J., Bruvoll, A., Cariño-Olvera, M., Fullerton, D., Gollier, C., Hanemann, W. M., Hassan, R., and Jotzo, F. 2014. "Social, Economic and Ethical Concepts and Methods," in *Climate Change 2014: Mitigation of Climate Change. Contribution of Working Group III to the Fifth Assessment Report of the Intergovernmental Panel on Climate Change*, O. Edenhofer, R. Pichs-Madruga, Y. Sokona, E. Farahani, S. Kadner, K. Seyboth, A. Adler, I. Baum, S. Brunner, P. Eickemeier, B. Kriemann, J. Savolainen, S. Schlömer, C. von Stechow, T. Zwickel, and J. C. Minx (eds.), Cambridge: Cambridge University Press, pp. 173–248.

Koopmans, T. C. 1960. "Stationary Ordinal Utility and Impatience," *Econometrica: Journal of the Econometric Society* (28:2), pp. 287–309.

REFERENCES 239

Koopmans, T. C. 1965. "On the Concept of Optimal Economic Growth," *Academiae Scientiarum Scripta Varia* (28:1), pp. 225–287.

Koopmans, T. C. 1967. "Objectives, Constraints, and Outcomes in Optimal Growth Models," *Econometrica: Journal of the Econometric Society* (35:1), pp. 1–15.

Koopmans, T. C. 1972. "Representation of Preference Orderings over Time," in *Decision and Organization*, C. B. McGuire and R. Radner (eds.), Amsterdam: North Holland Publishing Co., pp. 79–100.

Kotlikoff, L., Kubler, F., Polbin, A., Sachs, J., and Scheidegger, S. 2021. "Making Carbon Taxation a Generational Win Win," *International Economic Review* (62:1), pp. 3–46.

Kreps, D. 1988. *Notes on the Theory of Choice*, Boulder, CO: Westview Press.

Kreps, D. M. 2013. *Microeconomic Foundations I: Choice and Competitive Markets* (Vol. 1), Princeton, NJ: Princeton University Press.

Lamboll, R. D., Nicholls, Z. R. J., Smith, C. J., Kikstra, J. S., Byers, E., and Rogelj, J. 2023. "Assessing the Size and Uncertainty of Remaining Carbon Budgets," *Nature Climate Change* (13), pp. 1–8.

Lauwers, L. 1993. "Infinite Chichilnisky Rules," *Economics Letters* (42:4), pp. 349–352.

Lind, R. C. 1982. "A Primer on the Major Issues relating to the Discount Rate for Evaluating National Energy Options," in *Discounting for Time and Risk in Energy Policy*, R. C. Lind (ed.), Washington, D.C.: Resources for the Future, pp. 21–94.

Lindahl, E. 1958. "Just Taxation—A Positive Solution," in *Classics in the Theory of Public Finance*, R. A. Musgrave and A. T. Peacock (eds.), London: Macmillan, pp. 168–176.

Manne, A. 1999. "Equity, Efficiency, and Discounting," in *Discounting and Intergenerational Equity*, P. R. Portney and J. P. Weyant (eds.), New York: Resources for the Future, pp. 111–130.

Manne, A. S., and Richels, R. G. 2005. "Merge: An Integrated Assessment Model for Global Climate Change," in *Energy and Environment* (Vol. 3), R. Loulou, J.-P. Waaub, and G. Zaccour (eds.), New York: Springer Science+Business Media, pp. 175–189.

Marschak, J. 1950. "Rational Behavior, Uncertain Prospects, and Measurable Utility," *Econometrica: Journal of the Econometric Society* (18:2), pp. 111–141.

Mas-Colell, A., Whinston, M. D., and Green, J. R. 1995. *Microeconomic Theory*, Oxford: Oxford University Press.

Maskin, E. 1978. "A Theorem on Utilitarianism," *The Review of Economic Studies* (45:1), pp. 93–96.

Matthews, H., and Caldeira, K. 2008. "Stabilizing Climate Requires Near-Zero Emissions," *Geophysical Research Letters* (35:L04705), pp. 1–5.

McGartland, A. 2021. "Quality Science for Quality Decisions: Protecting the Scientific Integrity of Benefit-Cost Analysis," *Review of Environmental Economics and Policy* (15:2), pp. 340–351.

Miller, N. 2013. "Climate Change Controversy Takes a Philosophical Turn," *The Sydney Morning Herald* (October 12).

Mongin, P. 1995. "Consistent Bayesian Aggregation," *Journal of Economic Theory* (66:2), pp. 313–351.

Morgenstern, R., Newell, R., Pizer, W., and Prest, B. 2023. "RFF Comments on the Proposed Revisions to Circular A-4," Resources for the Future. https://www.regulations.gov/comment/OMB-2022-0014-0031.

Mulgan, T. 2006. *Future People: A Moderate Consequentialist Account of Our Obligations to Future Generations*, Oxford: Oxford University Press.

Myles, G. D. 1995. *Public Economics*, Cambridge: Cambridge University Press.

National Academies of Sciences, Engineering, and Medicine (NAS). 2017. *Valuing Climate Damages: Updating Estimation of the Social Cost of Carbon Dioxide*, Washington, DC: The National Academies Press.

Negishi, T. 1960. "Welfare Economics and Existence of an Equilibrium for a Competitive Economy," *Metroeconomica* (12:2–3), pp. 92–97.

Nesje, F., Drupp, M. A., Freeman, M. C., and Groom, B. 2023. "Philosophers and Economists Agree on Climate Policy Paths but for Different Reasons," *Nature Climate Change* (13), pp. 515–522.

Newell, R. G., Pizer, W. A., and Prest, B. C. 2022. "A Discounting Rule for the Social Cost of Carbon," *Journal of the Association of Environmental and Resource Economists* (9:5), pp. 1017–1046.

Nordhaus, W. D. 1994. *Managing the Global Commons: The Economics of Climate Change*, Cambridge, MA: MIT Press.

Nordhaus, W. D. 2007. "A Review of the Stern Review on the Economics of Climate Change," *Journal of Economic Literature* (45:3), pp. 686–702.

Nordhaus, W. D. 2008. *A Question of Balance*, New Haven, CT: Yale University Press.

Nordhaus, W. D. 2013. "Integrated Economic and Climate Modeling," in *Handbook of Computable General Equilibrium Modeling* (vol. 1b), P. B. Dixon and D. W. Jorgenson (eds.), Oxford: Elsevier, pp. 1069–1131.

Nordhaus, W. D. 2017. "Revisiting the Social Cost of Carbon," *Proceedings of the National Academy of Sciences* (114:7), pp. 1518–1523.

Nordhaus, W. D., and Yang, Z. 1996. "A Regional Dynamic General-Equilibrium Model of Alternative Climate-Change Strategies," *The American Economic Review*, pp. 741–765.

Office of Management and Budget (OMB). 1992. *Circular A-94*. https://obamawhitehouse.archives.gov/sites/default/files/omb/assets/a94/a094.pdf.

Office of Management and Budget (OMB). 2003. *Circular A-4*. https://obamawhitehouse.archives.gov/omb/circulars_a004_a-4/.

Office of Management and Budget (OMB). 2023a. *Circular A-4 (Public Review Draft)*. https://www.whitehouse.gov/wp-content/uploads/2023/04/DraftCircularA-4.pdf.

Office of Management and Budget (OMB). 2023b. *Preamble: Proposed OMB Circular No. A-4, "Regulatory Analysis."* https://www.whitehouse.gov/wp-content/uploads/2023/04/DraftCircularA-4Preamble.pdf.

Office of Management and Budget (OMB). 2023c. *Circular No. A-4*. https://www.whitehouse.gov/wp-content/uploads/2023/11/CircularA-4.pdf.

Office of Management and Budget (OMB). 2023d. *OMB Circular No. A-4: Explanation and Response to Public Input*. https://www.whitehouse.gov/wp-content/uploads/2023/11/CircularA-4Explanation.pdf.

Parfit, D. 1984. *Reasons and Persons*, Oxford: Oxford University Press.

Parfit, D. 1997. "Equality and Priority," *Ratio*, new series (10:3), pp. 202–221.

Pearson, C. S. 2011. *Economics and the Challenge of Global Warming*, Cambridge: Cambridge University Press.

Peterson, M. 2009. *An Introduction to Decision Theory*, Cambridge: Cambridge University Press.

Pigou, A. C. 1932. *The Economics of Welfare* (4th ed.), London: Macmillan and Co.

Pindyck, R. S. 2013. "Climate Change Policy: What Do the Models Tell Us," *Journal of Economic Literature* (51:3), pp. 860–872.

Posner, E. A., and Weisbach, D. 2010. *Climate Change Justice*, Princeton, NJ: Princeton University Press.

Ramsey, F. P. 1928. "A Mathematical Theory of Saving," *The Economic Journal* (38:152), pp. 543–559.

Rawls, J. 1971. *A Theory of Justice*, Cambridge, MA: Belknap Press of Harvard University Press.

Rennert, K., Errickson, F., Prest, B. C., Rennels, L., Newell, R. G., Pizer, W., Kingdon, C., Wingenroth, J., Cooke, R., and Parthum, B. 2022. "Comprehensive Evidence Implies a Higher Social Cost of CO2," *Nature* (610:7933), pp. 687–692.

Rennert, K., Prest, B. C., Pizer, W. A., Newell, R. G., Anthoff, D., Kingdon, C., Rennels, L., Cooke, R., Raftery, A. E., and Ševčíková, H. 2022. "The Social Cost of Carbon: Advances in Long-Term Probabilistic Projections of Population, GDP, Emissions, and Discount Rates," *Brookings Papers on Economic Activity* (2021:2), pp. 223–305.

Resnik, M. D. 1987. *Choices*, Minneapolis: University of Minnesota Press.
Rezai, A. 2011. "The Opportunity Cost of Climate Policy: A Question of Reference," *The Scandinavian Journal of Economics* (113:4), pp. 885–903.
Rheinberger, C., and Treich, N. 2016. "Catastrophe Aversion: Social Attitudes towards Common Fates," *Industrial Safety Cahiers* (Number 2016-02), pp. 1–43.
Romer, D. 2012. *Advanced Macroeconomics*, New York: McGraw-Hill.
Samuelson, P. A. 1950. "Evaluation of Real National Income," *Oxford Economic Papers* (2:1), pp. 1–29.
Samuelson, P. A. 1954. "The Pure Theory of Public Expenditure," *The Review of Economics and Statistics* (36:4), pp. 387–389.
Sandmo, A. 2000. *The Public Economics of the Environment*, Lindahl Lectures on Monetary and Fiscal Policy, Oxford: Oxford University Press.
Scanlon, T. M. 1982. "Contractualism and Utilitarianism," in *Utilitarianism and Beyond*, A. Sen and B. Williams (eds.), Cambridge: Cambridge University Press, pp. 103–128.
Scanlon, T. 1998. *What We Owe to Each Other*, Cambridge, MA: Harvard University Press.
Schelling, T. C. 1995. "Intergenerational Discounting," *Energy Policy* (23:4–5), pp. 395–401.
Scitovsky, T. 1941. "A Note on Welfare Propositions in Economics," *The Review of Economic Studies* (9:1), pp. 77–88.
Sen, A. 1977. "On Weights and Measures: Informational Constraints in Social Welfare Analysis," *Econometrica: Journal of the Econometric Society* (45:7), p. 1539.
Sen, A. 1979. "Utilitarianism and Welfarism," *The Journal of Philosophy* (76:9), pp. 463–489.
Sen, A. 1986. "Social Choice Theory," *Handbook of Mathematical Economics* (3), pp. 1073–1181.
Sen, A. 2017. *Collective Choice and Social Welfare: An Expanded Edition*, Cambridge, MA: Harvard University Press.
Sidgwick, H. 1907. *The Methods of Ethics*, London: Macmillan and Co.
Spear, S. E., and Wright, R. 1998. "Interview with David Cass," *Macroeconomic Dynamics* (2:4), pp. 533–558.
Starrett, D. A. 1972. "Fundamental Nonconvexities in the Theory of Externalities," *Journal of Economic Theory* (4:2), pp. 180–199.
Stern, N. 1977. "The Marginal Valuation of Income," in *Studies in Modern Economic Analysis: Proceedings of the Association of University Teachers of Economics, Edinburgh 1976*, M.J. Artis and A.R. Nobay (eds.), Oxford: Basil Blackwell, pp. 209–258.
Stern, N. 2007. *The Economics of Climate Change: The Stern Review*, Cambridge: Cambridge University Press.
Stern, N. 2008. "The Economics of Climate Change," *American Economic Review* (98:2), pp. 1–37.
Stern, N. 2010. "The Economics of Climate Change," in *Climate Ethics: Essential Readings*, S.M. Gardiner, S. Caney, D. Jamieson, H. Shue(eds.), Oxford: Oxford University Press, pp. 39–76.
Stern, N. 2015. *Why Are We Waiting? The Logic, Urgency, and Promise of Tackling Climate Change*, Cambridge, MA: MIT Press.
Sterner, T., and Persson, U. M. 2008. "An Even Sterner Review: Introducing Relative Prices into the Discounting Debate," *Review of Environmental Economics and Policy* (2:1), pp. 61–76.
Sunstein, C. R. 2004. "Valuing Life: A Plea for Disaggregation," *Duke Law Journal* (54), pp. 385–445.
Temkin, L. S. 2003. "Egalitarianism Defended," *Ethics* (113:4), pp. 764–782.
Tol, R. S. 2019. *Climate Economics: Economic Analysis of Climate, Climate Change and Climate Policy* (2nd edition), Cheltenham: Edward Elgar Publishing.
Tol, R. S. 2023a. "Social Cost of Carbon Estimates Have Increased over Time (Supplementary Information)," *Nature Climate Change* (13), pp. S1–E49.
Tol, R. S. 2023b. "Social Cost of Carbon Estimates Have Increased over Time," *Nature Climate Change* (13), pp. 532–536.
U.S. Ninth Circuit Court of Appeals. 2008. Center for Biological Diversity v. NHTSA, 538 F.3d 1172 (9th Cir. 2008).

Van Liedekerke, L., and Lauwers, L. 1997. "Sacrificing the Patrol: Utilitarianism, Future Generations and Infinity," *Economics & Philosophy* (13:2), pp. 159–174.

Varian, H. R. 1992. *Microeconomic Analysis*, New York: Norton.

Versar Inc. 2023. *External Letter Peer Review of Technical Support Document: Social Cost of Greenhouse Gas*. https://www.epa.gov/environmental-economics/scghg-tsd-peer-review.

Viscusi, W. K. 2011. "Policy Challenges of the Heterogeneity of the Value of Statistical Life," *Foundations and Trends in Microeconomics* (6:2), pp. 99–172.

von Below, D., Dennig, F., and Jaakkola, N. 2016. *The Climate-Pension Deal: An Intergenerational Bargain*, Unpublished manuscript. https://www.nottingham.ac.uk/climateethicseconomics/documents/papers-workshop-2/jaakkola-et-al.pdf.

von Neumann, J., and Morgenstern, O. 1947. *Theory of Games and Economic Behavior*, Princeton, NJ: Princeton University Press.

von Weizsäcker, C. C. 1965. "Existence of Optimal Programs of Accumulation for an Infinite Time Horizon," *The Review of Economic Studies* (32:2), pp. 85–104.

Voorhoeve, A. 2014. "Review of Matthew D. Adler: Well-Being and Fair Distribution: Beyond Cost-Benefit Analysis," *Social Choice and Welfare* (42), pp. 245–254.

Voorhoeve, A., and Fleurbaey, M. 2016. "Priority or Equality for Possible People," *Ethics* (126:4), pp. 929–954.

Wagner, G. 2020. "Why Oil Giants Figured Out Carbon Costs First," *Bloomberg.com*, January 22. https://www.bloomberg.com/news/articles/2020-01-22/why-oil-giants-figured-out-carbon-costs-first-gernot-wagner.

Weimer, D. L. 2008. "Cost-Benefit Analysis," in *The New Palgrave Dictionary of Economics: Volume 1-8*, S.N. Durlauf and L.E. Blume (eds.), Hampshire: Palgrave Macmillan, pp. 1167–1171.

Weyant, J. 2014. "Integrated Assessment of Climate Change: State of the Literature," *Journal of Benefit-Cost Analysis* (5:3), pp. 377–409.

Weyant, J. 2017. "Some Contributions of Integrated Assessment Models of Global Climate Change," *Review of Environmental Economics and Policy* (11:1), pp. 115–137.

Weymark, J. A. 2016. "Social Welfare Functions," in *The Oxford Handbook of Well-Being and Public Policy*, M.D. Adler and M. Fleurbaey (eds.), Oxford: Oxford University Press, pp. 126–159.

WITCH Team. 2019. "WITCH Documentation," February 26. https://doc.witchmodel.org/.

Yaari, M. E. 1965. "Uncertain Lifetime, Life Insurance, and the Theory of the Consumer," *The Review of Economic Studies* (32:2), pp. 137–150.

Yale Center for the Study of Globalization. 2007. Yale Symposium on the Stern Review. https://ycsg.yale.edu/climate-change/yale-symposium-stern-review.

Zuber, S., Venkatesh, N., Tännsjö, T., Tarsney, C., Stefánsson, H. O., Steele, K., Spears, D., Sebo, J., Pivato, M., and Ord, T. 2021. "What Should We Agree on about the Repugnant Conclusion?" *Utilitas* (33:4), pp. 379–383.

Index

For the benefit of digital users, indexed terms that span two pages (e.g., 52–53) may, on occasion, appear on only one of those pages.

Tables are indicated by an italic *t* following the page number.

abatement
  abstract technology for, 4–5
  emitters, 55–56
  marginal costs, xv–xvi
  optimal social choice social cost of carbon and, 32, 33
Adler, Matthew, 7–8
  on anonymity axiom, 97
  on deterministic prioritarianism, 161
  on Heartland case, 168
  normative abridgement and, 127–28
  on Pigou-Dalton principle, 163
  on prioritarianism, 127–28
  on reflective equilibrium, 163–64
  on weak welfarism, 129–30
  on well-being ratios, 155
aggregation. *See also* Harsanyi's aggregation theorem
  complete, 119–21
  general equilibrium theory and, 41–42
  Ramsey-Cass-Koopmans model and, 69
  same-lifetime, 115–19
  same-number, 114–15
Aldy, Joseph
  problems with argument of, 211
  on value of statistical life, 210
  on welfare weights, 210
anonymity axiom
  Adler on, 97
  strong, 97–98
  well-being, infinite paths of, and, 97
  well-being distributions and, 150
Arrow, Kenneth, 10–11, 36, 136
Atkinsonian social welfare function, 155
  leak tolerance of, 155–56
atmosphere rights, 55
average utilitarian social welfare function, 131
axiology, 181–82
axiomatic prioritarianism, 149–56
  approaches of, 149–50

baseline general equilibrium social cost of carbon (GE-BASE SCC), 77, 193–94
  Interagency Working Group and, 197
  problems with, 193–94
  summary, 193–94
baseline social choice social cost of carbon (SC-BASE SCC), 28–29
  conclusion on, 196
  project-level cost-benefit analysis and, 33
  summary, 193
Bernoulli's hypothesis, 109
betterness. *See also* general betterness
  alternative ordering, 39
  dated, 116–17
  defined, 39
  lifetime, 117–18
  paternalistic, 39–40
  ranking over lotteries, 103, 104
biodiversity, 6
Bliss (B)
  level selection, 91–92
  Ramsey on, 91
Blomquist, Glenn, 221
Brennan, Geoffrey, 124
Broadway, Robin, 82
Broadway paradox, 82, 195
Broome, John, xiv, 34, 126
  critical-level utilitarianism and, 182
  on expected utility theory, 104
  on intuition of neutrality, 182
  on Koopmans's axiomatic utilitarianism, 95
  on Koopmans's axiom of continuity, 95
  on normative obligation, 183
  on Pareto-improving climate policy, 230
  on people route to aggregation, 101, 115
  on snapshot route to aggregation, 101
  on zero level of well-being, 175–76

carbon budgets, 228
carbon tax. *See* pollution taxes

cardinality, 15, 16–17
Cass, David, 10. *See also* Ramsey-Cass-Koopmans model
catastrophe seeking, 171
character functions
    articulating, 42, 192–93
    dynamic general equilibrium theory and, 60–61
    methods to derive, 73
    Ramsey-Cass-Koopmans model and, 74
    schematic, 58
    social welfare functions differentiated from, 42, 46
    summary, 192–93
Circular A-4, 208
    Blomquist on, 221
    Cordes on, 221
    discounting and, 224–26
    "Explanation and Response to Public Input," 218
    peer reviews, 209–24
    Pizer on, 213
    Preamble, 224
    Public Review draft of, 208–9
    welfare weights and, 209, 218
claims-across-outcomes view, 161
Clear Skies Initiative analysis, 210–11
climate dynamics, 200–1
Climate Matters (Broome), 126
climate-policy ramp, 7
Cline, William, 135
compensation principle, 77.
    See also Kaldor-Hicks principle
    consistency and, 81
    defending, 81
    double criterion and, 81–82
    objections to, 80
    procedure, 78
    rejection of, 83
compensatory transfers, 59
competitive equilibrium, 37–38
    defining, 38
    endowment sets and, 46
    Negishi's Method for, 46
complete aggregation, 119–21
constrained optimization, 4–5
    components of, 5–6
    ranking scores, 5–6
consumption. *See also* intra-temporal consumption inequality
    elasticity of marginal well-being of, 22–23, 213–15
    household, 67

mitigation financing out of present, 30
    per capita, 12
consumption, generalized
    defined, 11–12
    Pigou-Dalton principle and, 153n.6
    role in Ramsey-Cass-Koopmans model, 67
consumption bundles, 11
    endowments and, 59
    final, 56–57
    market value of, 56–57, 58
    single indicator for, 11–12
consumption discount factors, 20
    rate of return, 20–21
    social welfare function underlying, 21
consumption paths, 12
    infinite, 90
    overtaking criterion, 92–93
continuity axiom. *See also* Koopmans's axiom of continuity
    defined, 152
    well-being distributions and, 151
Cordes, Joseph, 221
cost-benefit analysis, xiii, 196–227
    baseline social choice social cost of carbon and, 33
    federal, xiii–xiv, 196–97
    Pareto-improving, 195
    theoretical underpinnings of, 19–20, 77, 198, 221–22
Creedy, John, 146
critical-level utilitarianism, 178
    Broome and, 182
    derivation of, 186–88

Dasgupta, Partha, 96–97
    on responsibility, 142
    on social discount rates, xiv
    on social value of well-being, 141
    on social welfare function, 124
    on temperature scales, 154
dated betterness, 116–17
deontological approaches, 143, 228–29
deterministic prioritarianism, 150
    Adler on, 161
    uncertainty and, 165
DICE model, 199
    relationship equations, 4–5
    variations, 207–8
discounted utilitarianism, xvi–xvii, 89
    dual foundations of, 8–9
    moral philosophy and, 7–8
    Nordhaus and, 7
    parameter choice and, 7

rejection of, 7–9
Stern and, 7
discounting. *See also* consumption discount factors; pure time discounting; Ramsey discount rates; well-being discount rate
    Circular A-4 and, 224–26
    constant, 199
    Dasgupta on, xiv
    descriptive approach to, 201–2, 224
    Environmental Protection Agency and, 199–204
    interest rates and, 199
distributive weights, 28. *See also* welfare weights
    Harberger on, 145
dominance principle
    ex ante prioritarianism and, 157
    Fleurbaey on, 170

The Economics of Climate Change (Stern), xiv, 10
ECS. *See* equilibrium climate sensitivity
EDE. *See* equally distributed equivalent
emissions-perturbed path, 19
emitters
    abatement of, 55–56
    Lindahl equilibrium and, 53–54
    opportunity cost of, 54
    pollution tax and, 55
    rights and, 54, 55
    third parties and, 57
endowment distributions, 38. *See also* lump-sum transfers
    competitive equilibrium and, 46
    consumption bundles and, 59
Environmental Protection Agency (EPA)
    discounting and, 199–204
    justice and, 205
    Kaldor-Hicks principle and, 205
    model calibrations, 201
    omitted damages, 191–92
    preferences and, 201–2
    sensitivity analysis, 210–11
    social cost of carbon estimate, xiii–xiv, 200–1
    value of statistical life and, 206, 212
    welfare weights and, 204–5
    willingness-to-pay and, 204
equally distributed equivalent (EDE), 165
    expected, 166
equilibrium climate sensitivity (ECS), 199
    random values of, 199–200
equity weights, 28. *See also* distributive weights; welfare weights

ethics. *See also* population ethics
    branches of, 125–26
    Koopmans and, 91–92
    Nordhaus and, 7
    normative abridgement and, 196
    prudence and, 128–29
    social welfare function and, 164
    Stern and, 7
evaluative humility, 144–47
ex ante prioritarianism, 157
    dominance principle and, 157
    expected utility theory violation, 157
    independence axiom violated by, 159
    ranking, 158
exchange economies, 36–37
expected utility theory. *See also* von Neumann-Morgenstern framework
    aggregation and, 41–42
    Broome on, 104
    ex ante prioritarianism violating, 157
    Harsanyi's aggregation theorem and, 101
    preferences and, 104
    prioritarianism and, 156–57
    uncertain prospects, 103
ex post prioritarianism, 159
    ex ante strong Pareto condition and, 107, 160*t*
    Greaves on, 160–61
externalities
    harmonizing, 55–56
    inefficient outcomes from, 75–76
    Lindahl equilibrium and, 52
    negative, 51
    Negishi's Method and, 57–58
    Pareto efficiency and, 51–54
    personalized prices for, 52–53
    pollution, 54–55
extinction risk, 99
    endogenous, 99
    exogenous, 99
    total, 99

fairness
    debates over, 171
    prioritarianism and, 161
Fleurbaey, Marc
    on dominance principle, 170
    egalitarian arguments of, 170
    on social welfare function, 165
Foley, Duncan, 230
free-riders, 48–49
fundamental nonconvexities problem, 57–58

Fundamental Theorems of Welfare Economics, 35
  assumptions, 37
  First, 38–39
  Lindahl equilibrium and, 54–55
  public goods excluded from, 48–49
  Second, 38, 39, 54–55
FUND model, 28–29, 199

GCAM model, 3
GE-BASE SCC. *See* baseline general equilibrium social cost of carbon
general betterness, 107
  abridged perspective of, 185
  defense of, 185–86
  Hausman on, 184
general equilibrium theory, xv, 35, 75–76
  dynamic, 60–61
  preferences and, 35–36
  price and, 43
  static, 60
  summary, 192–93
  utility function and, 41–42
GE-OPT SCC. *See* optimal general equilibrium social cost of carbon
Gibbard, Allan, 132
goodness
  veil of ignorance and, 133
  well-being differentiated from, 105
Goulder, Lawrence, on social welfare functions, 124, 144, 148
Greaves, Hilary, 149, 158
  on ex post prioritarianism, 160–61

Hammond, Peter, 55–56
Harberger, Arnold C.
  on distributive weights, 145
  on Kaldor-Hicks principle, 145
  on public policy, 145–46
Harsanyi, John, 122–25
  on morality, 122
  social welfare function and, 89–90
Harsanyi-compliant prioritarianism, 108, 148–49
Harsanyi's aggregation theorem, 100–11
  expected utility theory and, 101
  population requirements, 174
  utilitarianism justified through, 100–1
Harsanyi's axiomatic utilitarianism, 99–121
Harsanyi's impartial observer argument, 130–35
  justice and, 131–32
Hausman, Daniel, 184

Heal, Geoffrey, 98
  on social welfare function, 124
Heartland case, 168
Hicks, John, 79
human migration, 6
hurdle rates, 13–14

IAM. *See* integrated assessment model
impartiality principle, 114–15. *See also* Harsanyi's impartial observer argument
  average utilitarian social welfare function and, 131
  Rawls and, 129–30, 131
  social welfare functions and, 131, 140–44
  temporal, 94, 97
impossibility theorem, 10–11
independence axiom
  defined, 106, 159
  ex ante prioritarianism violating, 159
infinite paths of well-being
  anonymity axiom and, 97
  strong Pareto condition and, 97
information invariance axioms
  defined, 152
  well-being distributions and, 151–52
integrated assessment model (IAM)
  cost-benefit, 4
  decision variables, 4–5
  detailed process, 3
  economic and climatic phenomena, 5–6
  Nordhaus on, 33–34
  normative, 33–34
  policy optimization, 3–4, 5
  positive, 33–34
  societal and climatic phenomena, 5–6
  types of, 3
  wealth levels and, 5
  what-if, 3, 5–6
Interagency Working Group on Social Cost of Carbon, 197–208
  baseline general equilibrium social cost of carbon and, 197
  goal of, 197
  Trump dissolving, xiii–xiv
Interagency Working Group on Social Cost of Greenhouse Gases, 197
intergenerational sustainability, 81
Intergovernmental Panel on Climate Change (IPCC), 28
  Second Assessment Report, 83
intertemporal marginal damage paths, 200
intra-temporal consumption inequality, 25–29
  global, 25–26
  across regions, 26

intuition of neutrality, 182
invisible hand, 47
IPCC. *See* Intergovernmental Panel on Climate Change
isoelastic well-being function, 22

justice, 125–26
    Environmental Protection Agency and, 205
    Harsanyi's impartial observer argument and, 131–32
    value differentiated from, 126
Justice 40 initiative, 219

Kaldor, Nicholas, 79
Kaldor-Hicks principle, 79, 82–83.
    See also compensation principle
    economic changes and, 193–94
    Environmental Protection Agency and, 198, 201–2, 205
    Harberger on, 145
    McGartland on, 193–94
    measurement bias in, 205
    normative abridgement and, 144
    objections to, 80
    summary, 193–94
Kamm, Frances, 132
Kaplow, Louis, 195n.3
Koopmans, Tjalling
    ethics and, 91–92
    social welfare function and, 89–90
Koopmans's axiomatic utilitarianism, 90–97
    Broome on, 95
Koopmans's axiom of continuity
    Broome on, 95
    time bias and, 96

leak tolerance, 155–56
lifetime betterness, 117–18
Lindahl, Erik, 50
Lindahl equilibrium, 50–51
    emitters and, 53–54
    externalities and, 52
    Fundamental Theorems of Welfare Economics and, 54–55
    with no lump sum transfers, 59
    Pareto efficiency and, 51
Lindahl-Pigou pricing scheme, 54
    compensatory transfers and, 59
lotteries, 103
    betterness ranking over, 103, 104
    ordering of, 104
    structural conditions, 116–17

lump-sum transfers
    defining, 56–57
    Lindahl equilibrium with no, 59

MAC. *See* marginal abatement costs
Manne, Alan, 70–71
marginal abatement costs (MAC), xv–xvi, 32, 227, 229
marginal utility, 43–44
    of unit of account, 45
Marschak, Jacob, 101
Maskin, Eric, 151
McGartland, Al, 193–94
methane, 28–29, 197
mitigation financing, 29–31
    example, 29
    with non-climatic investments, 29, 30
    out of present consumption, 30
morality. *See also* ethics
    discounted utilitarianism and, 7–8
    Harsanyi on, 122
    interpersonal, 122–23, 125
    Scanlon on, 125
Morgenstern, Oskar, 101
Mulgan, Tim, 181

National Academies of Sciences, Engineering, and Medicine, 197
    recommendations from, 200–1
Negishi, Takashi, 46
Negishi's Method, 229
    for competitive equilibrium, 46
    externalities and, 57–58
    Pareto-improving climate policy and, 57
    public goods and, 57–58
    requisite assumptions of, 57–58
Negishi weights, 47, 59, 69
net-zero date, 228
Neumann, John von, 101
von Neumann-Morgenstern framework (vNM), 103, 156–57
    uncertain prospects and, 156–57
nihilism, 184
nitrous oxide, 197
vNM. *See* von Neumann-Morgenstern framework
non-climatic investments, 4–5
    external costs of, 31
    financing mitigation with, 29, 30
    status quo assumptions, 30
Nordhaus, William, 4
    changes in approach, 76–77
    on climate-policy ramp, 7

Nordhaus, William (*cont.*)
  discounted utilitarianism and, 7
  ethics and, 7
  Nobel Prize of, xiv
  Pareto efficiency and, 76
  on policy optimization IAM, 33–34
  on potential improvements, 69–70
  on Ramsey-Cass-Koopmans model, 66–67
  on social cost of carbon, xiii
  on social welfare function, 33
  Stern debate with, xiv, 7
  on stringency of climate action, 7
  on temperature increases, 6
normative abridgement, 33–34, 83–84, 122–23
  clarifying conceptions of, 127
  ethics and, 196
  evaluative humility and, 144–47
  examples of, 125–30
  Kaldor-Hicks principle and, 144
  population ethics and, 180–86
  pure time discounting and, 135–40
  social welfare functions and, 140–44
normative domain divisions, 122–23

objective functions, 3–4, 5–6
  debate over, 7
  role of, 4
Office of Management and Budget (OMB), 208
OLG. *See* overlapping generations model
OMB. *See* Office of Management and Budget
opportunity costs, 31, 207–8
  emitter, 54
optimal general equilibrium social cost of carbon (GE-OPT SCC), 60–66
  conclusion of, 196
  summary, 194–95
  time series, 194–95
optimal growth theory, 10–15, 66–67
optimality
  overall choiceworthiness differentiated from, 123–24
  Ramsey rule and, 123
optimal social choice social cost of carbon (SC-OPT SCC), 31–34
  formula expressions, 31
  summary, 193
ordinal preferences, 74–75
overall choiceworthiness, 123–24
overlapping generations model (OLG), 70–74
  components of, 71
  initial conditions, 71
  Pareto weights and, 72
  Ramsey-Cass-Koopmans model contrasted with, 70–71
overtaking criterion, 92
  consumption paths, 92–93
  defined, 92
  temporal impartiality and, 94

PAGE model, 3–4, 199
Pareto condition, strong
  ex ante, 107, 160*t*
  infinite paths of well-being and, 97
  well-being distributions and, 150
Pareto dominance, 35–36
Pareto efficiency, 35–36, 38.
  See also compensation principle
  externalities and, 51–54
  Lindahl equilibrium and, 51
  Nordhaus and, 76
  normative criterion of, 36
  potential, 79, 82–83, 145, 206, 221–22
  Ramsey-Cass-Koopmans model and, 74
  term usage, 36
Pareto-improving climate policy
  Broome on, 230
  Negishi's Method and, 57
Pareto noncomparability, 36
Pareto weights, 42–46
  overlapping generations model and, 72
  positive, 47
  utility function transformation and, 46
  variable, 47
Paris Agreement, 227
paternalistic betterness, 39–40, 66
people route to aggregation, 101, 115
Pigou, Arthur C., 55–56
Pigou-Dalton principle, 108
  Adler on, 163
  generalized consumption and, 153
  well-being distributions and, 153
Pizer, William
  on Circular A-4, 213
  example from, 214*t*, 217*t*
  on welfare weights, 213
policy optimization types, 35
political obligation, 183
pollution taxes, 227
  emitters and, 55
  pollution externalities and, 54–55
population ethics, 174–75, 176–80
  normative abridgement and, 180–86
  Repugnant Conclusion and, 177
  Sadistic Conclusion and, 176

scenarios, 176–77
zero level of well-being and, 175–76
positive affine transformation, 15–16
Posner, Eric, 129–30
preferences
  of descendants, 67–68
  Environmental Protection Agency and, 201–2
  expected utility theory and, 104
  general equilibrium theory and, 35–36
  ordinal, 74–75
  utility functions and, 39
prescriptive growth theory, 66–67
prices. *See also* Lindahl-Pigou pricing scheme
  affordability and, 42–43
  anonymous, 50–51
  general equilibrium theory and, 43
  personalized, 50
  relative, 43
principle of avoidance of foreseeable regret, 158
prioritarianism, 100–1
  Adler on, 127–28
  alternative frameworks, 156–57
  expected utility theory and, 156–57
  fairness and, 161
  Harsanyi-(non-)compliant, 108, 127–28, 148–49, 156
  risk and, 156–73
  weak welfarism and, 129–30
private goods, 37, 48
private ownership economy, 37
probability agreement theorem, 111–12
production economies, 37
prudence, 128
  as non-ethical consideration, 128–29
public goods, 48–51
  dated, 60
  Fundamental Theorems of Welfare Economics and, 48–49
  Negishi's Method and, 57–58
  as nonexcludable, 48
  as nonrivalrous, 48
  personalized prices for, 52–53
pure time discounting, 13, 20, 67–68, 98
  Arrow on, 136
  normative abridgement and, 135–40
  rate, 13
  Stern Review, 99
pure time preference, 67–68, 71, 202

radiative forcing, 4–5
Ramsey, Frank, 11, 89
  on Bliss, 91

social choice theory and, 11–12
on well-being, 91
Ramsey-Cass-Koopmans model (RCK), 66–70
  aggregation and, 69
  character function, 74
  Nordhaus on, 66–67
  overlapping generations model contrasted with, 70–71
  Pareto efficiency and, 74
  special constraints, 75
Ramsey discount rates, 23
  region-specific, 27–28
Ramsey formula, 23, 141, 225
Ramsey parameters, 203
Ramsey rule, 32, 65, 75, 202
  consequences of, 32–33
  optimality and, 123
Rawls, John, 100
  impartiality and, 129–30, 131
RCK. *See* Ramsey-Cass-Koopmans model
reflective equilibrium, 163–64
REMIND model, 3–4
Repugnant Conclusion
  avoiding, 179, 180–81
  extended versions, 180–81
  formulation of, 177
  population ethics and, 177
Repugnant Obligation Conclusion, 181, 183–84
reversal paradox, 81–82
rightness function, 127
risks
  of extinction, 99
  prioritarianism and, 156–73
  value of reduction of, 212
  well-being and, 105
Roemer, John, xiv

Sadistic Conclusion, 176
same-lifetime aggregation, 115–19
same-number aggregation, 114–15
Samuelson condition, 50–51
Scanlon, T. M., 125
Scarce Drug thought experiment, 126
  source-sensitive ranking in, 129
SC-BASE SCC. *See* baseline social choice social cost of carbon
SCC. *See* social cost of carbon
Schelling, Thomas, 135
SC-OPT SCC. *See* optimal social choice social cost of carbon
Sen, Amartya, 10–11
  on welfarist rankings, 129

sensitivity analysis, 6
　Environmental Protection
　　Agency, 210–11
separability. *See also* independence axiom
　of outcomes, 159
　of people, 118–19, 151, 152, 159
　of times, 118–19
services reductions, 4–5
Sidgwick, Henry, 98
Smith, Adam, 47
snapshot route to aggregation, 101
social choice theory, 10
　applied, 66–67
　assumptions of, 11–12
　generalized consumption and, 11–12
　history of, 10–11
　Ramsey and, 11–12
　social cost of carbon and, 18–20
　summary, 192–93
　welfare economics and, 35
social cost of carbon (SCC)
　alternative formula, 20–25
　definition of, formal, 18
　Environmental Protection Agency estimate
　　for, xiii–xiv, 200–1
　families, xv, 192–93
　future implications of, 226
　general equilibrium theory and, 60–66, 74–
　　85, 192–93
　hybrid, 77
　Nordhaus on, xiii
　omitted damages, 191–92
　social choice theory and, 18–25, 31–34
　time series, 193
　underestimating, 191–92
social welfare function (SWF), 7–8
　assumptions of, 15–18
　average utilitarian, 131
　axiomatic foundations of, 89–90
　Brennan on, 124
　character functions differentiated from,
　　42, 46
　consumption discount rate and, 21
　Dasgupta on, 124
　discrimination and, 15
　ethics and, 164
　finite values of, 15
　Fleurbaey on, 165
　Goulder on, 124, 144, 148
　Harsanyi and, 89–90
　Heal on, 124
　impartiality and, 131, 140–44
　inequality-insensitive, 27

inequality-sensitive, 27
infinite sums, 13
　Koopmans and, 89–90
　Nordhaus on, 33
　normative abridgement and, 140–44
　optimal growth theory and, 10–15
　parameter disagreements, 8
　per capital consumption and, 12
　as rightness function, 127
　Williams on, 124, 144
Stern, Nicholas, 10
　discounted utilitarianism and, 7
　ethics and, 7
　Nordhaus debate with, xiv, 7
　on stringency of climate action, 7
STEW. *See* sums of transformed expected
　well-being
STWB. *See* sum of transformed well-being
sub-Saharan Africa, 28–29, 213
substitution, marginal rate of, 43
sum of, 50–51
sum of transformed well-being (STWB),
　166–67
sums of transformed expected well-being
　(STEW), 166–67
sup norm distance measure, 152
SWF. *See* social welfare function

technology, fertility of, 137
temperature increases
　global mean, 4–5
　Nordhaus on, 6
temperature scales
　Dasgupta on, 154
　well-being measures and, 154
temperature targets, 227, 228
temporal impartiality, 94, 97
Tol, Richard, 90–91
total utilitarianism, 179
transformation, marginal rate of, 50–51, 62
Transplant thought experiment, 126
　source-sensitive ranking in, 129
Transplant 2 thought experiment, 134
Treich, Nicolas, 7–8
　normative abridgement and, 127–28
Trump, Donald, xiii–xiv

uncertain prospects
　deterministic prioritarianism and, 165
　expected utility theory and, 103
　von Neumann-Morgenstern framework
　　and, 156–57
　states of nature and, 156–57

utility function
  assumptions, 40
  dynastic, 68
  general equilibrium theory and, 41–42
  increasing, 40
  lifetime, 71
  maximizing, 43–44
  Pareto weights and transformation of, 46
  preferences and, 39

value, 104, 125–26. *See also* goodness
  of death, 205–6
  justice differentiated from, 126
  marginal social, 141–42
  veil of ignorance and, 133
value of risk reduction (VRR), 212
value of statistical life (VSL), 205–8
  Aldy on, 210
  controversy over, 207
  Environmental Protection Agency on, 206, 212
  implicitly welfare-weighted, 211
  income-sensitive, 211–12
  population average, 210
  summary, 206
  willingness to pay and, 207
value of statistical life year (VSLY), 210–11
veil of ignorance, 100, 131
  goodness and, 133
  Kamm on, 132
  value and, 133
Voorhoeve, Alex, 170
VRR. *See* value of risk reduction
VSL. *See* value of statistical life
VSLY. *See* value of statistical life year

weak welfarism, 129–30
Weitzman, Martin, 34
welfare weights, 28. *See also* distributive weights
  Aldy on, 210
  Circular A-4 and, 209
  elasticity parameter, 222
  Environmental Protection Agency and, 204–5
  Pizer on, 213
well-being, 12–13, 150
  anonymity axiom and, 150

  cardinality, 15, 16–17
  continuity axiom and, 96, 151
  Dasgupta on, 141
  defining, 39
  efficiency in production of, 145, 148
  generational shortfalls in, 91
  information invariance axiom and, 151–52
  interpersonal comparisons of, 111–14
  lifetime level of, 11
  logarithmic, 22–23
  marginal, 21, 22–23
  Maskin and, 151
  Pigou-Dalton principle and, 153
  Ramsey on, 91
  ranking, 8–9
  relative magnitudes of, 15
  risk and, 105
  separability and, 151
  social value of, 141–42
  strictly concave, 21, 22–23
  strong Pareto conditions and, 150
  sum of transformed, 166–67
  temperature scales and, 154
  temporal, 101
  unit comparability of, 16
well-being, critical level of, 179
well-being, expected, 131
  sums of transformed, 166–67
well-being, infinite paths of
  anonymity axiom and, 97
  strong Pareto condition and, 97
well-being, zero level of
  Broome on, 175–76
  lifetime, 175–76
  population ethics and, 175–76
well-being discount rate, 15. *See also* pure time discounting
well-being ratios, 154
  Adler on, 155
  of differences, 15–16
Williams, Roberton, 124
  on social welfare function, 144, 148
willingness-to-pay, 66, 82–83
  Environmental Protection Agency and, 204
  future, 4–5, 78
  value of statistical life and, 207
WITCH model, 3–4